SHE MIGHT HAVE
BEEN QUEEN

January 5th 1953.
At the famous ball in New York.

A BIOGRAPHY OF THE DUCHESS OF WINDSOR

She
might have
been Queen

by GEOFFREY BOCCA

EXPRESS BOOKS LONDON

*Published in 1955
by
Daily Express Book Co. Ltd.
Fleet Street, London, E.C.4*

PRINTED AND BOUND IN ENGLAND BY
HAZELL WATSON AND VINEY LTD
AYLESBURY AND LONDON

Contents

Introduction

IT is not unusual for a man or woman to emerge in a particular moment of history, to dominate that moment, stir the passions of the world and then die in obscurity. Fame tends to evaporate quickly, and obscurity has a way of embracing even those who try most fiercely to avoid it.

Logically the Duchess of Windsor should today be an obscure woman or at best an occasional curiosity. Her place in history was set solely by the tumultuous events of a fortnight in December 1936, culminating and ending in the abdication of King Edward VIII. Historically speaking, she has accomplished nothing since. She passes from resort to resort, aloof, silent (even her voice is unknown to the public; is it high, low, English, American?). She occupies various rungs in the lists of best-dressed women. The disasters which have consumed the world in which she once flourished have passed her by.

Yet she has never ceased to fascinate. An aura of immortality illuminates her. She has never left the centre of the world stage, and from that first moment when her photograph was shown to the world as 'The woman the King loves', she has remained one of the most persistently controversial, complex and absorbing personalities of our day.

There are many answers to this paradox, and one of the aims of any biography of the Duchess of Windsor must be to trace them.

One of the most immediate, present-day reasons for interest in the Duchess, however, lies in the fact that she has aged so little. Had she become less handsome with the years, had the hair turned white, the back become less straight, the figure less slender, she might have passed from the spotlight, and time would have softened and dimmed her memory.

But she has broken the rules of time. She is one of the world's most elegant and unchanging women. She glows with an inner

fire which turns the past into the present and makes the Abdication seem like yesterday. Her face in the papers is still the face of
Mrs Ernest Simpson; the same prim hair-style, the intelligent,
watchful eyes, the tight smile. While other characters involved in
the Abdication grow older, become senile, and one by one die,
the Duchess is the victim of her own appearance, and to look on
her is to feel oneself back in 1936, in the cold, anxious nights of
waiting; back with an exhausted Prime Minister, Stanley
Baldwin, his head in his hands in his rooms at the House of
Commons; a distraught King crying out in Fort Belvedere, the
winter mists rising from the River Thames to hide the dreamy
turreted Fort and all its unbelievable secrets.

This is the face of a woman whose strange life might have taken
a strangely different course. Had the Abdication crisis ended
differently, Edward would still be King. The Duchess of Windsor
would be Queen, performing all the functions which Queen
Elizabeth used to perform. Would it, or could it ever, have been
a good thing? Who can tell?

The men who wrought the downfall of her husband are nearly
all dead now, but no one has tried to undo the work they did.

The reign of King George VI, the Duke's brother, came and
went. Queen Elizabeth II came to the throne, where she now sits,
a radiant figure commanding vociferous loyalties. Sir Winston
Churchill, champion of Edward VIII's cause in 1936, has been
Prime Minister twice. But the Windsors are left where they were
in 1937, and recognition of the Duchess by the British Court
seems to be as far away as ever.

The contrast between what was and what might have been
could be aptly seen on the night of January 5th, 1953, when the
present way of life of the Windsors was celebrated in festivities
that lasted until dawn.

It was one of those winter evenings unique to New York when
sub-freezing, forty-mile-an-hour winds meet from four different
directions at the corner of every city block, sending hats flying
and numbing the cheek-bones.

Weather so wild made it a suitable night for great indoor
occasions. Winston Churchill was in town, sitting before the fire

in the home of his old friend, Bernard Baruch, the American elder statesman, and at the Waldorf-Astoria Hotel on Park Avenue, the 'Duchess of Windsor Ball', organised by Elsa Maxwell, patronised by the Duchess of Windsor in aid of wounded American ex-servicemen, was held amid trappings that were breathtaking even by New York standards.

The grand ballroom at the Waldorf was hung with draperies of coral pink. The table-cloths were also pink and held in place by huge pink satin bows. Silver candelabra held pink candles, and there were centre-pieces of pink carnations. Suspended from the ceiling in a three-tiered perch, birds of paradise fought gallantly for life against the fumes of perfume, cigar and cigarette smoke rising in warm, exotic waves from the floor. The décor was by Cecil Beaton, the British court photographer and designer, and the whole thing setting off a special ball-gown which the Duchess of Windsor wore later in the evening.

In at least one respect a Mayfair ball would have been superior. In London the male guests would have been faultlessly tailored, down to the last man, in full evening dress. In New York, where even the wealthiest men tend to buy their clothes at £100 a time off the peg at such establishments as Brooks Brothers or Saks Fifth Avenue, those who wore tails at all looked self-conscious. More than half wore dinner-jackets.

But if the men were to be rated sartorially below the London standard, it had to be admitted that the women were almost stupefying in their beauty. In the second-floor cloakrooms they stepped out of millions of dollars' worth of rare fur, and stood sparkling in diamonds, shimmering French silks and aglow with that Florida suntan which, in a New York January, is as much the mark of the wealthy and privileged as a mink coat or a Cadillac.

The guests represented two distinct classes of American society. There were representatives of the nation's economic royalty, un-titled aristocrats from a century of pure American breeding, reinforced by generations of increasing dividends from America's railroads, oil-wells, motor companies and grocery self-service supermarkets. There were also representatives of a class lower down the social scale: American café society, a hoarser, more boisterous society, with faces well known in the gossip pages and divorce courts.

With a suitable nod to democracy, the one class rubbed shoulders with the other. There was Clare Boothe Luce, wife of the publisher of *Time* and *Life*, shortly to become American Ambassador in Italy, poised delicately on the eve of her fiftieth birthday and looking not quite twenty-three; Fleur Cowles, the driving force behind *Look Magazine*; Mr and Mrs Harry Winston (diamond man); Mrs French Astor; Mrs William Randolph Hearst Junior; Mrs Lytle Hull, formerly Mrs Helen Huntington Astor; Mrs Cornelius Vanderbilt Whitney, and the rest of the concatenation of crushingly fashionable surnames which go to make American high and almost high society.

They were there to pay £9 or so a head for charities to wounded soldiers, and at the same time to pay tribute in one degree or another to the two romantic exiles so frequently in their midst.

The table of honour in the ballroom was set close to the dance-floor and opposite the orchestra. The Duke and Duchess of Windsor sat opposite each other, side by side with half a dozen special guests. The Duchess was scintillating in a white ball-gown —the first of three which she would wear in the course of the evening. Her dark hair, as usual, was parted in the middle and pulled back with two small side-bows of wine-coloured velvet.

Slender as ever, the lines on her neck alone showed the mark of her fifty-seven years. But her light blue eyes shone. Her face was lively and dynamic. Her partner at the table was Jimmy Donahue, the boyish, balding playboy, heir to most of the Woolworth millions. Donahue has spent many of his thirty-seven years alternately amusing and horrifying American society, and he has been a great favourite in the past few years at the court of the Windsors.

Court-jesting on a large scale has been a Donahue stock-in-trade for years. As a boy he shocked his mother by dancing in the chorus of Broadway musicals.

In recent years he has put his genius for merry-making

extensively at the service of the Windsors, who appear to enjoy it. Not long ago he horrified the exclusive Colony Restaurant by bringing in three seedy violinists to serenade the Duchess and two other friends.

Such a thing had never happened at the Colony before, and the manager protested frantically to the laughing Duchess. Donahue airily waved away the protests, and the violinists, to the mingled delight and annoyance of the other guests, stood around the table and serenaded the Windsor party throughout lunch.

Donahue and the Duchess had their heads together, and were buried deep in conversation that made now one and then the other gurgle with laughter. The Duchess talked gaily, her hands moving in expressive gestures, favoured by nature in that, even while the flash-bulbs popped around her, however she looked, the cameras could do her no disservice.

The Duke across the table, sitting next to Mrs Lytle Hull, listened in desultory fashion to the gales of laughter, and seemed preoccupied. Now almost sixty, the Duke carried his years with grace in accordance with his age. He looked an elderly man, but the boyishness was still there; it is something which will probably never desert those antique-youthful features. He sipped only water and allowed his attention to wander. Sometimes he looked abstractedly at the dancers, whistled a bar or two of the music or clapped his hands once or twice in time to the beat.

'Say,' hailed one acquaintance, 'I'm glad to see someone else here in a white tie.'

'Have to wear it once in a while,' the Duke said briefly, which seemed to close the conversation.

The Duchess flashed him an understanding smile, and together they rose to join the packed mass of dancers. Cecil Beaton, who had carved a small space in the press for himself and was jitter-bugging energetically with Mrs Winston Guest, a blonde beauty, saw the royal couple and, smiling charmingly, cut in. Beaton should have known better. The Duke hates the American cutting-in practice. For a few bars the Duchess danced politely with Beaton, and the Duke with Mrs Guest; then the Duke and Duchess reclaimed each other and danced back to the table.

At the far end of the table of honour, Elsa Maxwell, the professional party-giver and hostess originator of the ball, kept an unblinking, guardian eye on the couple. But she was not in time to stop a middle-aged woman press-agent in extravagant décolleté, from flopping down at a vacant chair next to the Duke after cutting a swath through the dancers. The corners of the ex-King's mouth drooped apprehensively, but he managed to squint in the semblance of a smile, and said, obviously repeating a well-tried defensive formula:

'What is your name and whom do you represent?'

'My name is babble. I represent babble babble. I think you are wonderful. I think the Duchess looks just beautiful. The American people adore you both. Would you sponsor our product which is babbling . . .?'

Elsa Maxwell stamped and fumed and finally hauled away the interloper, hissing in her ear: 'The Duke does not like talking to publicity people.' But the woman was on her way, talking eagerly to an envious acquaintance. 'Did you see me? I sat with him. And I didn't call him your Highness or anything because we Americans don't do that sort of thing! And he asked me what my name was! Oh, he was so cute!'

Little contretemps like this are not unusual in the present existence of the Duke of Windsor. There is something about the Duke which makes some Americans feel more than usually democratic. The Duchess does not inspire the same emotions. Her personality is something too positive and diamantine for such familiarities, so the sensation-seekers and bobby-soxers always aim for the easier target.

Throughout the dinner of vol-au-vent, filet mignon and ice-cream, the Duke was as silent as the Duchess was voluble. First of the high spots of the evening came with the coffee, and it was provided by the society bandleader Meyer Davis, famous for a son, Garry, who once started a 'One World' Movement in Paris, attracting a lot of disciples before he got bored with the whole thing and returned to New York.

Davis had specially composed for the occasion a number called 'The Windsor Waltz', which went like this:

Beautiful ladies,
Dance to the Windsor Waltz.
As you whirl and glide
Let your eyes confide
The secret dreams of your heart.
If you wish for love warm and shining,
The one who's just for you,
Surrender your hearts when the Windsor Waltz starts
And make your wish come true.

A press agent had earlier asked the Windsors to dance it solo, and the Duke had said hastily that he didn't think it was the thing to do.

The official climax to the evening came with a fashion parade. Society celebrities acted as models, draping themselves in coy clusters at each end of the ballroom stage. Then Meyer Davis sounded a dramatic roll of drums, and Colonel Serge Obolensky, the suave, monocled, Russian-born, Oxford-educated socialite (once married to an Astor and now a New York hotel director) walked slowly across the empty dance-floor on to the stage ('The Windsor Waltz' *rallentando*). The curtains parted, and there was the Duchess of Windsor in a white taffeta gown heavily beaded in coral with coral panels. It was specially made for her in Paris.

It was undeniably impressive. The Duchess would have made a great model. She put her hand on Obolensky's arm and led the parade of society models on to the floor ('The Windsor Waltz' *allegro brillante*). She was completely poised, completely graceful, utterly confident. But her smile was strained.

The ball continued all night. The Duke and Duchess left comparatively early, and returned to their suite on the twenty-ninth floor of the Waldorf Towers; but the party did not end until close to daybreak.

* * *

It was all very enjoyable, the kind of thing that kept the Duchess of Windsor in the news, but it did have repercussions. It led some people to wonder whether the Duchess was acting correctly in posing as a model, and it led, for various personal reasons, to a widely publicised break in the long and famous friendship between the Duchess of Windsor and Elsa Maxwell. Still, it could not be considered an occasion of international importance, and it would be quickly forgotten if the world could forget that the Duchess is the wife of the former King of England. But neither history nor their way of life will allow the fact to be forgotten. Edward's reign of forty-six weeks is in the history-books; his portrait appears in any schoolboy's collection of 'Kings of England'; the Duke's struggle for the title of 'Royal Highness' to be given the Duchess; the Duke's Memoirs, his magazine articles and the topics of his conversation are a constant reminder of the past.

To solve the many mysteries of the Windsor story, a few premises must be established. One is that none of the parties directly concerned in the Abdication ever foresaw that more than half a generation later nothing would be solved or settled as to the Windsors' status, or that a night like the Duchess of Windsor Ball and its subsequent eruptions would come to play such a part in the Windsors' present existence.

Another is that this form of existence need not have been, and that the Windsors, with the large fortunes they have had at their disposal at one time and another, could have made a very different life for themselves if they had wished to do so.

This book stems from these standpoints, and tries to tell why the Windsors do not attend the Court which the Duke once commanded; why their exile continues; what are the might-have-beens in the Windsors' position in the world, and the part played by the Duchess of Windsor in bringing her husband to such a peculiar haven through the storms that have torn at this long and moving love story.

Home in Baltimore.
The house in Biddle Street where Wallis Warfield lived.

1912.
Wallis Warfield at a Princeton University social engagement.

PART I

'THE WOMAN I LOVE'

CHAPTER I

The Girl on East Biddle Street

———————

As the last century closed a little boy and a little girl, destined one famous day to be united, were playing their games in their own little worlds; the boy in the royal palaces of England and Scotland, watched by Queen Victoria and paternally proud princes of the blood; the little girl in a boarding-house on a tawdry street in Baltimore, Maryland, under the sad eyes of a widowed mother.

The gulf was, and is, almost incalculable in its vastness. Worlds of class and breeding, centuries of tradition separated them—it can only be described in the most aeonic terms. Yet the Duchess of Windsor has bridged it so skilfully that one tends to forget from what remote distances it all began.

A gulf equally great now separates the Duchess of Windsor from the impish child on Baltimore's East Biddle Street. Her playmates of those days have grown into Baltimore housewives, insurance men, lawyers, journalists and automobile dealers. Yet the spark must have been there even then, in the child and in the girl, the spark which was one day to inflame the ardour of the world's best-loved Prince. But in examining the Duchess of Windsor's childhood, where would one seek such a spark and how would it show itself?

The genius of a poetess or a novelist may be detected in childhood writings. Great reformers, such as Florence Nightingale, tend to pass their childhood in torment, gnawed by the hunger for their own destiny. But in the childhood of a woman famous only for the exquisiteness of her own womanhood, for her ability to inspire love of unique intensity in others, one must seek something different—and something less. One may be satisfied to uncover a childhood personality probably extrovert, uncomplicated and fundamentally normal. She would probably lack ambition, but possess a strong will. She would be remembered with esteem. The recollections of boy friends become more interesting than the recollections of girl friends.

Within this modest frame of reference Wallis Warfield, the little girl, shows up very well; more so because her childhood was not an easy one, and a less spirited girl may well have become melancholy and retiring.

Her geographic background, of course, was quite propitious. Wallis Warfield was actually the second Baltimore girl to marry a king. The first was the celebrated Betsy Patterson, who married Jerome Bonaparte, youngest brother of Napoleon. But when Jerome was pressed to choose between the throne of Westphalia and his wife, he chose, after the briefest reflection, the throne, and Betsy went back to Baltimore.

There is, without doubt, some special quality about Baltimore girls. Charles Dickens noticed it. Twenty-nine years before Wallis Warfield was born, he visited the city in the course of his reading tour of the United States, and commented, 'the ladies are remarkably handsome with an Eastern look upon them, dress with a strong sense of colour, and make a brilliant audience'. Possibly in Baltimore America comes closest to England. North Charles Street, the city's smart shopping centre, with its dignified antique shops, quiet couturiers and milliners, gives a sense of being nearer in spirit to Bond Street than to Fifth Avenue, and Baltimore's suburbs, with the neat houses sprouting Victorian bay-windows, are agreeably Bayswaterian.

Wallis's mother, like so many other mothers on the eastern seaboard of the United States, made impressive claims about her ancestry. She was born Alys Montague in Virginia, and confidently claimed ancestry back to William the Conqueror. Alys Montague Warfield had records which proved, to her own satisfaction at least, that her family was founded by Drogo de Monteacuto Montecute who landed in 1066. There is no question that the Montague or Montagu family of Virginia has links to the English Montagus, who today are one of the most thriving aristocratic families in England. This would make the Duchess of Windsor a very distant kinswoman to the Duke of Manchester (Alexander George Francis Drogo Montagu) and the Earl of Sandwich (George Charles Montagu).

Upton Sinclair, the novelist, was one of Wallis Warfield's cousins, and adored Wallis when she was a little girl. Sinclair asserted that Wallis had Indian blood in her veins and was a descendant of Pocahontas. The connection even with Sinclair's explanation was somewhat ephemeral. Wallis's great-uncle Powhatan Montague, whose brother, William Montague, was her maternal grandfather, had a family tree which sought to prove that he was a direct lineal descendant from the little seventeenth-century Indian heroine, Pocahontas, and from her father whose name was Chief Powhatan.

If this is a fact, it gives Wallis another unsuspected family link. Her old friend Lady Louis Mountbatten has also claimed to be a descendant of Pocahontas.

The record is at least plain on one point. Wallis came from sound, well-established American stock on both sides—on her mother's the Montagues of Virginia, and from her father's side the respected Warfields of Maryland. There are several Warfields today well-known in Baltimore affairs, mostly in law and insurance, and one member of the family, Edwin Warfield, a distant uncle of Wallis's, was State Governor from 1904 to 1908.

Family connections are all very well, but Wallis was born with very little else. Her father was Teackle Wallis Warfield, a retiring, ailing boy who worked insignificantly as a clerk in Baltimore.

He married Alys, a girl with blue eyes and the prettiness of a doll, when he was about twenty, and in time Wallis was born. In order to relieve the strain of Warfield's bad health and Alys's pregnancy, Warfield's mother, Mrs Henry Mactier Warfield, suggested a holiday for both at her expense, and they went together to the lovely Blue Ridge Summit resort in Pennsylvania, taking a room at the Monterey Inn.

Both Warfield and his wife wished passionately for a boy. On June 19th, 1896, Lewis Miles Allen, a twenty-two-year-old doctor just out of college, received an emergency summons to the Monterey Inn. Alys's regular doctor was away from the resort on another mission, and Allen brought Bessie Wallis Warfield into the world in her mother's hotel bedroom.

Allen, who later became a wealthy obstetrician and died in 1949 aged seventy-six, did not know for forty years that he was responsible for one of the world's most sensational women. But he did see her several times as a child, and later recalled her as 'quite pretty, with long hair and exceptionally magnetic in her personality'.

The Warfield family returned to Baltimore with a depressing burden of financial problems. Not long after T. Wallis Warfield was dead, and the problems became even more severe, so Alys, a child bride and child mother, now a widow, turned the house which she and her husband had taken on marriage into a boarding-house. It was a hard beginning for Wallis.

Today, 212 East Biddle Street, as the childhood home of the Duchess of Windsor, is possibly the most famous address in Baltimore, and thousands come to stare at it every year. This has made it a very speculative piece of property to own. A few months after the abdication of Edward VIII, a New York business-man bought the house and opened it as a Duchess of Windsor 'museum'. Several thousand people paid half a crown each to go through it, but it was not a commercial success. One disadvantage was that it had been completely remade inside since Wallis's day, and the only surviving items that could be connected with Wallis were the bath-tub she had used and an old gas-cooker intriguingly labelled 'Windsor'.

The house did not hold enough interest to make it a paying proposition, either as a museum or as a peepshow. At the same time it attracted too much interest among tourists and visitors to make it comfortable as a home. Consequently in the past fifteen years it has been occupied and vacated by a succession of dis-contented tenants, and has deteriorated into a battered, flaking building divided into flats.

In 1896 it was pleasant enough, in a district similar in tone to London's Chiswick. At the front it had the three marble steps peculiar to Baltimore's style of architecture. The habit of marble

steps continues, pleasingly, in Baltimore, but not at 212 East
Biddle Street. At some point along the past fifty years they disappeared, and have been replaced by steps of a more doubtful
geological origin.

Most of Alys's lodgers were relatives both near and remote.
Baltimore at the time of Wallis's birth was still affected in unique
ways by the American Civil War, even though by then it had
been over for more than thirty years. Although the State of Maryland fought on the side of the North, it had, and still has today,
strong emotional and family ties to the South. After the war,
when the South was prostrated by defeat, Baltimore became a
place to which the dispossessed, impoverished Southerners could
find refuge and escape from the miseries of the reconstruction
period.

Virginian families moved to Maryland in thousands. Alys herself was the daughter of one of these, and to others she let out
rooms. It was not a very commercial proposition. Many other
Southern women with Baltimore homes were doing the same
thing with little better success. She is reported by one old friend
to have made a little money by inviting friends or 'paying guests'
to lunch. In this way and by other feeble little ventures into the
business of sub-letting flats, Alys managed to keep going.

Life was both difficult and sad for Southern women like Alys,
and the children of these women, the girls especially, had a strong
tendency to inherit the mood of sadness. Which made Wallis all
the more noticeable as the outstanding exception to the rule.

From an early age she made up for her lack of conventional
prettiness with vivacity and magnetism. Even before she became
conscious of her own ambition and sense of self-preservation, this
dynamic, dark-haired girl was beginning to interest people of
influence and wealth.

This she did partly by her own nature and partly by rather
touching design. One of Wallis's Baltimore relatives believes that
Wallis as a child became very much aware of the insecurity of her
position, and that Alys, probably without even noticing it, kept
impressing on the child the fact that she would have to make her
own way in life, without money or assistance.

Whatever it was, Wallis quickly attracted guardians. Her rich uncle, above all, was enchanted by her. He was Solomon Davies Warfield, her father's brother, and a railroad magnate reputedly worth £1,000,000. Another friend was her grandmother, Mrs Henry Mactier Warfield, who took little Wallis under her wing and regaled her with stories of the Civil War and with sage advice. 'Never marry a Yankee,' she told Wallis, 'and never marry a man who kisses your hand.' (Her husbands consisted of one Yankee, one half-Yankee and one Englishman.) Her aunt, Mrs D. Buchanan Merryman—later famous as 'Aunt Bessie' of the Abdication period—also looked after the little girl fondly and became her life-long friend and confidante. Another aunt, influential, persuasive Lelia Montague, daughter of Powhatan Montague, lavished on Wallis much worldly wisdom, and in one way became largely responsible for her present personality.

It was S. Davies Warfield, Wallis's 'Uncle Sol', who decided that something practical had to be done about Wallis. Alys was too poor to educate her properly. Sol thereupon formally took over the responsibility of educating Wallis and introducing her to society.

Uncle Sol chose Arundel, a fashionable day-school which no longer exists, as Wallis's first school. Relieved of the responsibility of bringing up her daughter, Alys promptly remarried. Her second husband was a local politician named John Freeman Raisin; but a jinx seemed to pursue her domestic life, and Raisin also died only two years after their marriage.

After Arundel, Wallis went to Oldfield's, in Cockeysville, Maryland, a school of fifty-six girls so snobbish they did not even compete at games with other girls, preferring to play among themselves.

The young ladies of Oldfield's school went to bed early, rose shortly after dawn and were forbidden to have boy friends. Summers were a relief, when Wallis went to the freer and easier community of Miss Charlotte Noland's Summer Camp for Girls, a mile and a half from Middleburg, Virginia. Little as Wallis liked athletics, she loved her summers at camp, with picnics and lazy romantic days in the open air reading aloud volumes of poems by Kipling and Robert Service. She loved also the 'Indian Love Lyrics' of Laurence Hope and the adventurous stories of Bret Harte.

Burrland Camp was started in 1907, and Wallis first attended in the summer of 1909. She was one of the 'Big Four' girls there, the others being Martha Valentine (later Mrs John Cranley of Richmond), Eleanor Brady and Mary Kirk. They alone claimed the right to go into town and get the mail. Red-headed Mary Kirk was her closest friend, the daughter of Mrs Henry Kirk Junior, one of Baltimore's most prominent hostesses. Mary, a girl with a reputation for being a bit on the wild side, and Wallis together were a formidable combination. Mary was to play an unusual part in Wallis's later life.

The girls at camp went on hayrides, blackberry-picking expeditions and jaunts in coaches-and-four. Once they went on a coon hunt, which ended in maidenly terror when the coon turned out to be a skunk.

In Baltimore, after these expeditions Alys was beginning to notice a difference in her daughter. Once, according to a *New Yorker* writer, she threw a tantrum when her mother bought her a white dress for a party. 'I want a red dress,' she sobbed. When her mother, faintly, asked why, Wallis declared frankly, 'Because in a white dress the boys won't notice me.'

There seemed little danger of that, however. The recollections of Baltimore men who knew her give the impression of a person one did not forget quickly.

'She was the brunette type,' said one cousin from a rather younger age-group. 'Very witty and vivacious. She attracted men the way molasses attracts flies.'

Tom Shryock, later a Colonel in the American National Guard, became almost incoherent when he talked of her.

'Unless you know Wallis Warfield, it is impossible to describe her,' he said. 'She is one of the nicest, one of the grandest people in the world. Words cannot express the high regard I have for that woman. Why, when she went to the theatre she would turn to the usher, smile and thank him for showing her the seat. It didn't make any difference who it was who did anything for her—a policeman, a newsboy, anyone—she was immediately grateful and courteous." Shryock remained a close friend of the family.

In 1947 he and the Duke of Windsor met at a reception in Washington, D.C. The encounter between the husband and the old friend of the world's most romantic woman produced something noteworthy in the way of anticlimax.

'Bet you didn't buy those shoes in America,' said the Duke.

'No, sir,' said Shryock. 'Imported English leather.'

Another friend, Lloyd Tabb, kept some of her letters. One is enough to reveal the refreshing normality and energy of the girl. 'Well,' she wrote from Maine in answer to an invitation from Tabb, 'I must say I'm thrilled to death about coming to Glenora. It will seem like old times. I am leaving here tomorrow, Monday, and will get to Baltimore on Tuesday, so if it is convenient and your mother really wants me, Saturday would be a good time for me. When your mother writes to me, don't forget to give her 212 East Biddle Street as the address. This is certainly one peach of a place. Thursday night there was a big dance given for me. It was some party towards the end of the morning. Hope to see you soon. As ever, Wallis.' The date was 1912.

Wallis's social course was first set while she was in her teens by her persuasive and determined aunt, Lelia Montague, a beautiful woman whose relationship to Wallis was more like that of a cousin. This has been revealed in some of the writings of Upton Sinclair. Lelia, when she was very young, married a wealthy Baltimorean, Basil Gordon, who died. After that, Lelia, living between Baltimore and Washington, found herself wooed by two impressive suitors. One was Senator Alfred Beveridge of Ohio, and the other a distinguished Marine officer, George Barnett.

Lelia chose the Marine, and some years later, when America entered World War I, she used her considerable influence in Washington to get Barnett a major-generalship over the heads of others. Barnett, an erect, soldierly man of the British rather than the American school, commanded the United States Marines in France with distinction.

Lelia's father and Wallis's maternal grandfather were brothers.

Upton Sinclair was also related to the family in this line. He was Lelia's first cousin. Lelia played a big part in Wallis's début and in her life from then on. When the time came for Wallis to make her début, one of her hands rested on the arm of Major-General George Barnett, the other on the arm of a cousin, Henry Warfield Junior.

The Bachelors' Cotillon Club was the most fashionable and exclusive club in the city for the younger men. Twice a year, on the Monday of Christmas week and the Monday of New Year, the club gave balls, or 'germans' as they were called. They were the most spectacular affairs of the year in Baltimore. Gold damask hangings decorated the walls. Brocaded pillows were used as steps to the stage. The candelabra was silver, and the footmen wore splendid maroon coats with brass buttons.

A popular girl would be invited to both the Monday germans, but it was to the first that a girl considered she positively had to go, or die. It was an illustration of Wallis's popularity that she was one of the forty-nine débutantes invited to the first Monday german in 1914. In this particular year it was held on December 7th, and marked by a feeling of strain that had never been known before. The war in Europe had begun, and stirred an uncomfortable sense of unrest among America's younger smart set.

The Lyric Theatre, Baltimore, where the first Monday german was held, smelled rich with the perfume of green Southern smilax, that strange aromatic flower which so peculiarly catches an atmosphere of sunshine and leisurely living. Wallis and the rest of the débutantes looked appropriately radiant in white satin and chiffon dresses, which appeared so fetching at the time and seem so droll today.

For the next two years Wallis studied in between parties. She perfected her languages, learning to speak French and German extremely well. In later years her German slipped, but she maintained a reasonably good French.

In 1916, Lelia Barnett decided that for Wallis, now nineteen, it was time for a change. Mrs Barnett was enjoying her marriage to an eminent military man, and was inviting to dinner parties at Wakefield Manor, her Washington home, some prominent members of what was known as the 'Army-Navy Set'. Occasionally a politician or two would join the party, and the air after dinner would become electric with stimulating discussion. Lelia invited Wallis up from Baltimore, so that she could 'meet some interesting people'. Wallis came and was fascinated. She did not return immediately to Baltimore. With her studies over, Lelia decided that her exceptionally gifted and charming young cousin should look ahead. Obediently Wallis did, and never looked back.

CHAPTER II

'Win's Wife'

THE social whirl which now began under the guidance of Lelia Montague Barnett led to Wallis's first marriage. It was an odd business, standing out in the life of this remarkable woman as one incident of pure mediocrity.

The excuse for the marriage was simple and universal. Thousands of other girls were making the same mistake for the same reason. Somehow one would have expected Wallis Warfield, with her peculiar talents, to rise above prevailing circumstances. In this case she did not. The facts are she was too young and there was a war on.

It began early in 1916. Wallis had been a guest at the Washington home of the Barnetts for some time, when it was decided to travel south to Pensacola in Florida, a naval training establishment which, with Annapolis, is the American equivalent of England's Dartmouth or Osborne. Lelia's younger sister Corinne had married a naval lieutenant, Henry Mustin, whose particular job sealed for Wallis the excitement of this new experience. Mustin ran a new flying school opened by the Navy, and instructed young officers in the ways of bi-planes. Wallis was dated every night, and there was nothing unusual in the conversation she had with one especially attentive lieutenant in the Mustins' living-room. The lieutenant respectfully asked Miss Warfield if he might see her the following evening and make a party of four with Lieutenant and Mrs Mustin. Wallis, regretfully, said no, she had a date. The lieutenant respectfully suggested the night after. Wallis said no, she had another date. The night after that? Why yes, she would be delighted. And Lieutenant Earl Winfield Spencer with the elation of a young man in love went back to his quarters to try to live out the next few days with what patience he could.

Spencer was a dark, laughing, wild, chunkily built young man of twenty-seven, the eldest in an affectionate, closely knit family of four brothers and two sisters.

Spencer's father was a prosperous member of the Chicago Stock Exchange, and the family home was in Highland Park, Illinois, a fashionable Chicago suburb. His mother was British or, to be more exact, Norman-British. She had been born in Jersey, largest of the Channel Islands that lie between England and France. Spencer was a promising naval officer who was learning to become a pilot. The Navy was his one passion and interest. He was good-looking and smart, but wore that decoration which always worries English sailors when they see Americans wearing it, a moustache—an adornment forbidden in the Royal Navy.

Once he managed to command Wallis's time in the evenings, Spencer did his best to keep it; not always with success, for Wallis was a popular girl; but soon their relationship began to look serious. Wallis undoubtedly saw Spencer not as he was but against the background of his hazardous existence. She was moved and agitated by the atmosphere of war that was everywhere in Pensacola.

All at once it became too much for her. Wallis told her mother she was leaving and abruptly packed her bags; together they returned by train to Baltimore. Not long afterwards Spencer managed to get himself leave and followed. They met at Lelia Barnett's house in Washington, and a breathless courtship began. Three months after they first met, the paragraph that had become inevitable appeared in one of the Baltimore newspapers:

'An engagement just announced of unusual interest to society in Maryland as well as Virginia is that of Miss Wallis Warfield, daughter of Mrs John Freeman Raisin and the late Teackle Wallis Warfield to Lieutenant E. Winfield Spencer, U.S.N., of the Aviation Corps, son of Mr and Mrs E. Winfield Spencer of Highland Park, Chicago.'

The next few months for Wallis were spent in the exciting vacuum that comes to a popular girl between the moment of engagement and the fact of marriage. The Warfield relatives and

Wallis's friends entertained her well. There were parties for her in Washington and Baltimore by the Barnetts and Uncle Sol respectively. Mary Kirk's mother organised a large party for her at the Baltimore Country Club.

At the age of twenty Wallis was married to Lieutenant Earl Winfield Spencer at the Christ Protestant Episcopal Church in Baltimore. The time was 6.30 p.m., the date November 8th, 1916, five months before America entered World War I, and twenty years one month and two days before the King of England gave up his throne for her.

The wedding invitations were printed on the largest cards ever seen in Baltimore. Mary Kirk was among the bridesmaids, and so were Mary Graham and Mercer Taliaferro, other friends of Wallis's. The wedding was well up to Baltimore standards. Contemporary reports describe tall white tapers burning before an altar banked high with annunciation lilies. Candles and white chrysanthemums decorated the church, the candles flickering against the grey walls and stained-glass windows as the rain fell steadily outside.

The bridesmaids wore orchid-coloured faille and blue velvet gowns, blue velvet hats, and they carried yellow snap-dragons. Wallis, walking down the aisle on the arm of her tall unbending Uncle Sol, wore a gown of white panne velvet, a bodice embroidered with pearls and a velvet court train, one of the first ever seen at a Baltimore wedding. Under the skirt was a petticoat trimmed with old family lace. Her hat was a crown of orange blossoms with a veil of tulle, and her bouquet was of wild orchids and lilies of the valley.

As for Spencer, his good looks were to pass from him early, and he later became thick-set and jowly; but that night he looked as magnificent in his dress blues as one would expect of an adventurous young sailor.

One of the bridesmaids was Win's sister Ethel, and the best man was his brother Dumaresque Spencer. Hindsight gives the excellent Spencer family an uneasy, almost an interloping, place in the picture—like people invited to the wrong party. However, this was the Spencers' evening as much as it was the evening of the

assembled Warfields and Montagues; and having turned up from
Illinois for the wedding, they trooped immediately back again,
never to reappear in the story.

Yet the Spencer story was also an eventful one, for if ever there
was a family racked by tragedy it was the Spencers. Dumaresque
went to France to join the Lafayette Escadrille, the squadron of
the French Air Force manned by American volunteer fliers, and
was shot down and killed. Another brother, Egbert, was thrown
from his horse and died from the effects of the injury. A sister
committed suicide, and the mother was killed in an automobile
accident. Win Spencer, too, was heading for a personal tragedy
of his own.

That night a handsome young man and his bride, the girl in a
going-away dress, the man caped according to the winter uniform
of the Navy, arrived at White Sulphur Springs, Virginia, which,
then as now, was one of the most fashionable spots on this earth.
It was an interesting selection for a Wallis Warfield honeymoon.
As a little girl Wallis had spent holidays there with her grandmother, Mrs Henry Mactier Warfield. Later on, as Duchess of
Windsor, she was to return to White Sulphur Springs, and make
it, along with Palm Beach and the Riviera resorts, one of her
nomadic homes.

For a honeymoon Wallis and her husband took one of the trim
vacation cottages in the district. After a few days, they went north
for a week to garish Atlantic City, which probably was a relief
after the exclusive, conservative atmosphere of the Springs.

The war seemed closer than ever. The aviation training scheme
had been intensified, and between flights the men moped rest-
lessly and waited. After a few months of almost unbearable
anticipation, it happened. On April 6th, 1917, the United States
declared war on Germany.

It was as an instructor flier that Win Spencer received his wartime orders, and to his fury was ordered, not to Europe or to sea,
but to San Diego, California.

San Diego today, with the shift of world forces from the
Atlantic to the Pacific, sizzles with excitement, and it had a roar-
ing time in World War II. In 1917, however, it was a complete

backwater of the war. Spencer was in charge of the only up-to-
date organisation in the area—the North Island Aviation School.
The only units of the United States Navy based there were an old
cruiser—the *Oregon*, a veteran of the Spanish-American war—a
few sub.-chasers and a gunboat, the *Vicksburg*.

There was plenty to keep them happy, however, and the
atmosphere of California helped. It was warm, new and in many
ways strange. Years afterwards Wallis was still talking about it.
Once while she was Mrs Simpson in London she reportedly held
up one of her celebrated collections of jewels to a friend. 'See
this,' she said. 'Some day when I can't stand being away any
longer, I'll sell it and go and live in California.'

But even in California she had steady bouts of homesickness,
and kept up a fond and regular correspondence with her friends
and relatives in the East. The letter which probably made her pine
for home was the one of incoherent delight she received from
Mary Kirk, who was engaged to be married.

Mary's story was typical of several that were happening in
Baltimore. The hearts of the city's belles were currently skipping
whole series of beats. Into Maryland from Europe had come a
large group of young French officers. Their job was liaison and
intelligence work with the United States Army, and Baltimore
became their headquarters.

Mary had met and fallen head-over-heels in love with one of
them, a captain named Jacques Raffray, who in private life was a
prosperous insurance broker and jeweller. In 1918 they married.
Wallis would have dearly loved to attend the wedding, but the
distance was too great and her husband seemed established in San
Diego indefinitely.

Wallis and Spencer were still there in 1920, and at a ball at
Coronado, Wallis saw the Prince of Wales for the first time. It
was not in any way dramatic, and even long-standing friends
have seldom heard the Windsors mention it; but the fact of its
happening at all gives enough sense of fate and predestination to
delight the story-tellers.

Reports of the little incident vary, but it may have happened
more or less like this. The Prince, with Lord Louis Mountbatten,

was on his way in the battleship *Renown* to Australia and New Zealand via the Panama Canal. Six days steaming from Panama brought the *Renown* to San Diego, where she stopped for forty-eight hours to refuel. The Prince of Wales was just beginning his fabulous decade of travel, romance and popularity, and as usual, as soon as the local authorities heard he was in town, he was immediately hauled ashore for some impromptu fêting.

It was quite sudden and unannounced. Wallis and her husband were at the presentation. It was a crowded room, but no enchanted evening. There was no earthquake, no flash of lightning, no chill down the spine, no meeting of souls. It is almost impossible to imagine that Wallis, for all her ambition and will of steel, could imagine that she would ever marry this idolised Prince. At the moment she was penniless, miserably married to an honest but hard-drinking dullard, stuck in one of the most isolated corners of America.

By now Wallis and Spencer had been married for four years. Outside of flying and the Navy, Spencer had few interests. He liked to stay at home, and read a book or talk shop to other officers. Wallis was eager to be out and doing something different every night. While Spencer remained at home, Wallis had acquired the habit of going out alone and making friends of her own. Her circle grew and grew until she became the centre of a thriving social life all her own, a social life in which her husband played little part.

She made many friends. One was a pretty girl called Katherine Moore, who had served as a nurse in the French Red Cross during the war, and was later to become an important character in Wallis's life. Others were the Fullam sisters, Rhoda and Marianna, daughters of Admiral Fullam, commander of the San Diego base. The girls would meet at the smart, old-established Coronado Hotel, or travel up to meet other friends who lived in Santa Barbara.

Spencer was transferred to Washington late in 1920. This brought Wallis closer to her home and friends, but it brought her no nearer to marital happiness. The break came when Spencer was posted to Shanghai.

They were not divorced until 1927, and in 1926 Spencer was

still regarded as one of the Navy's better pilots. But the divorce coincided with a strange and unhappy degeneration in Spencer's life. He never rose above the rank of Lieutenant-Commander, and he married three more times. In 1936 he was executive officer of the aircraft carrier *Ranger*, but broke his leg on a shooting expedition in California and was relieved of his position. He was looked after by an old friend who, the following year, became his third wife. But like the first and second, this marriage did not last.

In a particularly unsavoury divorce action in 1940, by which time Spencer had been retired for two years through ill-health, his wife alleged he went on 'week-long sprees', and declared she feared for her life. She alleged in court that he was 'a mental case', and her daughters said that when he got drunk he would speak in Chinese. Spencer denied the whole thing. The divorce was granted. This wife died of a stroke in 1944.

In 1941 Spencer married his fourth wife. It was a happy marriage, but it was marred by a strange incident. In 1943, he was found on the floor of his home in Ventura, California, stabbed in the chest and bleeding profusely. Spencer said something to the effect that he had cut himself opening a tin.

Both wars passed Spencer by. In the first he was an instructor, and by the second he was retired even though he was not yet fifty. In 1950, aged sixty-one, he died, leaving a reasonable fortune of nearly £9,000 to his wife, but making no reference to Wallis in his will. For all his moroseness and the unhappiness of his life, Winfield Spencer in his own way was a gentleman, and never made an unworthy remark about his first wife. Usually he avoided the subject, but would say briefly, 'She was a wonderful woman' to people who brought her name up. He was expansive only once, to a reporter at the time of the Abdication. 'She was most attractive,' he said. 'She had one of the most powerful personalities I have ever known any person to possess. She was lovely, intelligent, witty—good company—stimulating I think is the word that best describes her. Our marriage lasted eight years, and I think Wallis was a wonderful woman. She will always command my admiration and respect.'

In 1920, with Spencer on his way to China, Wallis found herself alone in Washington, free and her confidence in herself fully restored. By now she was twenty-four and extremely attractive in a conventional way. She was small and quite plump, but her face had an unforgettable allure, with her high cheek-bones, her dancing blue eyes and ever-ready laughter. Her hands, which were large and strong, were her least beautiful part.

One of Wallis's greatest assets was her voice. It was summarised best by Janet Flanner (Genet of the *New Yorker*), who once called it 'two-toned, low and lower'. It was a voice with the natural charm of the South. People have accused Wallis of having developed an artificially husky voice. Actually the voices of educated Southern girls tend as naturally to go low as the voices of educated English girls tend to go high. Tallulah Bankhead is the most famous example, and her voice might be a caricature of Wallis's.

The woman described above is no conventional beauty. Nor was she rich. Her secret was her personality. The basic assumption in the life-story of the Duchess of Windsor is that no other person could have toppled the King of England from his throne, and that if Wallis had never appeared Edward VIII would almost certainly still be reigning. Whether Wallis guessed it or not, her arrival in Washington was the turning-point in her career. The interlude of mediocrity was over.

Monocled.
When Wallis Warfield was at boarding school.

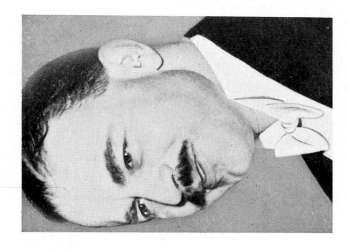

Mr. Ernest Simpson, her second husband.

Earl Winfield Spencer, her first husband.

CHAPTER III

Divorce and Remarriage

WASHINGTON, Europe, Shanghai, Peking, New York were all to see something of Wallis in the next few years as she progressed through the stages of reconciliation, divorce and another marriage towards her next and most important stop, which was London, England.

It would be unfair to assume that she was totally unmoved at the failure of her marriage. If she had been it is inconceivable that Spencer would have spoken so warmly about her in the years that followed. But Wallis soon accepted the inevitable, almost certainly because she realised an attempt at reconciliation was hopeless. The fact was that an extraordinary person had been briefly attracted to an ordinary person, and Wallis simply outgrew Spencer.

Left alone in Washington, Wallis met an old friend, Mrs Luke McNamee, wife of a naval intelligence officer who was frequently away on lengthy missions. Together they set up house as room-mates, sharing the expenses and the entertaining. They rented a small but tasteful house in Georgetown, a charming and Bohemian section of Washington which has always attracted a number of writers and intellectuals.

Both knew some interesting people, and Wallis had had a fine training in the skills of entertaining from Lelia Barnett. She was given assistance socially by her aunt, Mrs D. Buchanan Merryman. This amiable, forthright character—so well-known in Washington today that she can go into almost any shop, buy something, and say simply, 'Charge it to Aunt Bessie'—had many friends in Washington society.

A succession of parties began which beat anything Wallis could remember in Baltimore. This was the great American party era, brought on by Prohibition when everybody drank far more than

was good for them. Wallis, for her part, drank very little, sometimes nothing at all. Yet in spite of this, or because of it, she was
usually the heart and centre of the parties. She was not doing as
well as she was to do shortly, but she was still doing uncommonly
well.

Her circle of friends was both large and lively. One of her
intimates was Ethel Noyes, daughter of the President of the
Associated Press and later the wife of Sir Willmott Lewis,
Washington correspondent of *The Times*. There was also Don
Felipe-Alberto Espil, an ambitious young First Secretary in the
Argentine Embassy, and reputedly the best tango dancer in
Washington. Years later, when Mrs Simpson had become the
most famous woman in the world, Espil, now the Argentine
Ambassador, chuckled admiringly and commented to *Time*
magazine: 'My! My! Who'd have guessed our little Wallis
would come so far.'

In 1923 Wallis made her first trip to Europe. Later that year,
her post-war restlessness still upon her, she resolved to go to
China. Her decision was unexpected, and has never been
explained. Poor Alys, her mother, fretted and was upset at the
thought of such an undertaking, but Wallis and Alys had lived
apart for so many years that the daughter had lost the habit of
seeking the mother's guidance or advice. Wallis was now twenty-
seven. She packed and set out.

Her choice for her new home was curious. Her estranged
husband was stationed in Shanghai, yet Wallis appeared to have
no intention of rejoining him. Her subsequent divorce action
confirmed that there was no reunion between them. Spencer was
assigned to the Yangtze Patrol, which kept him away from his
base for long periods, and it is possible that he never even knew
that Wallis was in China. At any rate, in later years when he
reviewed their life together, he talked about San Diego and
Coronado and Washington, but made no reference to seeing her
in China. Few, if any, of the close friends Wallis was to make in
China even set eyes on him.

Almost as soon as she arrived Wallis travelled to Peking to visit
her old friend from Coronado days, Katherine Moore. It was one

of the eventful journeys of her life. Katherine had married a wealthy young American sportsman named Herman Rogers, who was later to play a key role in Wallis's matrimonial adventures. Rogers was a tall, athletic New Yorker, who had graduated from Yale in 1914 and from the Massachusetts Institute of Technology in 1917. World War I frustrated his ambitions of becoming a successful engineer, and as he possessed a substantial inherited income, he decided to go abroad to places where life was both fun and cheaper; always, however, asserting his loyalty to America by running up the Stars and Stripes above his house every day wherever he lived.

He took his bride to China, where he intended to learn Chinese and write a book. He succeeded in doing both, but later forgot most of his Chinese and found no publisher for the book. Sport and parties took up most of his time. He was an excellent polo player, tennis player, yachtsman and marksman. He gave some of the gayest parties in Peking.

Rogers and his wife now befriended Wallis, and introduced her to their own social life. For more than six months out of the year she spent in China, she stayed at the Rogers' house, and mixed with a smart, effervescent set of British, Americans and wealthy Chinese. She attended polo meetings. She played tennis —badly. She went on expeditions into the interior which started on horse-back, continued on donkey-back and ended by scrambling over rough country on foot. Wallis, who always impressed friends as a rather fragile figure of Southern grace and delicacy, surprised everybody by scrambling around with the best of them.

Early in 1925, however, Wallis decided that she had had enough of China. She said good-bye to the Rogers and sailed home, establishing herself for the purposes of divorce in the fashionable and 'horsey' area of Warrenton, Virginia, and a centre of yet more of the parties for which Wallis had developed a great hunger.

By the divorce laws of Virginia, she had to reside in the state for a year before her divorce could be heard. So she lived pleasantly in the Warren Green Hotel, consulting lawyers in the day-time and accompanying a string of dates in the evenings.

Life for Wallis at the age of twenty-nine had become a life of pleasure. She did no work, her pastimes were empty, her companionship vapid. But her attributes could be denied by no one. Her impact on men was extraordinary. Her popularity was great. She was clever. She was witty. She was high-spirited, good-natured and kind-hearted. All that could bewitch a prince she now possessed, and her charms were set off to their best advantage by the society in which she moved.

What were her dreams of the future? 'Don't worry, it might never happen' was one of her principles of life, and it is likely that Wallis, who had never had a proper home of her own, wanted more than anything to become a successful hostess, to have her parties talked about and her cooking appreciated. It was an honest ambition.

But Wallis was now being led by unsuspected by-ways towards her famous role in history. One day she went to Union Station in Washington to buy a return ticket to New York. Her reason was that she wanted to go to New York to see her friends, to escape from the drab stores of the capital and revel in the dress shops of Fifth Avenue. But fate was propelling her by degrees towards the Prince of Wales.

Wallis wanted to see Mary Kirk, still her friend and confidante, who was living in New York and worked for her own amusement in a specialty shop on West 57th Street. Mary and Wallis had corresponded frequently and saw each other whenever they could.

Mary's French husband had stayed on in the United States after the war to become a successful and wealthy American citizen with a flat east of Central Park. Their marriage was eight years old, but though they continued to live together it was dimming fast.

The reunion of Mary and Wallis was joyous, and Wallis stayed in New York for some time. Shopping always brought out the best of her taste and talent. She had very little money at the time, but she made up for it with her knowledge of clothes and her native sense of chic. Some of her friends ran little *boutiques* on the East Side, and Wallis would call on them. She would not buy, however, until the end of the season, by which time the prices had come down. She would take her pick, and then make alterations to the clothes she had bought until they were reborn as new creations. 'If I had thought of that in the first place,' one of Wallis's New York friends admitted, 'I could have sold them originally for twice the price.'

Mary Kirk often went shopping with her. They went to parties together, met for tea, and now Wallis entered an interlocking circle of friends through which she was to meet Ernest Aldrich Simpson of London and his wife. There is the usual confusion of recollection about how they first met. Some old friends believe they met at a party given for Wallis at Mary Kirk Raffray's house. Others say it happened through Mary Clement, a friend of Wallis's from China, who was also a friend of Mary Kirk's.

Mr and Mrs Simpson lived with their small daughter in Greenwich, Connecticut, and maintained a brownstone town house in the smart East Sixties of New York. They were very fond of bridge. Mary Clement, the wife of a naval officer, also liked the game and would call on them, often bringing with her a fourth. On one occasion she brought Wallis.

The Simpsons were on the edge of divorce. Mrs Simpson—she was the first of four—was an American, the former Dorothea Parsons Dechert, daughter of an ex-Chief Justice of Massachusetts. Simpson was part English, part American, and was one of those not uncommon types who stem from a double heritage yet lavish their loyalty on only one. His mother was American, and his father had lived in America for many years while retaining his British citizenship. In spite of all that, Simpson developed into an intensely patriotic Englishman, rejecting his claims to American citizenship when he was twenty-one. He went to Harvard, but England had entered World War I and he left before graduating to join the Coldstream Guards. He finished the war a second lieutenant, and through the irresistible influence of the Guards returned, more English than any Englishman, to America to complete his education and enter his father's shipbroking business.

Simpson was a pleasant English 'good sort', an able business-man, something of a Mayfair dandy, with good taste and a sensitive disposition. Nothing in the whole Windsor story is more incongruous than the fact that he has given the world a name that is a symbol for sensational love. So many years after the revelation of Edward VIII's love, the name 'Mrs Simpson' still touches the mind with a sense of mystery and excitement.

Wallis, who could see that the Simpson marriage would not last much longer, was attracted to Ernest Simpson at their first meeting. When Herman Rogers turned up in New York, she introduced them and told Rogers, 'I think I'm going to marry him.' But Wallis also had her mind on other things. Her divorce was coming up in Warrenton, and her Uncle Sol, the main source of her present well-being, was dangerously ill.

With these matters occupying her attention, she returned to Washington after fond farewells to Mary. On October 25th, 1927, the old railroad magnate died, and Wallis was among the many mourners at the funeral service held at Emmanuel Protestant Church in Baltimore. One of the pall-bearers was the famous American newspaperman, Arthur Brisbane. Warfield left a fortune estimated at £200,000, but bequeathed to Wallis nothing more than a £3,000 trust fund. Friends, knowing Uncle Sol's devotion to his niece, were surprised at the bequest, which would yield Wallis, already possessed of expensive tastes, nothing more than a few pounds a week. Sol's generosity to Wallis in the past had made it much easier for her to make a mark in Baltimore. The fact was possibly that Sol, a business-man to the core, felt he had done enough. As a Puritan, he may also have disapproved of the break-up of his niece's marriage and of her social journeys through Washington and China while still a married woman. There was a hint of defensiveness in the part of his will which mentioned his bequest to Wallis.

'My niece has been educated by me,' he wrote as if on guard against criticism, 'and otherwise provided for . . . in addition to provision made herein.'

Whatever was going on in old Warfield's mind, it did not seem to distress Wallis unduly. She cheerfully told friends that she would have to go out and get a job for the first time in her life.

But before she could consider work seriously there was the second complication which had to be undergone, the business of her divorce from Winfield Spencer.

It was the first of her two divorces, and it was as quiet as the second, nine years later, was to be sensational. It was heard on December 6th, 1927, Wallis appearing in the Circuit Court of Fauquier County, at Warrenton, Virginia, before Judge George Lathom Fletcher. Her charge was desertion.

The newspapers did not pay much attention to the divorce of so obscure a couple, but one significant fact emerged. Wallis, filing her petition, testified, according to the available reports, that her husband had deserted her on June 19th, 1922, and had contributed nothing to her support since. Several witnesses also testified. The date was important, not so much because it happened to be Wallis's twenty-sixth birthday, but because it signified that Spencer had deserted her *before* she went to China.

No objection was raised and the divorce was granted four days later.

Wallis, having cast off her first husband and finding herself with almost no income at all, paused to wonder what to do next. There was a suggestion that she might become a business-woman and sell construction elevators in Pittsburgh, Pennsylvania. A decision had to be made. Wallis, as she has done all her life when face to face with crises, decided to take a holiday.

She called Aunt Bessie in Washington and together they went to Europe. It was Wallis's second transatlantic holiday, and she went to London immediately. One of the first people she met was Ernest Simpson, who had transferred his offices to London and was working as a director of the ship-brokerage firm of Simpson & Simpson in association with his father's office in New York.

Simpson was alone now, his wife having left him and returned to New York with their daughter Audrey. He escorted Wallis everywhere, and by the time Wallis and Aunt Bessie were due to return to New York there was an engagement ring on her finger.

Wallis accompanied Aunt Bessie back to New York, but stayed only long enough to wind-up her affairs in America. Excitedly she told Mary that she was saying good-bye to her homeland, and intended to settle down in England for the rest of her life. On this as on other occasions Wallis's assessment of the future was quite wrong.

The wedding, at the Chelsea Register Office, was quiet. The announcement appeared in the *New York Times* and it took many of Wallis's friends by surprise. It read:

'Mr and Mrs Charles Gorden Allen, of Washington, D.C., announce the marriage of Mrs Allen's daughter, Mrs Wallis Warfield Spencer, to Ernest Simpson of London on July 28th, 1928, in London. Mrs Simpson is the daughter of the late Teackle Wallis Warfield of Baltimore, and niece of the late S. Davies Warfield, also of the city. She is the former wife of Lieut.-Commander E. Winfield Spencer of the United States Navy.'

So Wallis Warfield Spencer added another surname to the list, and set off on a honeymoon which took her to France, Spain, Majorca and Minorca. She was thirty-two and her husband thirty-one. The years were slipping by and the time was approaching when 'the most charming American woman in London', in middle-age, was to shake the world.

CHAPTER IV

Mrs Simpson Arrives

WHEN Wallis arrived in London she hardly knew a soul.
Three years later she was a leader in a thriving society. It
was a typical Wallis Warfield progression and, as in Baltimore
fifteen years before, she did it all by herself and made it look easy.

After Wallis and Simpson returned from their honeymoon they
found Simpson's flat at No. 12 Upper Berkeley Street too small,
and moved to a large apartment at No. 5 Bryanston Court,
Bryanston Square, Mayfair. At first Mrs Simpson was happy to
live fairly quietly, with an occasional theatre and night-club and,
for the rest of the time, evenings at home with her husband, who
loved to read histories and books about old ships.

There is no doubt that Wallis and Simpson were genuinely
fond of each other and remained so until the end.

Wallis soon began to meet people. Several secretaries in the
Argentine Embassy in London turned out to be old friends from
her Washington days, and Wallis and her husband were invited
to parties given by South American diplomats.

The English were less easy to know, and Wallis had bouts of
homesickness at first. She missed Washington, and she missed her
American friends. Within a year she found herself back in the
United States, though there was little consolation in the circumstances of the trip. Her mother was gravely ill.

Alys Montague Warfield Raisin Allen, at the age of fifty-one,
could not look back on a great deal of happiness. Two husbands
dead, the first little more than a boy, the second a gay blade after
two years of marriage. Mother and daughter had grown up more
like sisters. Wallis, taking the first train down to Washington
after landing, found that her mother had gone into a coma. She
died a week later. Sorrowfully Wallis returned to London.

As she emerged gradually from the shadows of mourning, she began to be surprised to see how many friends she had actually made. Through her Latin-American acquaintances she made new friends among the United States Embassy staff. Wallis was immediately popular among her fellow-Americans.

The time, the place, the atmosphere and the era were all becoming ripe for Mrs Simpson. If any one of these factors had been out of position in the London of the early 'thirties, history would have been startlingly different. The war had been over for more than a decade, but London was still tormented by a post-war lunacy. The old aristocracy had been eliminated, and into the vacuum they left behind poured the twittering society of bright young things. Royalty, isolated by the flood, could not remain aloof, and hardly tried. Instead it stepped down to join the fun. It was a period of social experiment and daring adventure. Such a situation had never existed in Britain before, and it exists no more. Ghosts alone remain of old days too garish to be remembered as either 'good' or 'bad': ghosts of night-clubs still standing but no longer peopled by dazzling celebrities; Mayfair mansions, the scene of unbelievable parties, now deserted or turned into offices; a few elderly ex-playboys still making the rounds, and out-of-date playwrights and novelists unable to make contact with the modern world; the dizzy Mayfair girls in hideous dresses, now transplanted in the austere masks of middle-age to New York or the more fashionable British colonial resorts.

In a society which valued the epigram as something of importance, Wallis Simpson, the expert, was in a position of advantage. It could never have been done in any other period, but times being what they were, Mrs Simpson shot like a rocket to the very top.

She began to entertain, and she immediately brought to that difficult art a flair that excited the society in which she moved. From the start her dinner-parties were original and provocative, spiced by many of Wallis's *bons mots* on the subject of cooking. 'Soup,' she said once, 'is an uninteresting liquid which gets you nowhere.' 'The idea,' she also said with her special talent for the calculated overstatement, 'that everything can be left to a good chef is one of life's most dangerous illusions.'

Wallis was true to her principles. In the kitchen as in the rest of the flat, Mrs Simpson was an efficient and busy mistress. Her cook, kitchen-maid, parlour-maid, chambermaid and part-time help were the first to come under the spell of eyes that never missed a speck of dust or a flower out of place. Always able to laugh at herself, Mrs Simpson has turned the sword on her own foibles. 'My doctor said he could fix me up if I'd stop moving ash-trays three inches,' she laughed. It was a genuine compliment to Mrs Simpson, however, that servants were prepared to take much more from her than they would from many other employers. Domestic servants are proud of their craft and they admire a perfectionist. Mrs Simpson was a super-perfectionist, and anything less than perfection infuriated her.

She introduced new ideas. Her Southern cooking is still re-membered, and she is believed by some to have started the now common habit of using a red handkerchief for her lipstick. These handkerchiefs she used to give to her women guests. The table in the dining-room at Bryanston Square was mirror-topped, and Wallis would entertain twelve to fourteen guests at one time, plying them with food and drink in an almost mathematical ratio designed to stimulate the best of their conversation.

She worked it out this way: two cocktails before dinner (a third would coarsen the palate). Food perfect but not too much (because that would make the guests heavy afterwards). As im-portant as the taste was the appearance. Mrs Simpson's food had to *look* attractive as well. 'Leave it to the chef and you can be sure everything he cooks will be the same colour,' she said. Then port or brandy as the guests wished. Every item had one object in view: talk, the best possible talk that could be arranged. 'I was always taught,' Mrs Simpson has told a reporter, 'that even a guest must carry his own weight. My mother taught me that you had an obligation in any gathering: to make other people happy if you could. As a guest or as a hostess, you must be sure that others have a chance to put their best foot forward.'

The food led to the conversation, and whenever the conversa-tion showed signs of flagging Mrs Simpson would drop a thumping polemic to startle the guests and start an argument. Thus were spent evenings in which the pace never slackened though it sometimes exhausted; in which the vitality of the hostess occasionally devitalised the guests; there were seldom any well-known people among the guests—just yet, anyway—but invariably they were parties to remember.

The qualities which made Wallis a good hostess made her an even better guest. She earned the undying gratitude of some of her friends by agreeing to come and help out when they had some especially turgid guests to entertain. Even the dullest guest could rarely maintain his gravity against Wallis's perpetual exhilaration and high spirits. Parties which seemed doomed from the start turned into triumphs when Mrs Simpson was there.

Ernest Simpson watched these *tours de force* bemused by his wife's genius. Like many others who knew something of Wallis's humble background, he asked himself where did she learn it all? Her schooling was only average, yet she chattered away in French so as to make one almost believe she was fluent at it. Never in her life until now had she had money to spare, yet her taste in clothes and in jewels was faultless; never too much nor too little of anything. Her cooking—both French and American—was a dream, and if she tasted a new dish in a restaurant she knew no rest until she had learned from the chef its secret. Her feeling for flowers was exquisite. Her love of music was profound and informed, so much so that on more than one occasion she rocked Sir Thomas Beecham on the subject when they met at parties. The volcanic maestro never felt he was talking down to a novice when he talked to Mrs Simpson, though nothing in her education or upbringing gave any clue as to where she acquired her knowledge.

Only in conversation did she tend to err by occasional indiscreet references to friends and acquaintances; but even that in the society in which she moved was little more than an occupational disease. She talked incessantly about everything, and people who first met her were impressed at the range of her interests. For conversation's sake Wallis developed the habit of reading all the newspaper headlines and skimming the latest books, but she was heard to better advantage if the conversation did not linger too long on the same subject.

In the course of her expanding relationships, Wallis became in time a particularly close friend of an American diplomat and his wife, Mr and Mrs Benjamin Thaw. Mrs Thaw was formerly Consuelo Morgan, and her sisters were the two much-publicised Morgan twins, Thelma and Gloria, who became respectively Lady Furness and Mrs Vanderbilt.

Via the Thaws, Mrs Simpson's name and her reputation as a party-giver reached the ear of the most important American in London, not the Ambassador, Charles Dawes, but the great Lady Cunard.

'Emerald' Cunard was famous for many things during her long reign in Mayfair—for her courage, her snobbishness, her personality, her eccentricity and her services to the arts. The musical soirées which she organised at her mansion at No. 7 Grosvenor Square were celebrated and awaited agog by the gossip writers on the London evening newspapers. She was a patron of music, a director of Covent Garden and an immortal in the passing world of London in the first half of this century. Her wealth was prodigious; among other sources of money, she possessed a fortune in shares in General Electric.

She was born Maude Alice Burke of California and New York. In 1895, when she was eighteen, she married Sir Bache Cunard, grandson of the founder of the Cunard Line. For the next fifty-three years she was to delight Londoners with her exploits. Disliking the name of Maude, she became Emerald to her friends —'because the name suits me'.

During World War II a balloon-barrage squad was stationed in Lady Cunard's back-garden, but Lady Cunard was gone. She escaped hastily to the United States when the war began, returning only when the blitz was over. She closed her bomb-damaged mansion, and moved to a suite at the Dorchester where, in 1948, at the age of seventy-one, she died.

Lady Cunard met Mrs Simpson at a party in 1930, and promptly invited her to one of her soirées. It was the highest pinnacle Mrs Simpson had reached in her steady social ascent, and people who were there that evening recall that Wallis's entrance was as impressive as might have been expected of her. In an assembly of guests dressed to kill and perfumed to obfuscate, Mrs Simpson was announced, and walked in with a beautiful carriage, wearing a simple black evening gown which she had made herself and no make-up whatever. The courage it took for an ambitious woman, far from pretty, to gamble on this effect of simplicity must have been great.

It worked. Wallis, with her personality and her engaging self-confidence, delighted Emerald Cunard. Wallis knew little about England or English affairs, but she did know human relationships, which are universal, and Lady Cunard's guests were as charmed with her as Lady Cunard was herself. Wallis and her husband found themselves invited regularly to Grosvenor Square.

Through this introduction she began to move into the society which made its headquarters at the Embassy Club in Old Bond Street. There are no equivalents today, either in London or anywhere else, to what this establishment used to represent.

It was made famous in the twenties by a restaurateur of genius called Luigi, and became the place where London's celebrities drew most of their sustenance and the gossip-columnists most of their news. Luigi died in 1930. Mrs Simpson made the Embassy Club her second home. She also became a familiar guest at the Kit-Kat, which had begun to rival the Embassy Club in the thirties but which was closed during the war.

One of the people she met through Consuelo Thaw and Lady Cunard was Lady Thelma Furness a friend of the Prince of Wales. Lady Furness married Lord Furness, the shipping magnate, in 1923. Later, in 1933, the marriage was dissolved. Much of an age and much of a temperament, Lady Furness and Mrs Simpson soon became close friends.

It all happened accidentally. Her circle of friends, though not really large, was now pretty choice, and comprised what was referred to as 'The Prince of Wales's Set'. Most of their conversation revolved round the Prince's almost legendary figure, and Wallis who had never met him would listen fascinated.

*   *   *

Thirty miles up the Thames from Westminster, the object of so much admiration and gossip ruled his 'court' from a romantic mansion near the river—Fort Belvedere. The Prince of Wales was a small, boyish man of thirty-six, with hair the colour of straw and an innocent face animated by sparkling blue eyes and a quick shy smile. He was eager in spirit, emotional, sincere, erratic, idealistic. For ex-servicemen and the unemployed he had a love and compassion the depth of which they could sense and return. And side by side with many princely qualities he had a disarming naïveté, enjoying electrical gadgets, jazz, the splash of a pebble tossed in a still pool. He had an unabashed admiration for America and the easy, monosyllabic give-and-take of Americans.

He had just returned from the Argentine, where he had graced a successful British trade mission. He was idolised in South America. He was adored in North America, in England, Wales and Scotland. Possibly no other personality of the twentieth century was so universally loved. The richest and the most desirable women in Europe jostled for his selection as the future Queen of England.

But there were flaws, almost invisible as yet, in the picture. Something in his personality sent out a wave that was almost like a cold shiver. The image of his father disturbed his rest. Old King George V, grey and ailing, could sometimes be laughed away as old-fashioned and strait-laced by the Prince of Wales's friends, but he could never be minimised or his immense stature as a king and a symbol be diminished.

The King bore heavily on the Prince of Wales, much more heavily than he did on any of his other sons, and he dominated a large part of the Prince's consciousness.

Probably in an effort to find a correct perspective for himself as well as to amuse others, the young Prince used to delight his English and American friends with streams of stories about his father, all the stories having one point in common: they showed the King in a warm light and in larger-than-life size.

Even at this time some of the Prince's selections as friends were disturbing the King, and the Prince told guests how he was driving home from Ascot with his father in the family Daimler.

'I saw you talking to some pretty disreputable people this afternoon, my boy,' the King said reprovingly. 'But, Father,' the Prince laughed, 'I distinctly saw you talking to a young person who has just been divorced.' 'I know,' the King replied thoughtfully, 'but she was such a damned pretty woman.'

The father obsession stayed with the Prince to the end of the old man's life. The Prince knew that one day he would have to take King George's place, and sometimes the future seemed to overwhelm him. Once, after a game of polo at Rugby, he threw down his helmet and burst out to his aides: 'Oh God! I dread my father dying! I dread the thought of being King!'

Soothsayers felt the waves he generated as he passed. The Hon. Ralph Shirley, a well-known occultist of the first two decades of this century, predicted as long ago as 1903 that Edward VIII would never come to the throne, or that if he did he would be rapidly succeeded by the Duke of York. This prophecy was actually printed in a periodical of the time called *The Horoscope*.

Cheiro, the famous clairvoyant and palmist, who had a vogue in London before World War I (his real name was Count Louis Hamon, and he died in New York in 1936, aged seventy) wrote this in his *World Predictions* in 1931:

'It is well within the range of possibility, owing to the peculiar planetary influences to which he is subjected, that the Prince will give up everything, even the chance of being crowned, rather than lose the object of his affections.'

Now, in the early 'thirties, King George V, a few senior servants of the State, and the Prince of Wales himself could feel the undercurrent of foreboding. But for the rest of the world the Prince's future seemed to shine with a blinding light.

The Prince's circle of friends was largely American or Anglo-American, and included the Thaws, Lady Cunard and Lady Furness. There was also Lady Honor Guinness and her husband Henry Channon, an American who took British citizenship and later sat as a Conservative in the House of Commons. Among his English intimates were Lord and Lady Louis Mountbatten, Mrs Frieda Dudley Ward, and Duff Cooper, married to the beautiful

Lorgnette-de-luxe.
At a fancy dress party in New York.

The Nahlin.
"We have come from nowhere. We are going nowhere!"

Lady Diana Manners, all gay company, and some with first-class minds.

It was through Lady Furness that the Simpsons first became good friends of the Prince though she was not responsible for the first meeting. That came about in the following way:

The Prince, one day, was entertaining Benjamin and Consuelo Thaw at The Fort. As they were leaving, he asked them to come back to dinner. Regretfully Thaw was obliged to decline because, he explained, he and his wife had a date that evening to meet Mr and Mrs Ernest Simpson.

'Bring them along,' said the Prince.

That afternoon he went to Sunningdale to have nine holes of golf with an equerry. The equerry, at the end, suggested another nine, but the Prince declined.

'I can't,' he said, 'I've got some people I've never met coming to dinner. An American couple called Simpson.'

CHAPTER V

The Prince Falls in Love

THIS account of the first meeting of Mrs Simpson and the
Prince of Wales differs from that described in the Duke of
Windsor's Memoirs. In his book the Duke tells the story in this
way:

'It was during the winter after my return from South America
in 1931. I had gone to Melton Mowbray with my brother George
for a week-end's hunting. Mr and Mrs Simpson were guests in
the same house. . . . Mrs Simpson did not ride and obviously had
no interest in horses, hounds or hunting in general. She was also
plainly in misery from a cold in the head. Since a Prince is by
custom expected to take the lead in conversing with strangers, and
having been informed that she was an American, I was prompted
to observe that she must miss central heating. . . . A mocking
look came into her eyes. "I am sorry, Sir," she said, "but you
have disappointed me."

' "In what way?"

' "Every American woman who comes to your country is
always asked the same question. I had hoped for something more
original from the Prince of Wales." I moved away . . . but . . . the
passage lingered. . . .'

The story which the Duchess herself has told to some of her
most intimate friends arises from the invitation which the Prince
of Wales extended to the Simpsons to come to Fort Belvedere.

The Thaws brought the Simpsons along. Lady Furness was
there, and introductions were made to the Prince and the few
other guests present. After that there were cocktails and a dinner
totally lacking in imagination.

The dinner over, some of the guests settled down to a game of
bridge, while the Prince and Thelma Lady Furness busied them-

selves with petit-point, which was one of the Prince's hobbies. The evening dragged on, with even Wallis's vivacity hardly proof against the insufferable dullness. Finally she rose to her feet and said in effect:

'What kind of a party is this?'

There was a fascinated silence.

'Well,' Mrs Simpson persisted, 'can't we dance or something?'

'A very good idea,' said the Prince of Wales. He put down his needle and rang the bell.

Immediately footmen entered. Some bore away the bridge tables. Others rolled back the carpets. The guests, in the sudden release of tension, rummaged happily among the Prince's large collection of low-brow gramophone records, and the dancing began. It continued far into the night. It was not the first time that Mrs Simpson had saved a party from death, but this was a party that changed her fortune.

Whether this version of the first meeting with the Duke is correct is not really important, though the Duke admits to some confusion by saying 'not long after our first meeting at Melton Mowbray we were at a party in London and I am supposed to have asked my hostess, "Haven't I met that lady before?".'

It was Lady Furness who made the suggestion which would once have seemed beyond the dreams of even the ambitious girl from Baltimore. 'You should be presented at Court.'

At first Mrs Simpson laughed away the idea, but it quickly caught hold of her. She thought it over, and put to Lady Furness her two difficulties, one of them a small one, the other possibly insurmountable. For one thing, she said, she hadn't anything suitable to wear, and she balked at buying a gown to wear once and never again. For another, it would be difficult for her to be presented at Buckingham Palace because she had divorced her husband. Thelma Furness said that she could borrow a gown; it was pointed out to Wallis that guiltless parties in divorce were frequently presented at Court. So she agreed, and the American Ambassador agreed to put Mrs Simpson's name down on the United States list for presentation to King George V and Queen Mary on June 10th, 1931.

Lady Furness lent her a train, and the three white plumes, traditional symbol of the Prince of Wales, which every woman had to wear when she was presented at Court. Wallis acquired a dress and wore at her breast an aquamarine crucifix.

It was as impressive an occasion as Court presentations always are, the King in Court dress sitting solidly on his throne, Queen Mary by his side, under the great Durbar Canopy which they had brought back from India. The scarlet and gold ballroom was brilliant with banked flowers. While a Guards band in the background softly played the latest popular melodies, scores of guests from every corner of the Empire stood around to watch or lined up for their turn to be presented. Behind the throne stood the royal Princes each in Court dress scintillating with Orders, the Prince of Wales, Prince George, the Duke of Gloucester, each on the look-out for his particular friends. With them were the Princess Royal, and the Duke of Connaught, exceedingly old but still appreciative of a pretty face and shoulder.

A number of people were presented, though the list now looks rather undistinguished. Only two people still prominent today are easily traceable—one Mrs Ernest Simpson, the other Mrs Ernest 'Buffie' Ives, sister of Mr Adlai Stevenson, unsuccessful Democratic candidate for President in the 1952 American elections.

The Prince certainly noticed Mrs Simpson, because he is recalled as acknowledging an approving chortle on the part of the Duke of Connaught by telling him who she was and commenting on her grace.

It was the second presentation of Mrs Simpson's life, the first at the Lyric Theatre, Baltimore, Maryland, U.S.A., the second at Buckingham Palace. Her old free-and-easy boy friends in Maryland would have been surprised if they could have seen this smart woman, completely self-possessed, make her deep, reverent curtsies to the King and Queen, they with gracious inclinations of the head responding to the woman who was to lead their son away from his royal duties and shake the strongest monarchy on earth to its foundations.

'I wouldn't have missed it for the world,' she said excitedly that night when Thelma Furness gave a party at her home to celebrate the occasion. And there she met the Prince of Wales again, who complimented her on her appearance. Already the Prince was finding Mrs Simpson pleasing, although some time was yet to pass before he looked on her with the eyes of love.

By 1933, however, he was beginning to grace the Simpsons' table at Bryanston Court. One society gossip columnist, who was present once or twice, wrote 'it was noticed for the first time how solicitous the Prince of Wales was of her every need, be it a match, a coat she might have wanted to take off, or some refreshment.'

In September 1934 the Prince invited Mrs Simpson on a yachting holiday on the Riviera, and the first record of the Prince's new love crept into the American press, *Time* magazine reporting:

'Such fun was Edward of Wales having at Cannes last week with beauteous Mrs Wallace Wakefield [*sic*] Simpson, that he sent back to Marseilles an airplane he had ordered to take him to Paris.'

The Prince was at a farewell party given for Wallis before she set out on her first visit to the United States since the death of her mother. While in America she saw Mary Kirk Raffray again; she travelled down to Washington to stay with Aunt Bessie, then she attended the Maryland Hunt Cup in Baltimore. Several old friends recognised her, and at least one ex-beau greeted her with an excited 'Hi, Wally! What have you been doing all these years?' Mrs Simpson smiled slantingly, replied cordially, but generally kept to herself and her family.

In 1934 a whole series of events combined to bring Wallis and the Prince of Wales together. Lady Cunard, who could look deeper into men's souls than most other people, saw what was going to happen before either the Prince or Mrs Simpson realised it. Whenever she invited the Prince to dinner, Mrs Simpson and her husband would also be among the guests, and Wallis would be seated close to the Prince. They were amusing dinners, no other salon being more conducive to conversation and romance, with the soft colourings of the walls and carpets, and candlelight everywhere flickering on Emerald Cunard's charming collection of pale Marie Laurencin paintings.

Then Thelma Furness's sister, Gloria Vanderbilt, in October 1934, became involved in one of the celebrated court cases of the decade, one which became known in time as the 'poor-little-rich-girl' case. Gloria had been feuding for some years with her mother, Mrs Laura Morgan, and her aunt, Mrs Harry Payne Whitney. One night, Mrs Whitney spirited away Mrs Vanderbilt's ten-year-old daughter, Gloria, heiress to a fortune worth millions of pounds.

Mrs Vanderbilt sued for her return, lost the case and, with it, custody of her daughter.

Hearing a call for help from Gloria's mother, Thelma Furness and her sister, Consuelo Thaw, immediately made reservations back to New York so that they could appear in support of their sister.

A few days before she left, Thelma and Wallis lunched together at the Ritz. Mrs Simpson commented that the Prince was going to be lonely.

'Well,' said Lady Furness, 'be sure you look after him for me while I am away.'

'Of course I will, darling,' said Mrs Simpson.

And, as Lady Furness was to comment with rueful frankness in later years, 'she did'.

        *   *   *

That was how it happened. Mrs Simpson was now the closest friend of the golden-boy Prince. But if luck had helped to carry Mrs Simpson to her new position of royal favour, her abilities alone would have to keep her there above all those beautiful gentlewomen of Europe, bristling with aristocratic connections, pulsating with blue blood, determined to trample with their dainty little feet all over her.

The Prince of Wales, probably for the first time in his life, was now really happy. He enjoyed the company not only of Mrs Simpson but of Ernest Simpson too. In fact, for a while the two were close friends. They found a lot in common, swapped stories of their experiences in World War I, and discussed fascinating matters like ships, economics, flowers, trees.

For a while a pleasing and not too emotional relationship existed. Several week-ends in a row were spent by the three together at Fort Belvedere. Simpson and the Prince would put on heavy boots and tramp round the estate, attending to the rhododendrons and chopping down any occasional tree that displeased their fancy.

Not sharing their enthusiasm for the raw English out-of-doors, Mrs Simpson would stay at The Fort assisting the chef and the servants, and lunches and dinners were often spent together by the Prince, the Simpsons and two or three other guests, all warmed by fine Scotch and water. After all his wanderings, the Prince was at last enjoying having a home of his own.

The friendship between Ernest Simpson and the Prince of Wales was genuine enough. Unfortunately for Simpson, before the year 1934 was out the Prince of Wales was hopelessly in love with Mrs Simpson. It was now Wallis's turn to feel the weight of a force over which she had no control—the Hanoverian capacity for intense love, the kind of love that Queen Victoria had for Prince Albert. Once Mrs Simpson set the love alight, she couldn't extinguish it even if she had wanted to, and all the King's Ministers and all the King's bishops couldn't extinguish it either.

The Prince's London friends were baffled. To worldly men, conscious of all the beauties surrounding the Prince, his love for a happily married, mature American woman was incomprehensible. Prince Christopher of Greece, turning up in London in November 1934 for the wedding of his niece, Marina, to Prince George, later the Duke of Kent, was seized at a party by the Prince of Wales, who said, 'Christo, I want you to meet Mrs Simpson.'

Christopher asked, 'Who's she?'

'An American. . . . She's wonderful.'

Christopher noticed how heedlessly the Prince pushed through the other women at the party. He was introduced to Mrs Simpson and when the crisis broke he explored his mind and recalled 'a pleasing but not beautiful woman who never stopped talking'.

Sir Samuel Hoare also met her, and later remembered 'not only her sparkling talk but also her sparkling jewels in very up-to-date settings . . . very American with little or no knowledge of English life'.

In February 1935, the Prince went to the little Austrian resort of Kitzbühel. Mrs Simpson was in the party frolicking with the Prince in the Alpine snows, but Mr Simpson was not. From there the royal party, which numbered a dozen people altogether, visited Vienna and Budapest. Aunt Bessie Buchanan Merryman acted as chaperon, and Mrs Simpson behaved so unobtrusively that there were few opportunities for serious gossip. She was always in the background, and never intruded when officials paid their respects to the Prince. Indeed, to the outside world she appeared less intimate with him than several other people in the party. Only on occasional evenings were they able to relax. Freed for a few hours from official protocol, they escaped to the night-clubs of Budapest, and danced gipsy czardas, some observers recalling the brilliant which sparkled in Mrs Simpson's hair.

Mrs Simpson slowly became a power in the land, a subtle and unobtrusive power, not so much concerned with influencing domestic or international policies, of which she knew little and cared less, but important because of the happiness which her presence gave the Prince of Wales.

As such she inevitably became an object of interest to men whose job it was to get acquainted with the people behind the throne. International agents are tough fellows who work and do not play at power.

To one group of people more than most others, unusual happenings in high places had an acute attraction. This was the ruling clique of Nazi Germany. The Prince of Wales was very popular in Germany, and it must have seemed to the Nazis that Mrs Simpson was a person to cultivate in order to advance their own interests. The man who came to try to perform the cultivation was Joachim von Ribbentrop, German Ambassador Extraordinary, later German Ambassador in London, later Foreign Secretary of Germany, later hanged.

Visiting England, Ribbentrop persuaded the German Ambassador, Dr Leopold von Hoesch, to effect an introduction. Von Hoesch organised a dinner at which the Prince of Wales and Mrs Simpson were invited. Ribbentrop was seated next to Mrs Simpson, and pulled out all the stops of his not inconsiderable charm.

Mrs Simpson might or might not have been pleased by Ribbentrop's attentions. She was now living in a world of which she could hardly have dreamed. She was courted and wooed by statesmen, flattered by English noblemen who laughed hard at her mildest epigram. If some of her friendships were later to turn out catastrophically, it had to be emphasised that Baltimore had not trained her for such an existence.

As for Ernest Simpson, he liked the Prince of Wales and revered his position as the future King of England. He did not realise how deeply the Prince was in love with his wife, but the Prince's friendship for Wallis was beyond his comprehension. He could find no weapons in the reserves of his simple philosophy to combat it. Neither indignation, fury, amusement, acquiescence nor sorrow would seem to fit the realities of the situation.

Mr and Mrs Simpson were present at one of the most dramatic scenes of the century, the scene at Friary Court, St. James's Palace, when the Prince of Wales was proclaimed King. The date was January 22nd, 1936. King George V, his last months clouded with anxiety over his son's impossible love affair, was dead.

George had ascended to the throne on May 6th, 1910, and his task had been a severe one. 'An unwritten constitution (such as Britain's),' wrote Harold Nicolson, his biographer, 'although possessing all the merits of elasticity and although hampered by none of the defects of rigidity, inevitably contains some zones of uncertainty. When the ship of state enters these uncharted waters, then the most impartial authorities begin to differ on what the correct constitutional procedure really is. King George . . . was often driven by the winds and tides of events into these zones of uncertainty, and was obliged to determine with little more than the stars to guide him, which was the true constitutional course to pursue.' King George brought to his job a gift for conciliation, straightforwardness and an ability to see the truth through the veils that separated him from the rest of his people. In the quarter of a century during which he reigned, the world witnessed the disappearance of five emperors, eight kings and eighteen minor dynasties. Despite the convulsions of war and foreign revolutions, the British monarchy, to which Edward VIII ascended, was more firmly established than ever.

Four proclamations were heard in London of the accession of the new King; one by the Garter King-of-Arms at St James's Palace, and by Heralds at Charing Cross, Temple Bar and the Royal Exchange. The King had invited a few close friends to the Palace to witness the ceremony, and the Simpsons were among them.

Four state trumpeters in gold-laced tabards paraded on the balcony of St James's Palace, followed by the Serjeants-at-Arms carrying Maces. In the courtyard were guardsmen and bandsmen with their drums muffled in black crêpe. Cued by a fanfare of trumpets, the Garter King-of-Arms stepped forward and raised a huge scroll. On either side of him stood other Kings-of-Arms, Heralds and Heraldic Pursuivants, with cockaded hats of gold and silver. The proclamation was intoned sonorously.

It was the stuff of centuries. The ceremony over, Mrs Simpson brought the matter back to the twentieth century and to earth. 'Very moving,' she said to the new King, 'but it has already made me realise how different your life is going to be.'

Mrs Simpson was not the only person to keep her feet on the ground amid the uplifting pageantry. In his offices at No. 10 Downing Street, Stanley Baldwin, the Prime Minister of England, had before him a complete dossier on the life of Mrs Simpson, which he read with increasing gloom. He knew that a major crisis might be on the way, and so did other people. Dr Cosmo Lang, the Archbishop of Canterbury, had a good idea of what was going on. The various press lords knew it, too. Baldwin and Edward VIII had disliked each other intensely ever since 1927, when they had been obliged to cross Canada together. Their personalities were mutually antagonistic and the trip was a trial to both of them. Baldwin was obliged by convention to hide so far as he could his real feelings when he was in the presence of the

Prince of Wales, and Edward was misled to some extent by the Prime Minister's avuncular manner. Had he known just how profoundly Baldwin detested him, he would have been both startled and at the same time better prepared for the events to come.

Long before the old King died, when Baldwin first heard of Edward's love for Mrs Simpson, he had made a significant comment. He had been discussing with Opposition leaders the future of the monarchy, and he said meaningly, 'The Yorks will do it very well'; referring to the Duke and Duchess of York who were next in line to the throne after the Prince of Wales.

At the Accession Council where the new King was presented to Princes of the Blood Royal, present and former Cabinet Ministers, Privy Councillors and others, Baldwin was plainly unhappy. He muttered to Clement Attlee his grave doubts about the future, and doubted whether the new King 'would stay the course'.

Stanley Baldwin was nearly seventy. He was popular in the country, the astutest politician alive, with an unerring sense of timing. He enjoyed being considered the physical embodiment of John Bull, professed to dislike politicians, and liked to imagine himself as a simple countryman, although in fact he hardly knew one tree from another. This artifice produced in his attitude to events a sort of double focus—one public, one private. His public attitude was bluff, honest, forthright. His private attitude was distrustful. His private aims were often good, sometimes not so good, and in order to achieve them he did not hesitate to deceive the public, deceive his friends, deceive everybody, in fact, except himself. To his Cabinet Ministers and in time to the public, he became the man determined officially to do all in his power to help the King solve his personal crisis 'even if we have to see the night through together'. But when the crisis broke, friends of his who could see behind the mask realised that his private aim was exactly and diametrically the reverse. He was determined to remove Edward and install his favourites, the Yorks, in his place.

In the privacy of Fort Belvedere the King and Wallis were making plans of their own, plans that looked ahead to one glorious moment when the crown of the Queen of England would be

placed upon Mrs Simpson's head. It must have seemed that the
philosophy of the song of François Villon which had sustained
them through eighteen enraptured months of love had at last
come true.

> *If I were King, ah love, if I were King*
> *What tributary nations I would bring,*
> *To stoop before your sceptre and to swear*
> *Allegiance to your eyes, your lips, your hair.*
> *The stars would be your pearls upon a string,*
> *The world a ruby for your finger-ring,*
> *And you should have the sun and moon to wear*
> *If I were King.*

But the King was an amateur at political intrigue. He had been
the idolised Prince too long, and it was the only existence he
knew how to fill. But did not Mrs Simpson suspect? She was a
creature of the earth and the world, and knew its yielding swamps
as well as its ivory towers. Did not the nostrils quiver, the scalp
tingle, in the heavy atmosphere of menace?

Apparently not. The lovers walked hand in hand through the
gardens of Fort Belvedere made silent by the leafy autumn
carpets of yellow and rust and gold. There was danger in every
step, danger in the air and in the waving branches of the trees.
But they sensed—nothing.

CHAPTER VI

Mrs Simpson's Short but Memorable Reign

'MRS Simpson's invitations came to rank as commands. . . . Her position in London is without precedent for an American. Nor have those who politically preceded her been remotely like her.'

Janet Flanner of the *New Yorker* thus caught up the mystery of this hush-hush love affair when, with a remarkable piece of literary virtuosity, she managed to tell the story of Mrs Simpson's relationship with the King without mentioning either the King or the relationship.

It described Wallis in the full bloom of her success. From the Baltimore boarding-house on East Biddle Street she had now risen to the point where her foot was on the first step of the British throne. The question being asked by politicians, courtiers, foreign ambassadors was—what next?

The King had become two persons, one person when the enigmatic figure of Mrs Simpson was at his side, and another person altogether when she was gone. Edward, at his desk, was difficult to handle by his Ministers. He antagonised especially his private secretary Major Alex Hardinge, the most unbending of all his counsellors. Another private secretary, Lord Wigram, resigned on account of the King's uncertain temper and habits. Only in her presence was he happy.

After the manner of lovers, his ways matched hers. He watched her happily as she laughed, joked, talked, spreading her strong expressive hands in acute, sharply defined gestures. Then the King would be restored to his old ebullient self. Caught in a downpour he was overheard to shout, 'Come on, Wallis, let's dodge the raindrops', and he sprinted for his Daimler, dragging along the protesting Mrs Simpson.

In private they made their plans. The object was clear, definite and admittedly remote. It was to establish Mrs Simpson as Queen of England. No compromise was contemplated. It would be done gradually, treading carefully, a step at a time, winning bit by bit the favour of the country, the Empire, the Church, Queen Mary and Parliament. The difficulties in the way were great, but the King held the one trump card. He was the King and a Coronation was coming up; England would never get rid of her King.

The first step was to make Mrs Simpson socially acceptable. To do that he invited her and her husband to a dinner party at St James's Palace, and on May 27th, 1936, Mrs Simpson's name was dignified for the first time in the Court Circular. The guests were an unusual combination. They included Lord and Lady Louis Mountbatten and Lady Cunard, friends and courtiers of the King and Mrs Simpson; Mr and Mrs Stanley Baldwin; Colonel Charles Lindberg, with his wife, just back from an eye-opening tour of Germany, and even now warning British officials that England could never stand up to Germany's air might.

The King had not told the Baldwins that Mrs Simpson was coming. The idea was to break the barrier between Mrs Simpson and Baldwin. It failed. They could find nothing in common, and Baldwin's dislike of the King was too deep to be bridged at a dinner party.

The King persisted. On July 9th Mrs Simpson's name appeared in the Court Circular again, very modestly and this time alone. It was the occasion of another dinner party, and a more formal one than the first. The Circular read:

'The King gave a dinner party at York House this evening, at which the Duke and Duchess of York were present. The following had the honour of being invited:

'The Marquess and Marchioness of Willingdon, the Lady Diana Cooper, the Earl and Countess Stanhope, the Countess of Oxford and Asquith, Major the Hon. Alexander and Mrs Hardinge, the Right Hon. Winston Spencer-Churchill, M.P., and Mrs Spencer-Churchill, the Right Hon. Sir Samuel Hoare, Bt., M.P., and the Lady Maude Hoare, the Right Hon. Sir

Philip Sassoon, Bt., M.P., Captain the Right Hon. David Margesson, M.P., Sir Edward and Lady Peacock, Lady Colefax and Mrs Ernest Simpson.'

Ernest Simpson was absent. Twelve days later on July 28th, the eighth anniversary of their marriage, he went to the Hotel de Paris in the village of Bray, near Maidenhead, according to subsequent court evidence, and spent the night there with a lady named Buttercup.

The parties took Mrs Simpson no further than she had already come, but still the initiative rested with the King.

Baldwin understood the importance of the King's affair, but he was a man who hated to make decisions before he had to, and not for the first or last time in his career decided to do nothing. He took the train to Aix, where he went religiously every year, and settled down to a happy holiday, taking the waters.

The King decided to take a holiday, too, and it proved to be an eventful one. The traditional royal vacations enjoyed by his father at Balmoral had little attraction for him, and he chose, instead, the Mediterranean. Originally he had planned to stay on the Riviera at the home of the American actress, Maxine Elliott, but France was being torn by strikes and the British Ambassador in Paris advised against it.

The King then decided on a cruise, but instead of using the royal yacht, the *Victoria and Albert*, he acquired the use of the *Nahlin*, a luxury yacht owned by Lady Yule. It was semi-officially explained that the 4,700-ton *Victoria and Albert* could not negotiate the shallower waters of the Mediterranean as well as the 1,600-ton *Nahlin*; all the same, a lot of eyebrows, those sensitive arcs of public opinion, were raised at this latest decision of the modern-minded King. Many felt that Edward was once more turning his back ostentatiously on the set ways of his father. The *Victoria and Albert* was slow and old-fashioned. The *Nahlin* was the last word in luxury yachts. John Brown of Glasgow, makers of the 'Queens', had built the ship six years before at a cost of £240,000. It had a gymnasium, a dance-floor, a bathroom for each of its eight staterooms. It could do more than twenty knots.

This went part of the way to explaining the King's preference, but the *Nahlin* had another advantage less widely known. Its fifty crew members had been particularly selected for their sense of discretion. Lady Yule, regarded until her death in 1950 as the richest woman in England, detested publicity, and she had a captain who once went so far as to tell an Australian reporter: 'We have come from nowhere. We are going nowhere.'

The cruise of the *Nahlin* was a milestone pointing in many directions. It marked the high point and the end of Mrs Simpson's social reign in London. It coincided with the final break-up in the marriage between Simpson and Wallis. It precipitated the crisis which from then on progressed non-stop to the Abdication.

Mrs Simpson was invited to join the party. Ernest Simpson—occasionally referred to inside the privileged circle as 'the unknown gentleman'—was not. The home in Bryanston Square was broken up, Simpson moving quietly into the Guards Club, and Mrs Simpson negotiating for some other place to live on her return.

The guests were the King's closest friends, in effect his social court. They included Dickie and Edwina Mountbatten; Duff Cooper and Lady Diana Cooper; Lord Brownlow, a Lord-in-Waiting and Lord-Lieutenant of Lincolnshire, and his wife Kitty; Sir John Aird, an equerry; Colonel Humphrey Butler, a handsome, well-known sportsman and his wife, the former Gwendolyn Van Raalte; Lady Cunard; Sir Godfrey Thomas, one of the King's assistant private secretaries; the Hon. Mrs Helen Fitzgerald, Canadian wife of Evelyn Fitzgerald, a London stockbroker; Herman and Katherine Rogers; and Mrs Gladys Buist, wife of Commander Colin Buist, R.N., an equerry, subsequently equerry to King George VI and extra equerry to Queen Elizabeth II.

When the crisis was over, this court was to be roasted in a broadcast by the Archbishop of Canterbury in terms so strong that one nobleman threatened him with a libel action. The Archbishop gave him a spoken apology, but refused to confirm it in writing and the matter was dropped. 'An exotic society' *The Times* was to call it. Actually, although the King, under the influence of Mrs Simpson, had largely broken with his father's

The " Hush-Hush holiday."
Publicity abroad . . . silence at home.

breach or non-performance of all
or any of the stipulations hereinbefore contained on the part of the Tenant then
the Landlord may re-enter and take possession without legal process and without prejudice to his   right to recover any sum which may be payable in
respect of rent gas electric light telephone charges and dilapidations (if any)
which may have accrued during the tenancy.

IT IS AGREED that the expenses of this Agreement and counterpart
shall be paid in moieties of Two Guineas each by the parties hereto together
with the stamp duty.

IT IS FURTHER AGREED that the Tenant shall retain the
services of the Landlord's Housemaid, Parlourmaid and Between-
maid paying their wages and insurances, so long as they faith-
fully fulfil their duties to the satisfaction of the Tenant.

IT IS LASTLY AGREED that the cupboard in the wall in the
Servants' Hall shall be retained by the Landlord and remain
locked during this tenancy.

AS WITNESS their hands on behalf of themselves, their heirs,
executors, administrators and permitted assigns.

SIGNED BY THE SAID   )
)
)
MRS. WALLIS SIMPSON   )   Wallis M. Simpson
)
)
In the presence of :-   )
)
        A. G. Allen,   )
           Johnson,   )
         3 French Row   )
              E.C.

An agreement made for the lease of 16 Cumberland Terrace.

intimates, his choice of friends was not very revolutionary. The subsequent wrath was directed mainly against Mrs Simpson herself, and Emerald Cunard, who was blamed by the Royal Family for doing most to bring the two together.

What probably damned this court above all was the simple secret that it shared. Everybody aboard the *Nahlin* knew that the King loved Mrs Simpson. They were aware of the delicacy of the situation, and must or ought to have foreseen the clouds of trouble piling up for them in England. But none could have guessed that within a few months the storm would blow both the King and Mrs Simpson out of England altogether, with a new King on the throne. For them this relationship clearly had some semblance of permanency, and some of them at least may have thought that in paying court to Mrs Simpson they were paying court to their future Queen.

On August 9th the King was flown by his pilot, Wing-Commander Edward (now Vice-Marshal Sir Edward) Fielden, from a private field in Middlesex to Calais. He travelled incognito, as the 'Duke of Lancaster'. This was an illuminating choice of names. The King's grandfather, Edward VII, almost always called himself the Duke of Lancaster when he was travelling incognito in Europe, and, indeed, became so celebrated for it that the very word 'Lancaster' was enough to open up every royal suite across the Continent. It was given out that the destination of the *Nahlin* might be the Baltic. But nobody was misled for a moment.

The King was seen entering the Orient Express. He was seen and photographed with Mrs Simpson at Salzburg. He was seen to leave the train at Sibenik in Yugoslavia. The press followed him everywhere. Most of the party went on board the *Nahlin* at Sibenik, the exceptions being Herman and Katherine Rogers, who joined it at Athens.

The cruise became the biggest holiday attraction in Europe. The sight of the *Nahlin* in port, no matter where, was the signal for hordes of sight-seers to cram the quays. The Europeans had heard much more than the British about Mrs Simpson, and were eager for a sight of her.

One man noted the excitement with a troubled mind. Sir

Samuel Hoare, First Lord of the Admiralty, was also on a Mediterranean tour in the naval yacht *Enchantress*, with the object of
inspecting British bases at Gibraltar and Malta. At one point the
Nahlin and the *Enchantress* passed. Hoare noticed the excitement
of his ship's crew, which had also been picked for its discretion,
and he realised for the first time that Englishmen as well as
foreigners were beginning to learn the truth. He reminded himself to tell the Prime Minister on his return to England.

Cheering crowds followed the royal party every time they
stepped ashore. In the brown fortress town of Trogir in Yugoslavia a horde of students swarmed round the King and Mrs
Simpson as they walked hand in hand through the narrow streets,
cheering them on their way. In Dubrovnik Mrs Simpson and
Lady Diana Cooper, venturing out on a shopping expedition,
saw crowds of people sweeping Edward away down the street
amid cheers of 'Long Live the King'. The breathless, laughing
Edward managed to exchange waves with the two ladies, but
could not stop. At quieter moments the King and Wallis were
able to bathe together off the Adriatic shore (and were filmed
doing so). They rowed together (and were filmed again). They
strolled through quiet villages, sometimes unrecognised.

From Yugoslavia to Greece; they were driven in style through
the streets of Athens, Mrs Simpson in the same car as the King.
One night they made rounds of the Athens night-clubs and danced
until 3 a.m.

The King also paid one or two duty calls. He had visited Prince
Paul in Yugoslavia. Now he visited General Metaxas and King
George of Greece. He inspected the Greek Navy. At the next
stop, Istanbul, he was greeted by Kemâl Atatürk. Then they left
the boat and set out across Europe by rail.

On the way back, the party stopped at Vienna, went to the
opera and saw *Gotterdammerung*, starring Kirsten Flagstad. The
King, bored, left the box at one point. Mrs Simpson went after
him, and brought him back in time for the final applause.

In the European press as well as the American press every
activity of the King and Mrs Simpson was reported in detail.
The British press remained silent, even the photographs of the

King's progress through the Mediterranean showing him almost invariably alone. Cabinet Ministers and Foreign Office officials remaining at home were aghast at the publicity the King's holiday had received. On September 14th, the King returned to England the subject of serious gossip. The rest of the party followed unobtrusively. Stanley Baldwin was still at Aix, and the atmosphere was like the last moments of silence before a great offensive.

Mrs Simpson went straight to London to organise her life in a new home. She had taken, on an eight-months' lease at £20 a week, a furnished, eight-roomed house at No. 16 Cumberland Terrace, Regent's Park. It was a charming place, designed by Nash during the reign of George IV and owned by Cuthbert Stewart, a London stockbroker, with a huge lounge decorated in Italian style and a drawing-room overlooking the park.

The charged air which Mrs Simpson now breathed was not the most conducive to sober reflection. The *Nahlin* cruise had been the greatest incident of her life so far. She had progressed up the ladder until she had come face to face with vistas at which ambition reeled, a cloudland of thrones, kings, princes, empires. Kemâl Atatürk in Turkey and Metaxas in Greece had treated her like a queen. It was what she heard over and over again from some of her intimate friends. One woman, in particular, the American wife of a diplomatic official, had kept pressing into her consciousness long before the *Nahlin* trip 'you can be Queen. You are bound to be Queen'. It seemed to be King Edward's ambition coming true. Mrs Simpson was no longer in command of herself.

*   *   *

The King, sensing the Whitehall chill, dined quietly with his mother. Queen Mary gave no sign she was conscious of the trouble in the air, though she obviously knew all there was to know.

There was a moment during the dinner when spirits were lifted. The King told his mother he intended to spend the last two weeks of September at Balmoral, and he saw at once how pleased she was. The Queen probably felt that even David could not get into trouble at Balmoral. If she did, she was quite wrong. At Balmoral the King got himself into very serious trouble indeed, and Mrs Simpson was again the cause of it.

Wallis could not accompany the King to Scotland. She had been kept in London to deal with the business of moving into a new house and completing arrangements for a divorce. The King had been at Balmoral for four restless days before she was able to join him. She travelled north by train with Herman and Katherine Rogers, and at Aberdeen station she met the King, who had driven himself from Balmoral to meet them. He smoked a pipe and was muffled, but hundreds of Aberdonians watched him as he helped Mrs Simpson to sit down in the front seat beside him, and the Rogers climbed in behind. Meanwhile, only a short distance away, the Duke and Duchess of York, 'on the King's behalf', opened some new buildings of the Royal Infirmary.

It was this which enraged Aberdeen. The newspapers remained tactfully silent, but anger at the King for apparently neglecting his duties in order to meet his friend was city wide and profound. This anger, instead of subsiding, grew until months later, long after the Abdication, the Provost of Aberdeen issued a corrective statement which did something, not much, to appease the citizens. 'Months before the opening date of the Infirmary,' the Provost said, 'I was in communication with the King through the Scottish Office and the reply I received was to the effect that owing to Court mourning the King had decided he could not perform any such ceremony as the opening of the Royal Infirmary . . .'

'At the same time he was so interested in the opening that he deputed the Duke and Duchess of York to act for him. . . . The fact that Mrs Simpson arrived in Aberdeen on the same day as the Duke and Duchess of York opened the building was a mere coincidence, and whatever may be said about the King's action in coming to Aberdeen on that day it in no way involved any breach of agreement.'

At Balmoral the King let the word fall that he intended to cut the domestic staff, and his popularity waned still further, the fond Scottish image of 'Bonnie Prince Edward' became even more dim. The King had other things to think about. His *Nahlin* friends had gathered round him for the last time. Mrs Simpson, the Mountbattens, the Rogers, Mrs Gladys Buist and her husband, were all there. So was the Duke of Kent and his beautiful wife. The Duke and Duchess of York were also there. Nobody ever learned what *they* thought about it.

The King put on the kilt and played the bagpipes. With Mrs Simpson he tramped the moors round the castle, and one can guess the endless discussions they had about tactics and strategy, how to handle Mrs Simpson's divorce which was to come up within a month, and how they were to present their position to the British people when the time came.

Taking advantage of a post-war regulation enabling people for the first time in undefended suits to obtain divorces outside London, Mrs Simpson, on the advice of her lawyers, had taken a small villa called Beech House, near Felixstowe. By establishing residence there, she could have her case heard quickly and quietly in the less-frenzied atmosphere of Ipswich. Or so she hoped.

By the end of the month when the royal party was due to return south, a plan of campaign had gradually been evolved. It was a hazardous plan, but if it succeeded it would end with the crowning of Mrs Simpson as Queen. Tense but confident, the King and Mrs Simpson left Balmoral to face the battle in London. King Edward VIII never saw Balmoral again.

Mrs Simpson was installed at Felixstowe. From Fort Belvedere and Buckingham Palace the King sent her supplies of pots, pans and household accessories. Mrs Mason, the King's personal house-keeper, was dispatched from Buckingham Palace to keep her comfortable, and David Storier, of Scotland Yard, the King's personal bodyguard, to keep her safe. He also sent her something special in the way of presents. It was a big, black, Canadian-built Buick, the last word in speed and luxury. Inside it he installed his chauffeur George Ladbrook. Mrs Simpson was now royally provided for, and what is more she was never out of the sight of the King's servants. With the divorce so imminent, they dared not see each other. Even the King, who recklessly ignored every-thing and everybody to be near her, realised that, and he fretted alone at the Fort, calling her several times a day for her much-needed counsel and for the sound of her voice. Mrs Simpson never let him down. She was always encouraging, never despondent.

Now the strain was very great. Baldwin, they knew, had cut short his holiday at Aix, an important act for a man so set in his ways. They knew he had done so strictly because of the crisis they had created, but they did not know what he intended to do next. The day after he arrived the King summoned him to Buckingham Palace. It was a curious, perhaps tragic, meeting. Both King and Prime Minister waited for the other to bring up the matter that was on both their minds. Each thought that it was the other's responsibility. As a result neither man said anything and they parted with the matter undiscussed, each more resentful of the other than before.

Already Edward was beginning to sag. He performed his royal duties erratically and without enthusiasm. On October 19th he invited friends—all male—for the partridge shooting at Sandringham. Sir Samuel Hoare was invited. Hoare, a silent witness on more than one of the King's activities, noticed how nervy the King was. On the first night of the four-day party, the blow fell.

The telephone rang at Beech House, and the King told Mrs Simpson the news. Baldwin had asked for an audience. Baldwin realised that he had to make the first move. The King had invited him to join the party at Sandringham, but Baldwin had asked to be allowed to decline the invitation on the grounds that it would be too conspicuous. This was obviously the opening of hostilities.

The King agreed to meet him quietly at Fort Belvedere the following morning. He rose shortly after dawn. The other guests were still sleeping when he went down to his car. He left word that the party should go on without him, and set out without security escort across the flat countryside of East Anglia.

It was St. Luke's Day and the weather was glorious. All morning Mrs Simpson waited at Felixstowe for news of the meeting. It was nearly midday before she heard the King's voice, and the report he gave her was encouraging. The King had drawn some optimistic conclusions from the first encounter. He did not know how widespread was the alliance against him already.

Baldwin had spent the week-end at the home of Lord Fitzalan. Among the guests had been Alex Hardinge and Lord Kemsley, the press lord. Together they had discussed the King's affair. In consequence, Baldwin arrived not only with the latest information, but conscious also that he had the support of the King's private secretary and of the newspaper proprietor most closely identified with the interests of the Royal Family.

From the beginning Baldwin left no doubt as to the reason for the interview. 'You remember, Sir,' he said directly, 'when we came from Folkestone together you said I might speak freely to you about everything. Does that hold good when there is a woman in the case?'

'Yes,' said the King.

Baldwin's manner became fatherly. He said he knew the King did not enjoy his royal duties. He did not mention marriage, but suggested that the King persuade Mrs Simpson not to continue with her divorce action in view of the criticism in the American press and its effect on the Monarchy both in Britain and the Empire.

Edward's manner became casual and light-hearted. 'Mr Baldwin,' he said, 'I have no right to interfere with the affairs of an individual. It would be wrong were I to attempt to influence Mrs Simpson just because she happens to be a friend of the King.'

The reply sounded a model of judiciousness, rather as though the King and Baldwin were discussing the problem of two other people. Neither was letting his feelings show, and both were deluded to some extent by the other's attitude. Baldwin was delighted with his own courage in forcing the matter out, and he thought the King had taken his point of view to heart. The King thought he could keep the matter personal and away from the public. It was an odd conclusion for a man who had spent a lifetime in the centre of the world spotlight.

The King and Mrs Simpson were now ready for the second crisis which they felt would probably come after the divorce hearing. Next time they would be tougher and force Baldwin into a corner. They would have been much less optimistic if they had known what Baldwin was really thinking. The Prime Minister understood his own difficulties better than the King and Mrs Simpson understood theirs. When he left the King, he went first to consult his close friend, Geoffrey Dawson, editor of *The Times*. Then he called on Queen Mary. The Queen Mother had moved from Buckingham Palace, and was assembling her antiques in the more intimate atmosphere of Marlborough House. 'Well, Mr Baldwin,' she is reported to have declared as he entered to discuss the matter with her, 'this is a pretty kettle of fish.' And in the course of the subsequent conversation Stanley Baldwin was left in no doubt that the Queen Mother was on his side all the way.

CHAPTER VII

A Window is Broken

H ARDLY a word had appeared in the British press about Mrs Simpson. Not a single word had discussed her love affair with the King. Yet fable was advancing faster than truth, and some kind of jungle rhythm was spreading her name across the nation. Mrs Simpson found this out personally and for the first time when she took the risk of leaving her refuge in Felixstowe to return to London.

Her divorce hearing was imminent, and she decided it was safe to go to Bond Street and have her hair done in preparation for the ordeal. It seemed to be a reasonable risk, but just in case of trouble she took Storier of the Yard along with her. Ladbrook drove them both to town in the Buick.

She was justified in taking the precaution. A group of news-papermen had been warned in advance of her arrival, probably by some contact or other inside the beauty parlour, and were waiting for her outside. Some pictures were taken, but Storier was able to hustle her indoors without too much trouble. That was the start. Crowds began to gather in Bond Street. The word travelled quickly and accurately, 'Mrs Simpson's inside!' The name and its significance was only vaguely understood by most people, but it was familiar in a disquieting way and they knew it had something to do with the King. A few in the crowd were wise. In reply to the inevitable, puzzled question of the uniniti-ated, they said, 'She's our next Queen.'

Soon hundreds of people were waiting in the street for a glimpse of the mystery woman. Inside the beauty parlour, Mrs Simpson became frightened and asked Storier what he intended to do. The detective found that there was a back exit, and when Mrs Simpson's appointment was over an hour and a half later, he sent word out to Ladbrook to take the car round. Ladbrook did and the crowd followed. Mrs Simpson, unaware that Storier's plan had failed, emerged and there was a buzz of excitement. Flustered and taken by surprise, Wallis got hastily into the car. She remembered that her bank was just round the corner and ordered the car there. She stayed in the safety of the manager's office until the people finally dispersed. Then she was driven back to Felixtowe.

This was the first of many adventures during two cloak-and-dagger months in the life of George Ladbrook, chauffeur of the King, usually a job which stifles even the most respectable of drivers with its decorum. Ladbrook was a forty-year-old, six-foot, 200-pound giant from Essex, and he held for the King a philosophical English loyalty which he was to demonstrate many times in the years to come.

On October 27th, a few days after the incident in Bond Street, he was given as tough an assignment by the King as any chauffeur, outside a Hollywood movie, could be expected to take on. He had to drive Mrs Simpson from Felixstowe to Ipswich for her divorce, and away from Ipswich afterwards, avoiding newspapermen and keeping her out of trouble.

Several days before the divorce hearing was due, newspapermen, most of them Americans, had been arriving in town, crowding the hotels, inns and boarding-houses. English reporters were arriving, too. Both were preoccupied with unique problems.

In America interest in the attachment of the British King for Mrs Simpson was insatiable and was reaching a climax with the divorce action. All of a sudden the Americans had become experts on British divorce procedure. They knew that the King would be free to marry Mrs Simpson before the Coronation, and were agog to see what would happen next. In Britain, on the other hand, the press lords, for the first and last time in modern newspaper history, agreed to suppress all news of the affair, hoping to stave off or avert a crisis too strange and rare for them to visualise clearly. They had done so because the King had appealed to some of them personally. 'Mrs Simpson is being pilloried,' he said, 'because she is my friend'; and he asked that they treat her divorce as they would treat the divorce of any other American woman. The press lords believed him. No other public figure in this age has been treated with so much sensitivity. Speculation all through 1955 on the love problems of Princess Margaret in the British as well as the American press presents the most vivid comparison.

The British newspapermen arriving in Ipswich were there largely as observers, a decorous role that made little appeal to them. The American foreign correspondents had problems all of their own, and felt little enthusiasm for the advantage they held over their British cousins. Foreign correspondents all over the world rely heavily on local newspapers for information. Without local newspapers they are often lost. In this case they were not getting any news at all out of the British newspapers, and were having to go out and work for the story as they had not done since they were ordinary reporters.

To Ipswich townspeople nothing could have been more mystifying than this harassed, sombre gathering of British and American newspapermen. For them it was a holiday. Once more the mental tom-toms were at work, and the town was jammed with people who seemed to know by instinct that Mrs Simpson was going to put in an appearance.

Policemen were everywhere, scrutinising everyone who tried to get into the court-house. For the first time in memory members of the Bar were denied free access to the court-room, and even the Mayor, himself an Ipswich magistrate, was held up until he identified himself.

Newsreel cameramen who tried to set up their equipment near the court were moved away. One newsreel group had hired a room overlooking the court, but the police heard about it and took the room over. Tickets were issued to thirty reporters. One New York newspaperman arriving at the last moment was unable to get a ticket. Shortly before two o'clock in the afternoon he clambered over an eight-foot wall into the court precincts. A policeman was waiting underneath for him as he came down.

Inside the court-room the public seats had been rearranged so that all those which faced the witness in the box were left vacant. Admission was made only to a few seats to which the witness's back was turned. The press seats had also been changed. Normally in British courts the press seats are set so that the reporters face the witness-box. The reporters permitted to enter the court-room now found that they, too, had been placed so that they could only see the witness's back.

Mrs Simpson was wise enough not to come from Felixstowe in her tell-tale Buick. Instead she hired a sober but fast English saloon car. On the road to Ipswich a photographer's car lying in wait, started in pursuit, but by the time it reached sixty-five miles an hour Ladbrook had left it miles behind. Outside the court-house as the car slowed into the garage a photographer broke the police barrier. A policeman smashed the camera out of his hand, and a police boot kicked it into the gutter.

The Judge, Sir John (Anthony) Hawke, arrived at 2.17. Hawke had served from 1923 to 1928 as Attorney-General to the Prince of Wales, but this was strictly coincidental. He had seen and had clearly been disgusted with the security precautions outside. And he did not know what was going on inside. The door of the counsels' robing-room was locked on lawyers engaged in other cases, preventing them from entering the court-room. A cold in the head did not improve Hawke's temper. The case of 'Simpson *versus* Simpson' was called, and Norman Birkett, K.C., on behalf of Mrs Simpson, rose to say:

'I appear in this case with my learned friend Mr Walter Frampton. I call the petitioner at once.' Mrs Simpson, looking pale but controlled, in a blue suit and a small, jaunty hat, went into the witness-box. A chair had been provided for her, although by the normal practice of the times a woman testifying in her own divorce case was usually required to stand.

In deference to the King's wishes, the British press next morning gave the case a minimum of space. The American press covered it in detail, and it is from American newspaper files that the writer gets his picture.

Mrs Simpson repeated the oath after the clerk, and Norman Birkett began questioning her smoothly and gently.

'Your names are Wallis Simpson? You are now living at Beech House, Felixstowe?'

'Yes.'

'Is your town address, 16 Cumberland Terrace, Regent's Park?'

'Yes.'

'You were married to Ernest Aldrich Simpson on July 28th, 1928, at the Register Office in the District of Chelsea?'

'Yes.'

'And I think that afterwards you lived with him at 12 Upper Berkeley Street and 5 Bryanston Court in London?'

'Yes.'

'Has there been any issue of that marriage?'

'No.'

'Did you live happily with the Respondent until the autumn of 1934?'

'Yes.'

'Was it at that time the Respondent's manner changed?'

'Yes.'

'What was the change?'

'He was indifferent, and often went away week-ends.'

'On Christmas Day, 1934, did you find a note lying on your dressing-table?'

'Yes.'

The note was produced and handed to the Judge. Mrs Simpson then said that shortly after Easter she received a letter in an envelope addressed to her although the contents appeared to be intended for her husband.

'Having read the letter,' Birkett continued, 'did you then consult your solicitor?'

'Yes.'

'Upon your instructions, did they keep observations on your husband?'

'Yes.'

'Did they report to you on the result of their observations?'

'Yes.'

'Did you subsequently receive information on which your petition in this present case is based?'

'Yes.'

Birkett then asked Mrs Simpson to read a letter which she had written to her husband. She read it quietly but clearly.

'Dear Ernest, I have just learned that while you have been away, instead of being on business as you led me to believe, you have been staying at a hotel at Bray with a lady. I am sure you must realise that this is conduct which I cannot possibly overlook and I must insist that you do not continue to live here with me. This only confirms suspicions which I have had for a long time. I am therefore instructing my solicitors to take proceedings for a divorce. Wallis.'

Evidence was produced from employees of the fashionable Hotel de Paris at Bray. They said they had brought morning tea to Simpson, and a woman who was not Mrs Simpson was with him in a double bed. There must be no provable collusion in an English divorce case and judges usually demand the name of the 'other woman'. As the evidence continued and reporters waited in vain for the name to be produced, the atmosphere in the court grew more tense. When Birkett finally asked the court to grant the decree nisi of divorce, it was realised that Birkett did not intend to introduce the name at all.

Sir John Hawke, his handkerchief over his streaming nose, had not bothered to hide his distaste for the whole proceeding, and had plainly indicated his belief that the case had been brought to Ipswich just to avoid publicity.

'Well,' said Hawke, 'I suppose I must come to the conclusion that there was adultery in this case.' There was a pause.

Mr Birkett: 'I assume what your Lordship has in mind.'

Mr Justice Hawke: 'How do you know what is in my mind? What is it that I have in my mind, Mr Birkett?'

Mr Birkett: 'I think with great deference that your Lordship may have in mind what is known as "ordinary hotel evidence" where the name of the lady is not disclosed. With respect, I thought that might have been in your Lordship's mind.'

Mr Justice Hawke: That is what it must have been, Mr Birkett. I am glad of your help.'

Mr Birkett: 'The lady's name, my Lord, was mentioned in the petition.[1] So now I ask for a decree nisi with costs against the Respondent.'

Mr Justice Hawke: 'Yes, costs against the Respondent, I am afraid. I suppose I must in these unusual circumstances. So you may have it with costs.'

Mr Birkett: 'Decree nisi, with costs?'

Mr Justice Hawke: 'Yes, I suppose so.'

It was over in exactly nineteen minutes. Mrs Simpson was escorted to her car. The newspapermen started to leave, but a second case was brought in so quickly that they had no time to get out of the court-room. The ushers stopped them and called loudly for silence. The reporters complained later that the doors had been locked until Mrs Simpson's car was gone. As soon as they were released, they made a dash for the crowded street, and then they discovered they had missed nothing.

Ladbrook had taken the car out of the courtyard and had set off for Felixstowe. Press cars started after him, but a police car swung across the road and blocked the route. Mrs Simpson's get-away was clean.

No investigation was ever made into the unprecedented and unnecessary precautions taken in the Simpson divorce case, precautions seriously at odds with the traditions of British freedom. Nor was it ever officially revealed who gave instructions to the police to be so tough with the reporters. Sir John Hawke was not a party to it, and no official agencies were at the King's command in his private love affair. Theodore Goddard, Mrs Simpson's solicitor, was probably the man most directly responsible.

In the end, the police achieved nothing except to establish a somewhat sinister precedent. The Americans were not prevented from reporting the case in full, the police measures merely giving them added colour material. The British press did not report the case in full, not because of the police but because of policy.

And even if policy had been different, the British press would have been inhibited in its reporting of the case by the Judicial Proceedings (Regulation of Reports) Act, 1926, which banned the publication of anything other than a bare skeleton of the case. In

[1] It was a Mrs E. H. Kennedy, known as 'Buttercup'.

other words, had the police taken no precautions at all the British reports of the Simpson divorce case would have been exactly the same, and the American reports would have been less lurid. All the incident did was to give a misleading veneer of force to the King's cause, and this veneer was recalled with anxiety by some, a few weeks afterwards, when Sir Oswald Mosley and his Blackshirts were demonstrating against Baldwin and in the King's favour in the East End.

Now the divorce was over, the person of Mrs Simpson paralysed the administration of the country. In Buckingham Palace Major Alexander Hardinge was reading a letter which had been shown to him by Geoffrey Dawson, summing up the state of opinion in America. Hardinge was horrified. He, more than any other of the King's advisers, was baffled by Mrs Simpson's personality. Had she been an Englishwoman he would have known how to handle her. But for Hardinge, above all, her 'Americanness' was an impossible barrier. He did not understand her thought processes nor the things she talked about. Hardinge was so worried by the information given him by Dawson that he spent a fortnight drafting a letter to the King, a letter which was to have vital consequences.

Mrs Simpson's shadow also darkened the cabinet room at No. 10 Downing Street. Stanley Baldwin was face to face with an urgent and critical situation. The result of the divorce meant that the King would be free to marry Mrs Simpson in six months' time, when her decree nisi became absolute. This would only be about two weeks before his Coronation scheduled for May 12th. Baldwin's predicament was made worse by the fact that no one could be quite certain of the King's rights. Nothing like this had ever happened before in England's history, and even the greatest experts on constitutional law could do no better than grope uncertainly through the legal darkness.

It was possible, then, that the King had it in his power any time after April 27th, 1937, to marry Mrs Simpson without consulting anybody, then return to Buckingham Palace and summon his Cabinet to meet the empire's new Queen. It was one thing for Baldwin to deal with a King standing pat, as he was doing at the

No. 16 Cumberland Terrace at the time Mrs. Simpson was
living there. The entrance hall.

present time on a technical situation that might never happen. It was quite another to deal with a *fait accompli*, a King already married and on the throne. The problem as it presented itself to Baldwin's mind, presupposed, of course, that the King, in order to marry the woman of his choice, would not hesitate to resort to any means in order to get Mrs Simpson accepted as Queen.

The Prime Minister's dilemma was a discouraging one. A man of whom he was uncertain was King. A constitutional crisis in such dangerous times was a terrible thought. Baldwin was an old man and the King was a young man. The England that he, with the King, directed was beset by potential enemies; new dictators as mettlesome as puppies now, but swelling rapidly into great beasts, prowled abroad. Unemployment, selfishness and moral weakness prostrated Britain at home. At a moment when stability at the top was vital, Baldwin found himself with an irrational King, drunk with love, on his hands.

And Baldwin had no reason to think that this was a problem capable of solution. He did not know what to do. The instability, for all he knew, would persist in one form or another throughout Edward's reign, a reign which would stretch many years beyond his lifetime. Baldwin loved his England with all the emotion he possessed. He revered the monarchy. If only the Yorks were on the throne. . . . It was a heavy burden for an old man to bear.

Wallis returned to London. She had no more use for the house in Felixstowe. She was slightly unnerved, and at the same time exhilarated. She was bewildered by the furore in Ipswich and staggered by the attention her affairs were receiving in America. She realised, possibly for the first time, that she was attracting more publicity than any other woman on earth. It was a position where the most hard-headed and logical of women would be carried away. She was forty years old and had never been a celebrity before, and it was all new and unbelievable. The effect on her was mixed. She was alternately flattered and frightened by it; pleased one moment, appalled the next. But all the time the crown and the throne hovered a measurable distance before her. It was a fairy-tale come true.

Now she was able to see the King again. She moved to Fort

Belvedere with Aunt Bessie, and the two lovers walked the gardens of the mansion, combining in their conversation visions of romance, ambition realised and a glorious future.

Meanwhile the letter which Major Alexander Hardinge was assembling was completed. It was sent on November 12th, and reminded the King that if the Cabinet submitted advice and the King rejected it, the Ministers must resign. He appealed to the King to send Mrs Simpson out of the country. Baldwin knew that Hardinge was writing the letter, and encouraged it. Before he submitted it Hardinge showed it for approval to Geoffrey Dawson, an unexpected act in this case for a man who is supposed to be the King's closest personal aide; at the same time a courageous act for an honourable man deeply disturbed.

Dawson was a character who was moving closer and closer into a picture which would seem to involve him only indirectly, as a journalist, if at all. He was a brilliant writer, and as editor of *The Times*, a newspaper over which the proprietor exercises no policy control, he was the most important journalist in Britain. In 1952, sixteen years after the Abdication, Dawson's part in the crisis was made the centre of a controversy by a sensational broadcast which Lord Beaverbrook made over B.B.C. television. Beaverbrook was reviewing the fourth volume of the *History of The Times*, and basing his conclusions exclusively on statements made in the appendix on the Abdication, asserted that, after Baldwin, Dawson was chiefly responsible for forcing the King to abdicate; that he did it 'by methods many would comdemn', and that 'he pursued his quest with a vigour that seemed more like venom'.

Beaverbrook described Dawson as 'a man of middle height with a good head going bald . . . and a rather flushed face. He liked to dine in important company.' Dawson was sixty-one. He was Conservative in outlook, discreet, untiring at his job and snobbish. He seldom spoke to Labour M.P.s. He felt himself under no obligation to be polite to servants, and he was cordial only to people whose company he liked. But the most important single fact about Dawson's character was that he lacked the courage of independence, and he was at his strongest when he attached himself to people whom he considered knew more than he. His first mentor had been Lord Milner, former British administrator in South Africa, who died in 1925. Later he attached himself to Lloyd George, and subsequently he was to become the devoted and adoring disciple of Lord Halifax. At the present time he was lavishing his loyalty on two men, Stanley Baldwin and the Archbishop of Canterbury.

This habit was not unusual, of course, or even necessarily undesirable, for a newspaper editor. Dawson's great predecessor on *The Times*, John Thadeus Delane, had been Lord Palmerston's protégé, and the friendship of important men has always been found invaluable to an editor. In the crisis coming up, however, Dawson's devotion to Baldwin became something more. The alliance between the Prime Minister and the editor of *The Times*, with the Archbishop of Canterbury lending his support in the background, gave the impression sometimes of an invulnerable force, against which the pop-guns of the mass-circulation news-papers popped in vain.

Whether or not Beaverbrook was justified in his attack, Dawson was the latest character to join the select group of personalities in this drama. To the talents of King Edward, Wallis Simpson, Stanley Baldwin, Lord Beaverbrook, Queen Mary, the Arch-bishop of Canterbury, he added his own gifts of clear-thinking and the ability to write history in daily journalism, failing to add what, amid all this brilliance, was possibly most needed and certainly most lacking—a sense of Christian charity.

Wallis disliked and feared Dawson above all. She had already read the innuendoes which he was inserting in *The Times* for her eyes and the King's eyes alone. To the still-ignorant public his references could have had little significance. One of his editorials, for example, appeared to deal with nothing more than the philosophy behind the appointment of a Governor-General to South Africa. But to Mrs Simpson and the King the warning could not have been plainer:

'It is the position—the position of the King's deputy no less than that of the King himself—that must be kept high above public ridicule, and it is incomparably more important than the individual who fills it. The King's deputy, like the King himself, should be invested with a certain detachment and dignity, which need not at all preclude his contact with all sorts and conditions of people, but which are not so easily put on as a change of clothes.'

Wallis and the King were furious about Hardinge's letter and guessed immediately that he had shown it to Baldwin or Dawson or both. The battle, they knew, was getting hotter, and the King sent for Baldwin.

He played his trump card and handed the Prime Minister an ultimatum. 'No marriage, no Coronation,' he said, and added, 'I am going to marry Mrs Simpson and I am prepared to go.' Did a gleam come into Baldwin's eye? Edward VIII saw nothing, and he had no means to divine a heart which beat faster.

Baldwin said he found this 'grievous news'.

Edward, of course, had no intention of going. He knew something about the fate of ex-kings. Some of his closest European relatives had been tumbled from their thrones, and he had witnessed the living purgatory of their lives in exile in the dreary round of the continental seaside resorts.

There could seldom have been a stranger contest than that now going on between Baldwin and the King. They were like two men with their backs to one another firing at each other over their shoulders. The King was pretending that he was willing to go, and was in fact determined to stay. Baldwin was pretending that he wanted the King to stay, and was now resolved to make him go. The King believed that by his ultimatum he had put himself in an unassailable position. The opposite was true. He had put himself at Baldwin's mercy. Edward's battle slogan was 'No marriage, no Coronation'. Baldwin's was 'The Yorks will do it very well'. The two statements, instead of clashing, dovetailed. Added together they meant that the King was on the way out.

Stanley Baldwin drove straight from Buckingham Palace to the House of Commons, and asked Geoffrey Dawson to meet him there. Baldwin, Dawson reported later, looked exhausted.

The King, feeling himself surrounded by enemies, realised he needed help. He heard with dismay that Beaverbrook was on his way to the United States in the S.S. *Bremen* in his annual quest of winter sunshine, and appealed to him by cable to return. Beaverbrook replied that he would turn round with the ship. The King knew he could rely on the sober but powerful support of Lord Rothermere and his son, Esmond Harmsworth.

The King then called on his family one by one and told them the facts. George, the Duke of Kent, though he subsequently turned into an enemy of his brother's choice, was sympathetic. The Duke of Gloucester was dazed. The Duke of York, face to face with the strong possibility of becoming King, was appalled. The King, leaving his brothers behind, then told his mother and begged her to meet Mrs Simpson. The Queen refused and next day told Stanley Baldwin all about it.

A few days later the Prime Minister was made aware of the fact that it was not only the King's problem he had to deal with but Mrs Simpson's problem also. He confessed as much to a friend.[1] 'The King agreed to go quietly,' Baldwin declared on November 24th, 'and he afterwards told this to his mother and his brothers. But he has clearly now gone back on that. Mrs S. was down at Fort Belvedere over the week-end. . . .' At our interview the King said he could do nothing without the woman.' Once this realisation dawned, Baldwin's entire plan of attack changed.

The world's statesmen, briefed day by day by their London Ambassadors, were following the developments enthralled. One of the few foreigners indelicate enough to try to intervene was Joachim von Ribbentrop, by now the German Ambassador in London, who felt himself an interested party. He had heard 'from a reliable source' that Edward had declared he would consider the coming Coronation only together with, or side by side with (*zusammen mit*), Mrs Simpson. 'I was very depressed and racked my brains for a possible way in which to influence the course of events,' Ribbentrop wrote in his diary. 'King Edward VIII had

[1] Thomas Jones, C. H., see Bibliography.

shown himself a potential advocate of Anglo-German understanding, therefore it lay in our interests that he should remain
King.' He asked for an audience, but the Court advisers did not
appear to feel that it was any of Ribbentrop's business. He was
pointedly told—probably by Alex Hardinge—that the King was
not at home. The palace door was shut on outsiders, and the Nazi
Ambassador, having made his little effort to nose his way in,
bowed out.

Still the nation continued to go about its work unaware of the
battle going on around its King. The business of the monarchy
went on, the Court Circular announcing arrivals and departures.
The King went abstractedly to South Wales to tour the distressed
areas. To unemployed miners he made a comment. 'Something
must be done,' he said, to ease their misfortune. It was a dangerous
remark for a reigning King to make to desperate men, and it was
received with horror in Whitehall. Was the fellow trying to start
a civil war just to get his own way? The King protested. It was,
he said later, the very least remark he could have made in the
circumstances, but it was one into which could be read political
significance, particularly in view of his conflict with the Prime
Minister. Baldwin himself complained to a friend that the King
had never mentioned to him any anxiety he might have felt for
the unemployed.[1] Once more the King had blundered. Once
more he had shown how not to be a King.

King Edward VII had been a King of grace and sophistication.
King George V, according to his biographer, Harold Nicolson,
never once said or did the wrong thing in his reign of a quarter
of a century. He was responsible for the widespread impression
that being a King was easy. Now King Edward was making it
look too hard for a man to handle. The tactlessness of his remark
to the miners was soon revealed. First they felt elation at the
thought that the King himself had taken note of their plight; then
when he abdicated in order to marry, apparently uncaring who, if
anybody, did the something that 'must be done', they felt a
personal sense of desertion, and bitterness against the King in
South Wales became very deep.

[1] Jones.

There was one consolation. Ministers had developed the habit of blaming Mrs Simpson for all the King's mistakes. She could hardly be blamed for this one.

On the night of November 30th, 1936, London glowed red with an evil omen of spectacular proportions. The Crystal Palace, built for the 1851 exhibition by Prince Albert, went up in flames. It was a tremendous conflagration. The Abdication crisis had only a fortnight to go.

*   *   *

No one sensed the witchery in the air more clearly than Beaverbrook when he returned to England on November 21st. He found the King in terror of Geoffrey Dawson, whom he believed was holding an article attacking Mrs Simpson, waiting for the right moment to print it. (Dawson wanted to break the press silence and use it just before Beaverbrook's return in order to spike the *Express* proprietor's guns; Baldwin dissuaded him.) Mrs Simpson still careered in her emotions from the heights to the depths, but she continued to give heart and combativeness to the King. Baldwin under the strain of the double game he was playing was almost at the end of his tether, buoyed up only by Dawson's support. So long as Mrs Simpson went on holding up the King while Dawson held up Baldwin, the battle would go on indefinitely. The press lords, in fact, were briefing their editors to that effect, and were preparing to keep the story running up to end beyond Edward VIII's coronation.

But now the King and Mrs Simpson were full of a new idea, an idea which the author believes originated with Sir Winston Churchill although it was subsequently credited to other sources. It was characteristically Churchillian, and it was just the solution Edward was seeking. The King, acting as a private person, would marry Mrs Simpson morganatically. Mrs Simpson would not take the rank of Queen, nor would her children, if any, succeed to the throne. But she would be the King's wife, probably with some title like the Duchess of Cornwall or the Duchess of Lancaster. The practice of morganatic marriage had been common enough in continental countries, but what precedent applied in Britain was remote and vague.

The King sent for Baldwin on November 25th and put the idea to him. The Prime Minister had already heard about it from Esmond Harmsworth, and he was prepared for it. He warned the King cautiously that he did not give it much of a chance, but the King impatiently packed him off and told him to submit it to the Cabinet and the Dominions, anyway.

Baldwin's forebodings were deep, and he had no intention of letting the King get out of the trap this way. His dislike of Mrs Simpson was infinite. He guessed that she would never be content for long with the inferior position given her by morganatic marriage. He told the Cabinet of the King's proposal, and the same fear occurred to his Ministers. Neville Chamberlain, the Chancellor of the Exchequer, went home and wrote in his diary: 'I have no doubt that if it were possible to arrange a morganatic marriage it would be only a prelude to the further step of making Mrs Simpson Queen with full rights.'

Nevertheless, this was probably Baldwin's severest moment. If the King insisted on the morganatic marriage proposal, Baldwin would be obliged to resign. The King would then ask Winston Churchill to form a government. Churchill would have to go to the country, and there would then be an election which the King might well win, particularly if he presented his case as that of a lonely and modest man who wanted to marry and did not even seek to make the woman of his choice Queen. From any point of view an election on such an issue would be a disaster to the nation and the Monarchy.

The Archbishop of Canterbury had immediate views on the subject. Dr Lang was being careful to avoid any direct involvement in the situation, but he did not hesitate to assert in private that the circumstances in which the King hoped to be crowned would make the ceremony meaningless. It would, he said, be 'pouring all those sacred words into a vacuum'. If the King marries Mrs Simpson, he was saying in effect, I will not crown her.

Whatever else King Edward VIII had done, he had murdered sleep. Nightmares wriggled their weird jives through the dreams of Britain's leaders. Baldwin tossed on his bed at the idea of an election on such an issue. Chamberlain dreamed of an American society divorcee crowned and hailed 'Queen Wallis' with all the panoply of glory. The Archbishop of Canterbury saw in a dark corner some ambitious prelate defying the Church and crowning the King and Queen himself.

The Government, however, was given very little time to deliberate on the matter because on December 1st the secret was let out. Newspapers seized on an oblique criticism of the King's church-going habits at the Diocesan Conference in Bradford to break to the nation for the first time the full story of the crisis, the King's love affair and Mrs Simpson. The criticism was made by the Bishop of Bradford, the Right Reverend A. W. F. Blunt, who later denied reports published at the time that his speech had been approved in advance by the Archbishop of Canterbury.

Mrs Simpson and the King were rocked by the sudden appearance of the story in every newspaper. 'They don't want me' was the King's first mortified cry when he picked up the *Birmingham Post*. That night Beaverbrook, who has a relish for the dramatic, called and told the King that the Cabinet had turned down the proposal for a morganatic marriage, that the facts were known in Fleet Street, and that the London press would come out with 'sensational disclosures' on Thursday morning.

The world was now collapsing about the lovers, but there was still plenty of fight left in them. Mrs Simpson's worst fears concerned the intentions of Geoffrey Dawson, whom she knew was preparing to attack her in *The Times*. The King, as apprehensive as she was, and still completely at sea regarding the things that can be arranged and the things that cannot, rang the Prime Minister at No. 10 Downing Street, and imperiously ordered him to forbid Dawson to publish the article.

Wearily Baldwin tried to explain to the King that the press of Great Britain was free and he had no more authority over *The Times* than over any other newspaper. The King could not see it. Were not Baldwin and Dawson working as a team? He insisted.

In the end, Baldwin called Dawson apologetically and said that the King would be satisfied if he (Baldwin) read over the intended article. Dawson grumbled and said that the paper had been almost put away for the night, but he sent a proof of the article to Downing Street at midnight, by which time Baldwin had gone to bed. It was not, however, the article the King most feared.

Now that the story was out in the open, the King and Mrs Simpson found themselves with many powerful allies. The *Daily Express* and the *Daily Mail* were going all out in their support— Rothermere's *Mail* more forcefully in fact than Beaverbrook's *Express*. No one could accurately assess public opinion, but there was no doubt that sympathy for the King was widespread, and even *The Times* was forced to admit later that the overwhelming majority of readers' letters on the subject were in favour of the King's marriage. The King's position was undoubtedly strong, and he was determined to stay. In his Memoirs he represented himself as a man always half-prepared to abdicate. The facts would suggest more that he was ready to fight to the end for both the throne and the woman. If he played his cards right now, he was almost immovable.

But quite suddenly Mrs Simpson's forces crumbled. In almost every high moment of history there can be found some insignificant incident which gives the dynamic push towards the climax; and in this instance it may well be that the person responsible was not the Prime Minister nor any of his colleagues, but a skulking ruffian who hid in the darkness of Regent's Park.

A window was broken in Mrs Simpson's house in Cumberland Terrace. The troublemaker was never caught, and probably never suspected that his action may well have accelerated the crisis of the Abdication.

For, with the tinkle of breaking glass, Mrs Simpson took decisive action.

CHAPTER VIII

Plans, Plots and a Nocturnal Meeting

FOR some days even before this incident Mrs Simpson's daily life had been subjected to much strain. Threatening letters had been pushed through her letter-box. There was a report—certainly a crack-pot report but alarming, nevertheless—that terrorists planned to blow up the house.

Reporters, most of them Americans, kept watch outside and had forced her to abandon the front part of the house altogether. She entered and left by the kitchen, which had a door leading to the garage.

On the day of her departure she had planned a dinner party for some friends. Then the window was broken in the dining-room. And in the kitchen the servants were terrified to hear someone *inside* the garage beating with a club or hammer against the kitchen door. No one dared open the door and confront the intruder, but later, when he had gone, the servants ventured outside and saw distinct marks of his hammering.

Alarmed, Mrs Simpson cancelled the party. Ladbrook was called. A servant asked what was to be done with the food that had been prepared for the dinner.

'Eat it yourselves,' Mrs Simpson replied, and London's greatest hostess turned her back on the garlanded table and with Aunt Bessie left the house. She never returned.

At Fort Belvedere both she and the King were deafened and stunned by the world-wide storm their love had raised. 'I cannot stay here another day with all this going on,' she said. But the King had worked out plans which he went on to reveal to her. They were his own plans. He had consulted nobody. They were unworkable and had almost no hope of succeeding. But conceived in love, they were also boyish and inspiring.

The idea was to spirit Mrs Simpson very quietly out of the country to the safety of France undetected either by the press or the public. The job might have been handled better by Scotland Yard, or the Foreign Office working tactfully in co-operation with the French Sûreté. But the King preferred to do it in his own way, and had evolved an extravagant plan which resulted in one of the most futile but at the same time one of the most exciting flights of romantic history.

Mrs Simpson would travel to the Riviera, where they had friends. False names would be used and false trails would be spread to divert reporters. Any communications between Mrs Simpson and the King would be in code. If they talked to one another by telephone, or cabled one another, the King would be referred to as 'Mr James', after St. James's Palace; Mrs Simpson would be 'Janet'; Lord Beaverbrook was 'Tornado', Stanley Baldwin was 'Crutch'. According to the Duke of Windsor's story, Winston Churchill was referred to by his initials.

The King was aware that he had little time to lose. The uproar was increasing. He was due to see the Prime Minister again soon. A great debate was due in the House of Commons in which the King suspected his major support would begin and end with Churchill. After that, nobody knew what would happen.

At lunch-time that day the telephone rang at the Villa Lou Viei, the mountain home, near Cannes, of Herman and Katherine Rogers, who were at that moment entertaining an English guest. The butler announced that the call was from London. Surprised, but not realising the momentousness of the occasion, Rogers picked up the receiver in the lunch-room with both his wife and guest listening in. He nearly dropped the phone when he was told that His Majesty the King was coming on the line.

Without preamble the King asked if Rogers would take Wallis as a guest. 'I want to get her out of the country,' he said.

Rogers said of course he would.

The King went on: 'It might be necessary for you to move on from Cannes and get her even farther away from England. Would you be prepared to do that?' Rogers said yes, and the King then gave a guarded outline of his plans and when Rogers could expect Mrs Simpson.

Rogers was a thoughtful man when he put down the telephone. He had been reading the papers, and he knew he was letting himself in for something big. He did not realise yet how big. After his holiday at Balmoral some months earlier, Rogers had written thanking the King warmly on behalf of his wife and himself, expressing the sincere hope that if there were anything he could do in return, he was at the King's service. Now the King had taken him up on his offer. Rogers was pleased but disconcerted. 'I hardly thought I'd ever be in a position to help a King of England,' he later confessed to a friend.

First of all he swore the English acquaintance to secrecy—not too hopefully. Who, after all, could resist repeating a sensational conversation he had overhead with the King? In later years Rogers was impressed to learn that the acquaintance had kept his word and had not repeated a hint of what he had overheard to a soul.

Next he checked his wallet. There was not much money there. He agreed with his wife that he should go to his bank in Cannes, and get out all his cash and if necessary borrow more. 'I might have to go to Cairo and, for all I know beyond,' he said. And while he was sending for his car, Katherine Rogers went to prepare the bedroom.

Meanwhile in London the King considered his next problem, the selection of an aide to accompany Wallis on the difficult trip to the South of France. There were few people left in the Court that the King could trust any more, and almost automatically he turned to Lord Brownlow, one of his Lords-in-Waiting, and a close friend both to the King and to Mrs Simpson. Peregrine Brownlow was thirty-seven at the time, a witty, handsome, quick-thinking man whose worldliness did not affect his sense of idealism or his unquestioning devotion to the King.

Lord Brownlow was called by the King on the telephone, and told of the plans for getting Wallis out of the country. He was asked to come at once to The Fort and tell no one, not even his wife. The vigour and tempestuousness of the King's call left little time for contemplation. Brownlow put down the telephone and must have mused on the strangeness of human affairs. Less than twenty-four hours before the incident of the brick, he had been at a meeting called by Lord Beaverbrook to try to solve the crisis. At this meeting it had been agreed that the best method to adopt would be to persuade Mrs Simpson to give the King up. The crisis, it seemed to them, must die on the spot, and Baldwin would be frustrated in his showdown with the King. The big question at the time was how to approach and 'get at' Mrs Simpson, who was always under the King's watch.

This was later to be referred to—without too much bitterness— by the Duke of Windsor as 'the conspiracy'. And here was the King himself putting Mrs Simpson in the hands of one of the conspirators-in-chief. Although the aims of the men around the King seemed sometimes contradictory, there was no question of loyalty in their own minds. Everyone was united in his determination to keep the King on the throne at all costs, and above all other considerations.

Brownlow threw a few changes of clothes into his case, absently adding to the pile a novel which he seemed to think he might have time to read. The afternoon was grey and cold, and rain smacked against the windows of his dressing-room. He put on a heavy coat with an astrakhan collar, a style he had picked up from the King, and locked his bag. He was just checking his passport when his wife, the beautiful Kitty Brownlow, who died early in 1953, came into the room. It was a slightly embarrassing moment, as Brownlow had sworn silence to the King, but he survived it.

Lord Brownlow's Rolls-Royce was then called for, and he drove from his London house to The Fort, arriving in time for a tense tea. The lights were on because the afternoon was so dark, and this added to the air of gloom. Around the tea-table were the King, Mrs Simpson, Aunt Bessie and Major (now Sir) Ulick Alexander, Keeper of the Privy Purse, a loyal King's man who went on to serve both King George VI and Queen Elizabeth II in the same capacity until 1953.

Over tea the King eagerly outlined his plans. Brownlow and

Wallis were to leave straight away, not even stopping at Cumberland Terrace in case her flight was suspected by the newspapermen on watch there. With them would travel a smart and trusted young Scotland Yard detective named J. G. ('Jimmie') Evans and George Ladbrook.

In Dieppe they would pick up the Buick which had been sent on in advance, and from then on it would be south as fast as Ladbrook could make it to Cannes.

The story of the parting is told by the King. 'The separation was all the harder to contemplate,' he wrote, 'for the reason that there was no way of telling how long it would last. Nothing was said between us as to when or where we would meet again. . . . Long afterwards Wallis confided in me that only on this last day at The Fort did she begin to comprehend what abdication really involved. . . . Until then it had only been a word—a possible remote alternative. . . . When in the darkness she left The Fort with Perry Brownlow for France, it was with the hope that she would see me again, but never expecting that she would. I watched them go. With dimmed lights and the Scotland Yard man in front, the Rolls took the back drive down towards Virginia Water, and the public road through Windsor Great Park some distance beyond. . . .'

The King was left alone to attend to other business with as much concentration as he could muster. It had been an eventful day—more eventful than he was yet able to realise. And he still had to see Stanley Baldwin later in the evening.

It was now possible to review events that had been pushed into the background by Wallis's flight. For some days the King had been working on a new approach; to broadcast to the British people explaining his love. 'Neither Mrs Simpson nor I have ever sought to insist that she should be Queen,' he wanted to say. 'All we desired was that our married happiness should carry with it a proper title and dignity for her, befitting my wife.' He would go on to offer to withdraw from Britain for a while until the issue was settled.

Once at the microphone he understood his talents well enough to know that he could put his message across. The difficulty was how to get there in face of Stanley Baldwin's probable disapproval.

He had already made quiet overtures to the B.B.C. That morning he had sent Sir Godfrey Thomas to Broadcasting House to talk to Sir John Reith, Director-General of the B.B.C., about it. The King knew and liked Reith, and hoped he would be receptive to the idea. Reith at least proved sympathetic. He poured out a stiff whisky and soda for Thomas, who was close to collapse, having worked non-stop on the King's behalf since the crisis began. Thomas, rallying, asked Reith if the King could broadcast at short notice from Windsor.

Reith replied, 'Of course,' but asked, 'Has the Prime Minister agreed to it?'

Thomas was on his guard at once and said that so far as he understood, 'it could only so be done', and he left it at that. He returned to Fort Belvedere to report to the King.

Now the King thought about Winston Churchill, the one man, he knew, who would help him. But he was separated from that immense, wise and sympathetic figure by a great gulf. Baldwin again. The Prime Minister would have to give his permission before Churchill could be consulted, and the King could guess bitterly and in advance what Baldwin's answer would be to such a request.

Baldwin and Churchill had been adversaries too long, and it was unlikely that the Prime Minister would allow Churchill— 'my opposition' Baldwin sometimes called him—to join the fight with official blessing on the side of the King. Only that afternoon Churchill had challenged Baldwin in the House of Commons, and asked for an assurance that no irrevocable step would be taken before a general statement had been made to Parliament. Baldwin would not be drawn.

But if Churchill could not be consulted directly, he could always be consulted indirectly, and this the King had resolved to do. He sent a copy of his proposed speech that morning to Lord Beaverbrook at Stornoway House, asking him for his comments and requesting that he show it to Churchill. Beaverbrook immediately called Churchill, and suggested they meet and study the speech together. Churchill was obliged to decline. He had to

No. 16 Cumberland Terrace. The bedroom.

Dawson of the Times.
The man Mrs. Simpson feared most.

go to the Albert Hall in the evening to address a meeting of an organisation called Defence of Peace and Freedom, but he promised to join Beaverbrook immediately afterwards and go over the speech with him.

The meeting to which Churchill had been called had nothing whatever to do with the King's affair, but the national preoccupation with the crisis was so great that the most unrelated events seemed to be sucked into it. When the meeting was over the audience of 5,000 rose to sing 'God Save the King'. As the last notes died away a woman shouted 'Long Live the King'. There was a moment of surprised silence, and then a tremendous cheer shook the huge hall.

It was an incident which could not be ignored or underestimated. It showed that although the nation as a whole remained almost disturbingly quiet, a chance word could fire the masses and sweep events out of the control of the participants, with unimaginable consequences.

Afterwards the two close friends, Beaverbrook and Churchill, radiating between them more energy, dynamism and antic genius than any other two people in the world, settled down to apply themselves to the King's speech.

Meanwhile Baldwin had arrived at the Palace. His car pulled up outside promptly at nine, and he tried to slip in unseen by the back door. But people were everywhere and they watched in silence as he hurried inside. The King had already been furnished with one important piece of advice by Beaverbrook. It was:

'Don't show the speech to Baldwin.'

Tell him about it, urged Beaverbrook, and insist on your right to make it. But don't let him know what's in it. The important thing is to get the microphone at all costs and say your piece.

The King, illustrating once more why he was the despair of his friends, immediately read the speech to Baldwin. The Prime Minister listened bleakly. This was an ugly new development for him, and he did not like it at all. He commented that he would have to consult his colleagues, but he personally thought the broadcast was 'thoroughly unconstitutional'.

Now more than any other time in the crisis the two men's hatred rose to the surface. There was an outburst from the overwrought King, and a moment that came closest to frankness in all the dealings the monarch and the Prime Minister had had with each other.

'You want me to go, don't you?' the King cried. 'Well, before I go I think it is right for her sake and mine that I should speak.'

Baldwin was not deluded by this rhetoric. The King had said a lot about 'going', but nothing was clearer than his present determination to stay. The speech he had just listened to was no speech of farewell. It was a fighting speech aimed at getting public opinion on the King's side. Baldwin had not yet heard of the demonstration in the Albert Hall, but he knew that public opinion was precariously poised and ready to crash down in one direction or the other. He absorbed the King's words and replied to them with care.

'What I want, Sir,' he said, 'is what you told me you wanted, to go with dignity, not dividing the country, and making things as smooth as possible for your successor. To broadcast would be to go over the heads of your Ministers and speak to the people. You will be telling millions throughout the world—among them a vast number of women—that you are determined to marry one who has a husband living. You may by speaking divide opinion, but you will certainly harden it. . . .'

Baldwin went on to give the King a remarkable warning, which must have seemed to the King almost a threat. He reminded Edward that Mrs Simpson's divorce did not become absolute until the following April, and that if the King associated too closely with her before then it was possible that some 'muddle-headed busybody'—Baldwin's words—might seek to delay or prevent the divorce by some sort of intervention with the divorce authorities. It was to frighten the King away from making the broadcast that Baldwin made this statement. Later at another crucial moment when the King appeared to be making a comeback, the very thing that Baldwin warned might happen did happen.

King Edward began to see his hopes of the broadcast fade. He counter-attacked, and for once, miraculously, scored a point. 'May I consult Winston Churchill?' he asked abruptly.

Taken by surprise, Baldwin said yes. The interview was over. Baldwin went pensively home. The big events of the crisis were still to come.

CHAPTER IX

Mrs Simpson Departs

T HE car had quickly left the lights of London's suburbia behind and travelled through the rainswept darkness towards the coast. On the main highway to Newhaven the party had an unpleasant experience. A police car pursued them and indicated to Ladbrook to pull in to the side of the road. The policeman did not recognise Mrs Simpson in the back of the car, but a quick glance at Evans's Scotland Yard badge convinced him that he had put his nose into something that it would be healthier for him to ignore. He waved the car on. Had the King warned the Government of Mrs Simpson's flight, such an incident would have been avoided. As it was, it proved to be one of the lesser scares.

The party got on board the boat without trouble, and Lord Brownlow conducted Mrs Simpson to the cabin that had been reserved for them. At Dieppe, Ladbrook collected the Buick, and a grinning French Customs officer stuck the car's papers under Brownlow's nose. 'Mr Harris' realised that, with horror, they were still in Mrs Simpson's name. The secret was cracking already. The *douaniers* crowded round, and with knowing winks and wise nods led the partly discreetly through the crowds of waiting tourists to the street outside. Brownlow was relieved to be rid of this complication so easily, but he was not reassured. Too many French reporters and dock workers were looking on. Still, there was nothing he could do about it, and he ordered Ladbrook on to Rouen. As soon as the Buick moved out of sight through the streets of Dieppe, the porters, buzzing happily, dispersed to sell their information to the local press.

The car reached Rouen at dusk. The town was full of visitors, and Lord Brownlow had to make his way through a swarm of

French actors and actresses in the lobby of the Hotel de la Poste to get to the reservations desk. Brownlow was worried about Mrs Simpson, who was suffering acutely from the strain of parting, and he was relieved when he found that there were still vacant rooms. The hotel was pretty busy, he was told, because it was accommodating a touring company of the Comédie Française. Mrs Simpson was able to make her way to her room unrecognised, but she could guess what would be the King's state of mind without her, and she insisted over Brownlow's protests that she must call him.

This was responsible for the next crisis. The only available telephone was on the room clerk's desk in the middle of thick clusters of French actors. It was asking for trouble to phone from there, but Mrs Simpson insisted. After the usual delays, the call was put through and Wallis spoke to the King. The actors listened, fascinated, some of the girls in the company wept openly. Brownlow chafed anxiously and glared a Guardsman's glare at the actors. It might have petrified a Guard, but the actors were too absorbed in the conversation to take any notice whatever. The line was good, and Mrs Simpson, who probably never realised there was anybody else in the lobby, was much lighter in spirit after the call was made.

The party was up early next morning, but already a few Rouen reporters were in the lobby interviewing the actors, who were giving a splendid performance of the 'coup de telephone de Madame Simpson a son amour' with sighs, sobs and gestures. Through the mist of histrionic tears, Brownlow and Mrs Simpson were able to slip unnoticed out of the hotel.

Outside, however, the situation was bad. Labrook had driven up to the hotel in the Buick, which was immediately surrounded by excited passers-by. Of all the mistakes the King made in his plans for Mrs Simpson's escape, the Buick was undoubtedly the greatest. Already it was the most famous car in the world, even the number-plate, CUL 547, being as familiar to many newspaper readers as their own telephone numbers. In France American cars of any description attracted attention at this time, and the Buick was unmistakable.

Lord Brownlow had to push to get through. As he helped Mrs Simpson inside, a French girl, aged about eighteen, and dressed, so far as various memories can recall, as a girl guide, turned her Leica camera on Mrs Simpson. Evans sitting inside the car, reached out and splayed his hand over the aperture. 'It might have contained acid,' he explained later. The girl laughed and evaded his hand and aimed the camera once more at Mrs Simpson.

Reports of what happened next are confused by the speed in which incident succeeded incident. The crowd pressed round the car, and the camera fell from the girl's hand, smashing itself on the pavement. In a moment the general holiday good humour faded. There was a scuffle, and the situation was becoming ugly—desperate even—for Evans and Brownlow with their precious charge. Brownlow shouted at Ladbrook, 'For heaven's sake, get us out of here'.

The Buick butted through and to everybody's relief put the crowd behind. Soon it was on the high road and making good progress, and the incident faded gradually from their minds. Mrs Simpson's morale had been much higher since she had made the telephone call, but her concern for the King's welfare remained. Abdication, she knew, had been uppermost in the King's mind at their parting. As Brownlow was a confidant and intimate in the Abdication drama, they discussed the matter, and Mrs Simpson insisted once more on phoning the King on arrival at Evreux, which was the next town on their route.

Brownlow protested. 'It's asking for trouble,' he said, 'to keep phoning from hotels and restaurants. Let's go to the local police-station at Evreux. I'll explain to the police what's up and you can phone safely.'

But Mrs Simpson was determined to act under the instructions of the King, who had urged absolute secrecy, and she was fearful of bringing French officials into the adventure.

Lord Brownlow was obliged to agree to the call, and Mrs Simpson demanded some paper to write down the message. Brownlow had no paper but remembered the novel he had brought with him from England, fished it out of his bag and tore out the flyleaf. On it Mrs Simpson wrote the words, 'On no account is Mr James to step down'—Mr James being the pre-arranged code-word for the King.

The King was at Buckingham Palace when Mrs Simpson got through from Evreux, but the line was dreadful. However the King strained to hear what she was saying he could not catch a word, and what was worse he could not get through to her a message of his own. Earlier that day he had been called up by a friend, Bernard Rickatson-Hatt, then Editor of Reuter's, that the press was on to her, and although the Buick had given them the slip they knew roughly where it was, guessed the destination was Cannes, and were heading there as fast as she was.

How had the news leaked? The fact was that Wallis unwittingly broke the secret herself. A few days earlier she had entertained Newbold Noyes and another American journalist, Otis Wiese, to cocktails at The Fort. Over strong Old Fashioneds they had discussed the situation, and she promised them another interview later. But immediately afterwards the story had broken in the newspapers and the brick had been thrown through Mrs Simpson's window. Plans for flight followed, but Wallis, with Southern politeness, first called Wiese at the Ritz Hotel to cancel the interview. 'I don't have to tell you why,' she said, and told him why. That night American newsmen were on the watch at all British ports-of-exit for France. Though Wallis and Brownlow, with the confidence of ignorance, had slipped through unseen, the newsmen had rallied in France and were closing in relentlessly.

Neither Wallis nor the King could make any sense to each other at all through the atmospherics. No phone call since the instrument was invented could have probed more profoundly into the depths of human frustration. The King said in his book that he nearly hurled the receiver against the wall.

Nor was the anxiety limited to the King and Mrs Simpson. Brownlow and Evans were having a most embarrassing time of it. The party had stopped at the Hôtel du Grand Cerf at Evreux. There Brownlow found to his relief that there was an enclosed telephone-box in the lobby. His relief did not last long. The walls were like paper and Mrs Simpson, having to shout to try to make herself heard, was audible all over the crowded lobby. Many of the hotel guests were English and American, the hotel being a very popular resort place until the war: it was shelled flat shortly after D-Day.

To prevent Mrs Simpson's call becoming the public property it was in Rouen Lord Brownlow and Detective Evans, probably feeling utter fools, stood outside the box and talked loudly to each other. As the line inside proved helpless, the two men talked louder and louder. People present must have wondered for years and possibly still do today why two distinguished looking young Englishmen stood so long in front of a telephone-box talking gibberish at the tops of their voices.

Whatever the temporary loss to the dignity of the British aristocracy and the Metropolitan Police Force, Brownlow and Evans at least succeeded in jamming out Mrs Simpson's call from the guests. She left the box unrecognised and they headed for the car. But they could never seem to get over one obstacle before meeting a bigger one. Although it was many months before the sense of Mrs Simpson's message reached the King, the King's message to Mrs Simpson was made too desperately clear within a matter of minutes. As she was leaving the hotel the first British newspapermen began to arrive and spotted her.

This was the advance guard. Ladbrook bustled and in no time at all the party was in the Buick and away, and the reporters were left behind. For two hours they drove on a superb highway at one of Ladbrook's fastest licks. Brownlow was pleased at escaping the reporters so easily. The party had become quite a cheerful one by this time. Mrs Simpson in the excitement of the flight was regaining some of the famous verve that had been unhappily missing in the last few trying weeks, and kept everyone in the car amused at her comments on the passing French scene.

Then two catastrophes hit them simultaneously. 'Blimey,' said Ladbrook, 'I've hit the wrong road.' And Mrs Simpson said, 'Oh, I've left the note behind.' Here were two serious problems dumped into Lord Brownlow's lap, of which the more serious by far was that of the note, 'Under no circumstances is Mr James to step down.' The first solution would be to drive back to Evreux, pick up the note and get on to the right road, but Brownlow and

Mrs Simpson agreed that such a move would be to invite utter disaster, as the town by now would be infested with newspaper men of all nationalities.

It was agreed after a brief conference to abandon the note. Optimism reasserted itself. It was, after all, a cryptic and not particularly incriminating message, and even if a reporter did find it, it might not mean anything to him. And probably it would be found by an hotel employee and destroyed.

They under-estimated the wit of the hôtelier, who, shortly after Mrs Simpson's departure, went into the telephone-box and found the note. He read it, having already recognised his visitor, and saw the significance. He framed it and kept it to show his favourite customers. A year or so later Harold Nicolson, the writer, stopped briefly at the hotel for lunch, discovered and retrieved the hôtelier's prize and returned it to Mrs Simpson, who by that time was the Duchess of Windsor.

Having made his decision, Brownlow told Ladbrook to carry on until they got back on the right road. They found themselves back on their planned route just north of Blois. The little town was deserted when they arrived, for which discovery they were most thankful, and they booked rooms at the Hôtel d'Angleterre. But some form of mental radar was attracting their pursuers, and less than half an hour after their arrival the first press cars were nosing speculatively into the town.

The first to spot them was the detective, Jimmy Evans. Of all the King's selections none had been better than that of Evans. He was experienced at keeping royalty out of trouble. He was good-looking, sophisticated and totally unlike the typical British policeman.

While the rest of the party went to their rooms, Evans went to the bar and was enjoying a glass of wine when the first reporters burst in. They were British and they did not recognise him. Evans, fascinated, listened in to their conversation.

They had Mrs Simpson cornered. They had bribed the concierge and all the servants. Every move Mrs Simpson made would be reported to them immediately. They also said something about the Buick; blocking the Buick. . . .

Evans paid for his drink and went upstairs. He warned Lord Brownlow and Mrs Simpson of the situation, then looked in on George Ladbrook who was lying on the bed fully-clothed even to his French beret. A large cigar was stuck in his round face. Evans told him to be ready for an emergency departure. Ladbrook sighed and stirred.

By late evening there were more than thirty newspapermen in the hotel, most of them British and eager to make up with as much sensation as possible for all the months of enforced silence. There were also a fair number of Americans and Frenchmen.

The first arrivals booked rooms, and by the time the others turned up the hotel was full. None wanted to move to any other hotel, so those unable to get rooms cheerfully elected to sleep on chairs all night in the lobby and wait for any appearance Mrs Simpson might care to make.

Brownlow had to think hard. He worked out a tentative plan. To the concierge he said quietly—but sibilantly enough to be overhead—'We will have breakfast at eight. It is very important that we are out of this hotel at nine o'clock.' As he waited for the *ascenseur* to take him to his room, he heard a Fleet Street newspaperman on the telephone to London. 'Don't worry,' he was bellowing—and Lord Brownlow began to see virtues in wafer-thin walls—'We've got them trapped. They are leaving at nine.' Impassively optimistic, Brownlow returned to the hotel room at the door of which Evans stood guard and told Mrs Simpson the news.

In time all the reporters made their calls to London and New York, and as even the latest sleepers made their way to bed silence finally enclosed the hotel. The scene in the darkened lobby was like a refugee centre, with newspapermen lolling on chairs and couches. The luminous watch on the wrist of the unsleeping Detective Evans said three o'clock when Lord Brownlow, heavy-eyed, crept silently along the corridor to awaken Mrs Simpson. His call was unnecessary. She was ready and she emerged a revelation. Not a hair was out of place. She looked bright and wide-awake, and appeared as if she had stepped from the bath and the attentions of a score of maids. Her clothes were as chic and as faultless as if she were about to go to a Mayfair cocktail party. She gave Brownlow an alert smile, and together the three adventurers set out to run the gauntlet of the snoring reporters.

They tiptoed downstairs and through the lobby, stepping over motionless bodies. If one reporter had awakened they would have been lost. Almost too easily, it seemed, they were outside in the bitterly cold night, behind them not a single newspaper man had been disturbed in his slumber. They congratulated one another with triumphant winks, then crept round to the back of the hotel where the Buick was garaged. They had cheered too soon.

Parked directly in the path of the Buick the reporters had set another car with the hand-brake firmly applied and every door locked. Mrs Simpson's party seemed effectively stymied.

'What,' Mrs Simpson wanted to know, 'do we do now?'

Ladbrook, who was scratching his head at the scene when they arrived, said, 'Leave it to me.' He ordered the other three into the car and started the motor. The car moved forward and pressed its bumper against the locked vehicle. In the still night air the racing engine seemed to make the sound of fiends, but there was still no move from the hotel. Very slowly the car began to budge. Ladbrook kept pushing, and in the end, the reporter's car, bumped, dented and seriously diminished in saleable value, had been pushed out of the way. Once more they were off and racing south into the dawn along empty highways, complimenting themselves on their victory with a fervour that was all the more heartfelt because they knew that it could not last.

The weather had turned out bad. Snow was falling and the roads were treacherous, but the Buick kept going. For most of the time Brownlow and Wallis sat in the back and chatted, mostly about the crisis they had left behind them and how the King was making out alone.

An important change was coming over Mrs Simpson. The King had sensed it in the last words they had together when she told him she was realising for the first time what Abdication meant. The woman whose almost inhuman sophistication never failed to stagger childhood friends when they saw her again, seemed to be rediscovering the fact that she was once Wallis

Warfield, remembered as one of the nicest girls in Baltimore.

Wallis Simpson had a kind heart and her sympathy was easily touched. She was beginning to understand that the King's cause was hopeless, and that renunciation by her might be the only way left in which he could remain on the throne.

Brownlow for his part must have been thinking of his second mission on this expedition, about which the King knew nothing, but though the thoughts of both people were almost certainly running along the same lines the moment had not yet come when they could be discussed openly. Mrs Simpson had recovered her good spirits along the road, and was now trim and in possession of herself.

She laughed through one incident which came close to farce. Brownlow was muffled against the cold in his heavy overcoat when a sudden bump threw him against the side of the car. There was the sound of breaking glass. The bump had broken a small bottle of whisky in his pocket and the fumes spread everywhere. At first it was a joke ('Before breakfast too!') ('Hope the reporters don't catch us now!'), but the aroma quickly became too overpowering for laughter. Finally Mrs Simpson put her foot down.

'Perry,' she said, 'I cannot stand this. You'll have to put your coat somewhere.' Lord Brownlow protested weakly about the cold, but Mrs Simpson was not moved, so he stuffed the coat in the boot of the car. He spent the rest of the journey wrapped up in a couple of rugs.

When Ladbrook tired, Brownlow took the wheel. There were no signs of reporters as they flashed through village after village, but Brownlow and Mrs Simpson guessed that they had not shaken them off for long. However, their luck held good as far as Moulin, where they stopped for an early breakfast. Here Lord Brownlow composed a telegram to send to the Rogers, whom he knew would be waiting for them in the greatest of anxiety at Cannes.

He reworded it more and more vaguely until he was finally satisfied with it that it would arouse no suspicion. It said something like: 'Having wonderful time. You might see us tonight but don't wait up.' He put no signature on it and handed it in to the telegraph office. Once more he under-estimated the capacity of the French to read between the lines even in English. Rogers received the cable all right—after he had read it in print in the local Nice paper that afternoon.

Brownlow did not hear of that until later. The roads continued free of press cars and the fugitives were in excellent spirits all morning. Ladbrook at one point was seeking the 'Route Bleue' to make a turning. As they passed a crossroads Mrs Simpson said absently, 'Isn't this it, the Route Royale?'; then collapsed in laughter at the joke which she insisted was on her.

About fifty miles before they reached Vienne, the press hit them again in huge numbers. And this time they could not be shaken off. Local inhabitants in the Rhone valley villages poured out to watch the mysterious caravan of cars tearing through, a big black American car in the lead, and a stream of other cars of all sorts and nationalities following.

Probably the best-known thing about Vienne is the Restaurant de la Pyramide, sometimes called Chez Point, the world's most famous eating-place. Lord Brownlow and Mrs Simpson decided to stay there for lunch, and Ladbrook drove the car into the garage while the press remained outside. They entered the restaurant via the wine cellar and Brownlow asked for a private room. The head waiter was desolate, but all he had that was not occupied was the banqueting hall.

'It'll do,' said Brownlow, and he and his charge were conducted to a huge echoing room. They sat at the long dining-table, posting Evans outside, and had an excellent light meal consisting of paté, salad, fowl and white wine. Brownlow and Mrs Simpson were both excellent conversationalists with a highly developed sense of humour. The press men waiting outside became something of a joke, and lunch was spent merrily, the absurdly large room adding to the somewhat hysterical laughter.

They had managed to enter the restaurant without much embarrassment. But the sight which greeted them as they left was positively terrifying. The struggling crowds of reporters and photographers had now been reinforced with newsreel camera squads, and Mrs Simpson's appearance was the sign for the cameras posted on the tops of cars to start whirring.

As the Buick started up, all the other cars got into line behind. At Aignon later that afternoon they paused for a snack in the car. Obligingly the press cars pulled behind them, and all the newspapermen also took advantage of the occasion to have snacks, too.

They did not stop again. At 2.30 the following morning they arrived at the foot of the narrow winding mountain road leading from Cannes up to the Villa Lou Viei. It was an appropriate sanctuary. It had once been a monk's residence, and parts of it were 650 years old. The Rogers had bought it some years ago.

No one, of course, in the brightly lit house was thinking of sleep. The Rogers had had a harassing time. For more than twenty-four hours they had been watching more and more newspaper men arrive until now there were more than 500 encamped just beyond the small private road that led from the house to the main mountain road. Rogers knew that Mrs Simpson was going to have a hard time breaking through. The road from Cannes is so winding that it needs a constant use of the wheel, and even at comparatively slow speeds the tyres scream on the corners.

He took comfort, however, in the gendarmes at the end of the pathway, who were keeping the reporters at bay. And out in Cannes harbour other friends of the King and Mrs Simpson had rallied. The *Nahlin* was there and so was the yacht *Sister Ann*, property of the French sewing-machine heiress, Mrs Reginald Fellowes. Both kept steam up in case Wallis was obliged to escape further by sea.

Lord Brownlow was the first in the Buick to spot the reporters now reinforced by hundreds of sight-seers, and he realised that at the end of the 650-mile dash this was going to be the severest test of all.

'Wallis,' said Brownlow, 'if you don't want to be photographed the only thing to do is to get down on the floor.'

Mrs Simpson did so and Brownlow told Ladbrook to outdo himself and head for the house for all he was worth.

The accelerator went down hard. The Buick leaped forward and hurtled into a vivid white blaze of flash-bulbs. Reporters scattered. Ladbrook swung the wheel right, left, right at the succession of sharp bends.

To the watchers the faces of three grim, determined men appeared and were gone as the car went careering by. No Mrs Simpson! Then the Buick, with unslackening speed and with tyres screaming, shot into the private road leading to the house. Reporters and photographers dashed through the dust in pursuit, but the gendarmes sprang out in the wake of the car and formed a barrier. Mrs Simpson was safe at last.

*   *   *

The anxious Rogers hurried out of the house to greet them but first he had a nasty shock. He opened the door of the car. 'Hallo, Perry,' he said, then, 'My God, where's Wallis?'

'Here I am,' said Wallis, somewhat dishevelled but cheerful as she climbed from under a car rug. With great relief Rogers led his guests inside, where Katherine Rogers was waiting with food and badly needed stiff drinks.

Outside, the newspapermen and photographers, deprived of their coup, dispersed with not very good grace. No one had succeeded in even seeing Mrs. Simpson. A few of the more unscrupulous characters in the newspaper business in London, however, were not going to be defeated as easily as the men on the spot had been. Noticing in the cabled pictures that there was no sign of Mrs Simpson, at least one art editor decided it was a mistake and cheerfully introduced one by composite photography. It duly appeared the following day. It showed Mrs Simpson wearing different clothes from those she was wearing at the time; but, after all, one couldn't have everything.

The reporters, whose equipment is the written word rather than the visual image, had rather a better time of it, and a very moving picture of Mrs Simpson's arrival was recorded. As long after the event as 1948 one London newspaper biographer of Mrs Simpson was still under the impression that watchers at the gate would 'never forget her tragic face, pale under the Mediterranean moon, and her half-closed weary eyes'. Actually Mrs Simpson was crouched on the floor, and if her emotions have been correctly remembered, she was rather enjoying it.

Sleep came with varying ease to the people besieged that night in the sixteen-room Villa Lou Viei. Ladbrook and Evans slept the sleep of men satisfied with a job accomplished as well as it was within their power. Mrs Simpson, on the other hand, was as wide awake and alert as she had been throughout the flight. She was still apprehensive, however, for her personal safety, and asked Lord Brownlow to sleep in an adjoining room. This was a dressing-room which the Rogers had turned into a makeshift bedroom, and Mrs Simpson arranged for the connecting door to be left half open.

The story of what happened after everyone in the house had gone to bed was repeated with hilarity at breakfast next morning, and has been repeated many times since by mutual friends.

Both had retired, Brownlow so weary that he did not even take his clothes off. He simply threw himself fully dressed on the divan bed. As he smoked a last cigarette he called Mrs Simpson.

'Wallis,' he said quietly in case she was asleep. A sound from the next room indicated that she was not and Brownlow said something to this effect:

'We've had a tough journey together and I'd like to ask you a favour. I think you might feel I'm entitled to a little privileged information. Tell me the story. How did it all happen? What made the King fall in love with you? How did you do it?'

Brownlow's cigarette was out, and he was fighting against sleep even while he spoke. After a while Wallis said:

'All right, I'll tell you.' She started to speak.

The next thing Brownlow remembered was the sudden start of awakening. For a moment, as so often happens after the first sleep of utter fatigue, he did not realise where he was; then he heard Mrs Simpson's voice saying:

'And that, Perry, is the whole story. What else could I do?'

So the world's strangest love story was told freshly and purely, as, after all the subsequent years of fact and rumour, it can never be told again, possibly not even by the Duchess of Windsor her-

The famous black Buick.

1. SPECIFICATION. (Original.)

To be filled in by the Owner and stamped by the Export Officer of Customs and Excise before exportation, and detached and retained by the Export Officer.

Issued to *Mrs Ernest Simpson*

Address *16 Cumberland Terrace. London N.W.1.*

DETAILS OF VEHICLE AND EQUIPMENT.

Chassis : Make *Buick*	Body : Type *Limousine* (Touring, Saloon, etc.)
Year of Manufacture *1936*	Colour *Black*
Country of origin *Canada*	Make *Fisher*
No. *648990232*	Colour of upholstery *Fawn cloth.*
Engine : Make *Buick*	Tires : Total No. *6*
No. *2943888*	Size *700 x 16*
No. of Cylinders *8*	Make and Tread *Goodyear.*
Horse Power *33*	
Weight of Vehicle, cwts. *44*	Registration No. *CUL 547*
Value ,, ,, £ *600*	

EQUIPMENT.

Wheels or Rims *6*	Pumps *1*	Speedometer *1*
Tools and Jack *act*	Mirror *1*	Horns *Dual*
Clock *1*	Windscreen Wiper	*Dual*
Lamps (electric, oil or gas) *6 + 2*	Luggage Grid	

WIRELESS.

Make	Weight
No.	Value

Insert any item of equipment Not specified above.

Shipped per s.s. or Exported at *Newhaven*   Signature of Owner *Ernest Simpson*

Examined and certified correct.

Signature of Export Officer *A.H.Beard.*

CUSTOMS AND EXCISE: Date *4.12.36*

The document on which the Buick travelled to France. Note "Signature" of owner.

self. It was meant for the ears of one loyal friend who slept through it all.

Brownlow, awake again, was somewhat vexed with himself. But being a gentleman he could hardly say, 'Sorry, would you mind starting at the beginning again?' Instead, regretfully but philosophically he turned over and went back to sleep.

CHAPTER X

The Lovers are Tricked

THE night of Thursday, December 3rd, 1936, was the turning-point in the crisis. That was the night when Wallis left, the night 5,000 people in the Albert Hall cheered the King and a 'King's Party' appeared to be forming, the night when the King confronted Baldwin with his intention to broadcast. At midnight that night Godfrey Thomas had called Sir John Reith on the telephone and told him that the King might broadcast on the following evening. It was the high-water-mark of Edward's fortunes.

Twenty-four hours later he was a beaten and a broken man.

What happened to cause such a change? The first pregnant hours of Friday gave no indication of the great break to come. In fact, it seemed as if the King's cause was strengthening by the hour, and at 10 Downing Street the news looked bad. The Cabinet had heard with gloom of the Albert Hall demonstration and of the nation-wide sympathy for the King as revealed in readers' letters to *The Times*. An alarming rumour had reached the Ministers that Windsor Castle was being wired for sound by B.B.C. engineers. They received yet another shock when Baldwin opened his business of the day.

The Prime Minister had guessed he was in for trouble when the time came to admit to his colleagues that he had given the King permission to see Winston Churchill, a man both feared and disliked by the orthodox Conservatives who formed the bulk of Baldwin's Cabinet. Having foreseen trouble, he decided to forestall it in a manner peculiar to his tangential personality.

'I made a bloomer last night,' he said sheepishly, and told the Cabinet what had happened. Duff Cooper, the War Minister, an acute observer of the Stanley Baldwin character, watched the performance fascinated. 'He adopted, with the vocabulary of the schoolroom, the appearance of a penitent schoolboy "owning up" to a delinquency,' Duff Cooper later recalled.

As Baldwin had admitted his error, his colleagues could hardly take him to task about it. But a week later, when the drama was completed and the Prime Minister had finished making his triumphant speech to the House of Commons describing the Abdication, Duff Cooper provoked a sequel. He congratulated Baldwin and said to him: 'So it wasn't a blunder, after all.'

Baldwin was flushed and elated. He laughed. 'My dear Duff,' he exclaimed, 'I never thought for one moment that it was a blunder, but it seemed to me the best way of presenting the matter to my colleagues that morning.'

Baldwin immediately felt he had gone too far. 'The laugh faded, the mask fell, and he hurried down the corridor in solemn silence.' At that moment Duff Cooper remembered a Frenchwoman whom he had once met at a party and who did not recognise Stanley Baldwin standing nearby. 'That man must be an actor,' the Frenchwoman had commented.

The Prime Minister's cause sagged even further that afternoon. Once more Churchill demanded an assurance that no irrevocable step would be taken. This time he was cheered—an ominous sound, following the cheers in the Albert Hall the previous evening. Churchill had been informed that the King had permission to consult him. It was a conflict to give him obvious joy . . . Cavalier against Roundhead; Royalist against Puritan; dashing rebel against relentless constitutionalist.

He dined that evening in Fort Belvedere. The situation, as it was explained to him, shocked him. About Mrs Simpson he prudently said not a word. He concentrated on the constitutional aspect, enfolding his judgment in words so complete that they seemed beyond argument. His audience, the King, Walter Monckton, Ulick Alexander, George Allen, listened, rapt. No crisis could possibly arise, he said, until Mrs Simpson's divorce was confirmed in April. Baldwin had no authority to confront the King with a choice of Abdication. If there was disagreement, it was the Government not the King whose responsibility it was to resign. His argument had only one weakness, and the King apparently did not enlighten Churchill on it. The alternative of Abdication had been introduced not by Baldwin but by the King, not once but repeatedly, and as a threat. Baldwin was merely holding the King to his word.

Winston Churchill travelled back to London that night stimulated and heartened by the situation as he found it. He drafted several messages. One was a letter to the Prime Minister stating that the King was in no fit state to give a decision. It would be 'cruel and wrong', he said, to extort one. He wrote out a statement to give to the press, pleading for 'time and patience', and urging tolerance and delay in reaching a decision over the King's affair. Finally he wrote a letter of 'half-humorous advice' to the King, suggesting, according to the Duke of Windsor's Memoirs, that he should withdraw into Windsor Castle, pull up the drawbridge and admit no one.

Churchill wrote his notes in good heart and good conscience. He was looking forward to a fight and a long fight. It is certain from the tone of his messages that he did not think for one moment that the King was on the point of giving up.

Yet even as he wrote, Stanley Baldwin, at No. 10 Downing Street, seemed to receive a telepathic flash. From sources which even now cannot be disclosed, the author has proof that Baldwin on Friday night knew that the King was licked and the crisis was over. Something or someone had told him that a secret ravage was working on the King, a ravage that had escaped Churchill's notice, but which was making Edward sag like a pricked balloon. Mrs Simpson's departure had wrecked him.

The following day the King sent Walter Monckton to Baldwin with the news that he intended to abdicate. The King's friends were amazed, but Baldwin was ready for it. At once he established a Cabinet Committee, under Sir John Simon, the Home Secretary, to draw up the Abdication documents; then he went off to tell the Duke of York to stand by.

The King's friends witnessed his collapse and were in despair. The greatest blunderers of all were now proved to be the conspirators, and they had blundered in the most foolish way imaginable.

They had ignored the personality of the woman in the case. They thought they could be loyal to the King alone, and seemed to consider Mrs Simpson little more than a nuisance, someone to be got rid of or otherwise put out of mind. The fact was that not one of the King's supporters liked or bothered about Mrs Simpson, and this weakened their argument fatally. Churchill scarcely mentioned her. His entire campaign was for delay and the avoidance of irrevocable decision. If he gave any opinion at all on whether or not the King should marry, it seems to have been a guarded hope that the King would get over his infatuation once the crisis died down.

Beaverbrook's simple solution for many difficulties over the years had been 'never resign, wait until you are fired'. Now his theme was, keep the King on the throne, because once he was off it he could not get back on to it. He knew that there was a core to the crisis far more important than the personalities of Edward VIII and Mrs Simpson. It was nothing less than the future of Great Britain and the Empire. But having understood that, he then took up an illogical position. Idealism has driven Beaverbrook in many strange directions in his career, but none stranger than this. His passion was the British land and the British people. His obsession was a policy of British Imperial isolationism, and he identified Edward with his own cause, partly because Edward was the personification of his beloved Empire, partly because he could just not bring himself to trust the Empire to Baldwin.

One of the tragedies in the conflict lay in the fact that Baldwin and Beaverbrook might have been allies had their personal dislike of one another been less strong. The essence, as seen by the author, is that Baldwin's fight, however he fought it, was the preservation of the kingly symbol, the unity of the British nation, the dignity of Parliament, the loyalty and reverence of the British Empire. Victory for Lord Beaverbrook's man would have meant at best a nation sullenly divided, and an Empire that might have cut its ties rather than pay homage to Wallis Warfield Spencer Simpson Windsor as Queen, or even as first lady.

Baldwin, in fact, was fighting Beaverbrook's fight. Such is the sadness of rivalry in small matters that Baldwin even today, nine years dead, is the one man Beaverbrook seems unable to recall with magnanimity.

The King's supporters thought that once Mrs Simpson was out of the way, King Edward would become more amenable to their advice. Instead, he lost all reason and thought only of following her. Baldwin, as usual, was wiser than his enemies. He had learned much about Edward's personality from the miserable tour of Canada nine years earlier. Working from an unsure position, he based everything on his assessment of Edward's temperament. He never made a mistake, and he saved the Monarchy.

Baldwin had realised more quickly than anyone else the vital fact that the King was beaten from the moment Mrs Simpson left his side. Edward lost his courage, morale and his will to fight. This total collapse was without doubt the most important single factor in his Abdication after 325 days as King of England. And its very suddenness illustrates more clearly how closely Wallis and the King actually came to victory. If Wallis had kept her nerve and continued to stay close to him, invigorating him and giving him encouragement, he might have gone on fighting indefinitely, and possibly won. It would have been a bitter, empty victory, but he might have forced his will on the country.

Even now the die was not completely cast. The King could reverse his decision before the Cabinet Committee got seriously to work on the complicated and unprecedented construction of the Act of Abdication. But Edward, after many months of day-dreaming about what he would do for himself and his intended bride, was now face to face with many unpleasant truths. Forty years of popularity that came close to idolatry, built up by every device of propaganda and wishful thinking, had evaporated in a week.

No matter where he plunged in search of solution, he could only penetrate deeper into the essential truth of his own utter defeat. Snatch aside the curtain of the unrelenting Baldwin and he could see the horrified faces of the churchmen who sat around the green table at No. 10 Downing Street. Tear that aside and there was Geoffrey Dawson scribbling into the early hours words of resistance, condemnation, doom. Escape from Dawson and behind him was the Archbishop of Canterbury, his head averted, lips down-turned. Behind the Archbishop was the Church. Behind the Church was the British people flung at first like a glass ball full of artificial snow, into a flurry, now settling inexorably behind Parliament, the Government and the Prime Minister.

As far as Edward VIII was concerned, once he reached the throne with his domestic life unresolved, the avenues that were available to him were few and distasteful. He could remain celibate, something which is demanded of priests but never of kings, who are indeed required to be just the opposite. He could make a 'cold' suitable marriage which would have revolted him. He could tread the not untrodden royal path of forming a semi-permanent relationship with a mistress. A sufficiently dedicated King would have taken the first or second course. A practical King might have chosen the third. A King better organised in his own life would never have let himself get into this position in the first place.

But King Edward VIII was in love as few men in history had been in love. Mrs Simpson was the one light in an existence that otherwise was unbearable to him, and both he and she indignantly rejected a relationship without marriage. Having come so far, there was no way out. Abdication, the grenade which the King hoped to pitch into Baldwin's tent, was stuck in his hand. Baldwin had cleverly left the King without the freedom even to do what Baldwin was ostensibly urging him to do; to change his mind and stay on the throne. To renounce Mrs Simpson would have been to brand himself, not only a weakling, but also as the most foresworn man who ever sought the hand of a lady.

Spiritually he was left without comfort or guidance. The Archbishop of Canterbury knew how deeply Edward resented him, but he knew, too, how desperately alone the King was. The Archbishop was troubled. He was aware, at least to some extent, that he had left undone things he might have done. 'I am disposed to think,' he wrote later in his diary, 'I might have written to Edward VIII if only to liberate my conscience.' After some soul-searching, however, the Archbishop decided he had done the right thing, after all. 'Almost certainly,' he added, 'this would have invoked, even if any reply had been given, the sort of slight which *I* personally would have understood, but to which the Archbishop of Canterbury ought not to be exposed.'

So Dr Lang left Edward to deal with his soul in his own way.

*   *   *

The King had made his decision. He intended to quit and marry Mrs Simpson. But instead of putting an end to the intolerable strain, it merely unleashed new disasters to pile up on the old.

On the morning of Saturday, December 5th, when King Edward formally announced his intention to abdicate, he held in his hand a letter from Sir John Simon containing the most ghastly intelligence. It reminded him that Mrs Simpson's divorce would not be made absolute until April, and that any close association might induce someone to get the King's Proctor to intervene and stay the divorce.

This was a new and unsuspected blow for the King, who had not up to now realised he would have to remain separated from Mrs Simpson even after the Abdication. Sir Walter Monckton, who was negotiating between the King and the Prime Minister with a skill which aroused the admiration of all parties, suggested the only way out. Parliament could do anything if it wanted. It could confirm a divorce. Monckton advised an approach to Baldwin.

When the Abdication Bill was presented to Parliament would the Government also introduce a second Bill to make Mrs Simpson's divorce absolute forthwith?

If that could be done Edward could leave England and be reunited with Mrs Simpson immediately. If it could not be done, then the curtain was about to rise on a period of the most intense distress and danger.

The Prime Minister was surprisingly receptive to the idea. He was positively enthusiastic. The news which Mrs Simpson heard in Cannes seemed almost too good to be true. The King told Mrs Simpson that Baldwin had pledged himself to getting the

Divorce Bill through Parliament. He had staked his career on it and had promised to resign if he failed.

Baldwin had played many quick-change roles in this crisis, but his one-night stand as the friend and champion of the two lovers was his masterpiece. The greatest tribute to his performance was that he convinced all who heard him. To convince his enemies, Edward and Mrs Simpson, was clever enough, even though they were inexperienced and fair game. But tough fellows like Sir Walter Monckton and Sir George Allen were fooled no less.

'I believe,' Walter Monckton said gleefully, 'that now we shall be able to tidy everything up.'

Baldwin departed from The Fort well pleased. Without the Divorce Bill the King might have changed his mind in a hurry. Tomorrow was another day. Tomorrow would be too late. There can be no doubt that the last person the Prime Minister was thinking of at this moment was Mrs Simpson, or of the brutal blow he was about to inflict on her. The Prime Minister—unlike Geoffrey Dawson or the Archbishop of Canterbury—never appeared to feel any personal animosity towards Mrs Simpson. We have no record that he ever spoke of her viciously or even appeared to think of her much at all. She was an impersonal thing, a pawn incapable of human feelings or the capacity to suffer.

Even if he did think at this time of Mrs Simpson's feelings, he would have been compelled to ignore them. The future of the Monarchy was in his hands. He dared not fail. Any suffering caused to the outgoing King and the woman he loved was unimportant compared with such a vital cause.

On the following morning (Sunday), Baldwin, the actor, took a day off and became himself. At the morning session of the Cabinet called to consider the King's proposal, Baldwin simply put the matter before his colleagues and sat back, inert, indifferent, listening to them howl.

The Divorce Bill scandalised the Cabinet. It was attacked on legal, moral and religious grounds, and because it looked as if the Government were striking a bargain with the King over the Abdication.

Loudest objections came from Sir Thomas Inskip, a member of

the Church Assembly and the strongest churchman present. If the Bill went through, he would have to resign. Ramsay MacDonald worried about the time element, and Neville Chamberlain grumbled about the effects of the crisis on the Christmas trade. Sir Walter Monckton was called in after a two-hour wait outside the Cabinet-room and listened to the chorus of protests. He turned to Baldwin for support, for a reiteration of his threat of resignation, a threat which would quickly whip the Ministers into line.

All Baldwin said was: 'This must be settled before Christmas.'

That was the end of the incident of the two Bills. It had blossomed and withered in twenty-four hours, but while it lived the King was filled with new hope, and when it died his anger surpassed all that had gone before.

Then the King pleaded with the Prime Minister to be fair to Mrs Simpson. When the time came for Baldwin to review the Abdication to the House of Commons would he please pay tribute somewhere in the course of his speech to her impeccable behaviour in times that were trying to say the least. Baldwin did not say he wouldn't, but he didn't.

The King began to go to pieces. He was, he felt bitterly, a King who was ruler of nothing, lord of nobody, a King who could do no right. Contemporary accounts of him speak of a man who raved, wept, called himself a fool, and then in moments of quiet said, 'My brother will make a better King than I'. He waited helplessly for Baldwin to push him off the throne.

The last hope of the King's supporters now rested in the success of the 'conspiracy', which had widened to the extent that it was a secret to almost no one except the King and Mrs Simpson. Nearly all the King's friends had been put into the picture, and most of his enemies, too. Even the Prime Minister knew all about it: Beaverbrook had kept his friend Sir Samuel Hoare informed, and Hoare, in turn, told Baldwin, who was reported—by Hoare —to be 'sympathetic'. Hoare revealed this development many years later, and nothing illustrates more vividly the unexpected ways in which personal loyalty carried the various participants in the crisis.

For a moment we actually have the opponents Beaverbrook and Baldwin, men working for opposite ends, now partners in the same plot. Baldwin then carried the confusion even further by calling Theodore Goddard, Mrs Simpson's solicitor, to Downing Street for a secret conference. The probable truth was that while Baldwin gave Hoare the impression that he was not opposed to the 'conspiracy', he was really very uneasy about it, and to Goddard he outlined a plan which was shortly to become clear.

CHAPTER XI

The Prisoner in the Villa Lou Viei

WALLIS SIMPSON in her retreat at Cannes was in truth needing very little persuasion. She was beginning to see the issue more clearly than she had ever done before.

The hours following her arrival had been hours of dismay and despair. The exhilaration of the madcap flight across France had to some extent driven the crisis from her mind. But now she was left with her own thoughts. The celebrated, imperturbable Mrs Simpson was deserted and perturbed indeed; perturbed, torn, distressed. Her great court had disappeared. Only Herman Rogers and Lord Brownlow were left of all that scintillating Anglo-American aristocracy that had loved and sported around Fort Belvedere and St James's Palace.

Round and round the problem went in her mind. 'What can I do? What else could I have done?' But in spite of every strain she was keeping her head. However history judges her part in the *impasse* to which the British Monarchy was brought in December 1936, these last few days of the reign of Edward VIII reflect on her nothing but credit.

For herself she sought nothing. In the five, six, seven, sometimes eight, telephone calls she had every day with the King, she repeatedly told him to hang on, not to abdicate whatever he did; unaware or refusing to believe that it was too late.

News of Stanley Baldwin's turn-about on the proposed Divorce Bill was responsible for her blackest despair of all. If the King were really to abdicate, marriage was her only sanctuary from the crisis. To bring the King down and then be unable to marry him would bring on her such furies of public opinion that would dwarf what she had endured already. She would be utterly forsaken.

Until April she would have to tread the knife-edge path which leads from a decree nisi to a decree absolute. She must stay rigidly separated from the King. Reunion was prohibited. She was trapped, the stealthy watch of the King's Proctor behind her and the implacable gates of a puritanical law in front of her.

To this drama of tortured love, acted out on a telephone between Fort Belvedere and Cannes, the French switchboard operators listened in eagerly. At first they were delicate enough just to listen in a little from time to time. Gradually they grew bolder, and listened in to everything, romantically ignoring other calls. Then they would trade the entire conversation—inaccurately —to the French newspapers.

Finally Brownlow, who was still in charge of Mrs Simpson's safety and welfare, lost his temper and stormed out by car to call on the Prefect of the Alpes-Maritimes Department. The Prefect, who controls the district politically, was immediately fearful of repercussions and called Paris. Within a matter of hours the French Foreign Office replaced with skilled and trusted telephone operators the over-romantic eavesdroppers, and the King and Mrs Simpson were able to hold their last conversations before the Abdication in privacy.

The little party of friends in the Villa Lou Viei were now literally besieged. The British and American correspondents outside had banded together to hire the largest car they could find, which happened to be a gigantic Hispano. This they kept with the nose sticking out across the Rogers's private path. Unless the Hispano backed up no vehicle could get into or out of the grounds. The engine was always kept running, and the correspondents' aim was to scrutinise everyone leaving or coming to the house. If Mrs Simpson or Rogers ventured out the Hispano would let them pass, then keep on their tail everywhere they went.

The reporters were trying every trick they knew. Gendarmes had to winkle out from neighbouring houses photographers with telephoto lenses, and one newspaperman was hauled down from the roof of the villa on to which he had somehow managed to climb. The villa at the time was being redecorated and had the plumbers in. Two reporters dressed themselves as plumbers and tried to bribe the real plumbers to let them into the house. They then discovered that Provençales are the hardest of all Frenchmen to bribe. They failed, and to the accompaniment of the guffaws of the rest of the reporters, the two men returned sheepishly to their hotel to change back to the ordinary clothes.

One American woman correspondent, using the names of mutual friends, put Herman Rogers under a social obligation to see her. She suggested an interview at her hotel and he reluctantly agreed. The correspondent had arranged it cosily and informally with a log fire, a bottle of whisky and two glasses. She was attired, for comfort, in filmy negligée. Rogers, who was a particularly handsome man, had been feeling rather distrustful of the whole business, and spoiled the effect by bringing his wife along. . . .

Extra postmen were put on the round to carry the flood of letters arriving at the Villa Lou Viei by every mail. They represented every shade of opinion from encouragement to threats of death. It was hopeless trying even to sort them.

In 1952 Rogers moved from the Villa Lou Viei to a smaller house nearby, and in an attic found a dozen crate loads of letters, which he burned. He estimated that it amounted in all to about one tenth of the volume of mail which arrived all told.

It was the never-ending mountain of mail as much as any other single item that was influencing Mrs Simpson. She was terrified by the abuse and opprobrium which she was receiving, and she began casting around in her mind for some way to divert the anger away from her. Renunciation had already occurred to her, but she could not face this except as a last desperate resort. She did not realise how hopeless the King's cause had become, and she still hoped.

The idea came to her to make a tentative statement of withdrawal from the King's life, not a renunciation, but a cautious plea to ease her present unsympathetic position, in which she appeared to be solely responsible for toppling a King from his throne. In one of her telephone conversations with the King, he agreed that she should issue the statement. Edward, absorbed in his mental problems, as well as the Act of Abdication now near completion, did not realise that Mrs Simpson was on the threshold of saying good-bye to him for ever.

On Monday, December 7th, Brownlow called a press conference at the Hôtel Majestic in Cannes. He announced crisply in his best Guardsman's manner: 'What I have to say tonight is divided into two sections, separate and distinct. First a denial, secondly an official announcement. The denial, is as follows: Mrs Simpson has given no interviews of any sort or kind or made any statements to the press whatsoever other than the statement I now make on her behalf.' (This in answer to a few wild French claims of 'exclusive interviews'.) 'The following is the official announcement of Mrs Simpson: "Mrs Simpson throughout the last few weeks has invariably wished to avoid any action or proposal which would hurt or damage His Majesty or the Throne. Today her attitude is unchanged, and she is willing, if such action would solve the problem, to withdraw forthwith from a situation that has been rendered both unhappy and untenable." '

The reporters faded away, and Mrs Simpson was left with a few hours of peace in which she could explore the miseries of her position. The confines of the Villa Lou Viei were suddenly too small for her. She asked Lord Brownlow to start the car and get away from it all for a while. The reporters' Hispano slid into position behind them, but Lord Brownlow was prepared. He twisted and doubled back over the mountain lanes and gave them the slip. For the first time for days Mrs Simpson was freed from pursuit, from siege and from the telephone.

The Riviera roads were deserted at this time of the year, and as the car sped aimlessly through towns and villages Mrs Simpson and Lord Brownlow talked it over. She asked him his opinion. He replied frankly that he thought she had put herself in a position whereby the British people, rightly or wrongly, would never forgive her.

Wallis could well believe him. The vision of the crown and the throne at last faded into nothing. So did morganatic marriage. The man who loved her could not even keep the throne for himself if he married her. The masquerade was over and the love affair was heading for a classically unhappy ending. Wallis War-field had started from nothing and reached the society of emperors. She had achieved what few women of history had achieved, but at the moment of crisis her bourgeois upbringing had let her down and she was lost from the moment she fled England.

Only one thing would save the King and preserve his throne. Renunciation, followed by flight. At long last Wallis Simpson saw it all. Few people today realise how deeply the plans were laid for what was to be the second and final escape of Mrs Simp-son, or how closely they came to be carried out. They were evolved in great detail. Mrs Simpson would issue a formal state-ment of renunciation, via Perry Brownlow. In the meantime Evans, the detective, would be sent on ahead into Nice and make reservations in the Blue Train to Genoa or Brindisi, whichever port could offer earlier ship bookings. They would then sail to-gether somewhere too remote for her to be recalled by the King. Ceylon was discussed, and even China, where Wallis had lived thirteen years earlier. Once Mrs Simpson was safely installed on the other side of the globe, Brownlow would return home.

They agreed that the King must hear news of the renunciation from Mrs Simpson herself. It would be a painful moment, but it was intolerable to think that the monarch should first hear the news from the press.

In the setting sun the car turned its nose back towards Cannes. It was dark by the time the two friends returned to the villa. As soon as she re-entered the house the pressure of the crisis closed in on her once more.

Here, as usual, there was confusion and anxiety. The King had called. When he spoke to her, he was frantic and gave her a perplexing message. Theodore Goddard, her solicitor, was flying down to see her. 'But don't see him,' the King warned imperiously, and added that he was carrying a message from Baldwin.

This was baffling. Her own solicitor 'a Baldwin man'; of all the strange happenings of the Abdication this was to be one of the strangest, and in his Memoirs the Duke of Windsor himself seems to have had only a vague notion of what it was about.

What had happened was this. Earlier on Monday, December

7th, Mr Baldwin had summoned Goddard to Downing Street, and they had discussed Mrs Simpson's statement which had just been received.

Mild though the offer had been, it had filled Baldwin with apprehension. He was so busy working for the abdication of the King that he had not paused to consider the possibility that Mrs Simpson might abdicate first.

As a result of their conversation, the Prime Minister put a Government plane at Goddard's disposal. Goddard was to fly to Cannes, and on the Prime Minister's behalf urge Mrs Simpson to give up the King.

This poses an immediate question—why? Baldwin was determined to get rid of the King. Of this there can be no argument. If Mrs Simpson accepted Goddard's plea, the King would stay on the throne and Baldwin might come face to face with the necessity of abdicating from his own office.

The answer was that the message was an excuse. Baldwin wanted information. He did not know what was going on in the Villa Lou Viei, and he was anxious. He needed to have a man inside the house who could send him news. The man he chose was Theodore Goddard.

It is unfortunate, historically speaking, that Goddard died without revealing much of his part in the Abdication story, for his finger was in the oddest of pies. It was certainly he who was responsible for the precautions taken at Ipswich when Mrs Simpson was granted her divorce. Now he was Baldwin's emissary.

He did not, of course, tell the King he was going, but the King found out from his own solicitor and was horrified. His first thought was to warn Wallis.

But Mrs Simpson's reaction was different. As puzzled as the King about the significance of Goddard's mission, it nevertheless filled her with excitement. What message could the Prime Minister possibly have for her? Was it some move to put an end to the crisis, and at the same time save her from fulfilling her own drastic decision? A last-minute change of policy perhaps; a break in his nerves; surrender even; an agreement for a morganatic

marriage rather than have the King abdicate? She awaited
Goddard's visit eagerly.

Meanwhile Goddard, accompanied by his doctor—he had a
heart condition—was enduring a nightmare journey. Bad weather
had delayed the take-off, and in the air the plane was severely
buffeted. Goddard had never flown before, and he was in intense
discomfort. The plane force-landed at Marseilles, but Goddard's
resolution held. He acquired a car and drove non-stop to Cannes,
arriving exhausted, in time for breakfast. Reporters, seeing Mrs
Simpson's solicitor with a doctor, went dashing off with all sorts
of crazy rumours.

For Mrs Simpson the meeting was a sad anticlimax. Goddard
told her frankly that he was on a mission from her enemy, and
expressed the hope that she would do what she had already made
up her mind to do.

Mrs Simpson then proved her sincerity and good faith. In
Goddard's presence, she called the King and told him of her
decision. Edward was staggered. Beset on all sides and intent on
the act of sacrifice, this was the most crushing blow of all.

'It's too late,' he cried, 'the Abdication documents are being
drawn up.'

Mrs Simpson, though wrung dry of emotion, persisted.
Edward overwhelmed her arguments, and she yielded although
only momentarily. But Goddard had heard enough. He faded
away, turned up in Paris where he rang Baldwin. Then, on arrival
in London he was met by car and taken immediately to the Prime
Minister. The news was very gratifying to Baldwin, who was
about to address the Commons.

The Goddard visit was a severe psychological blow to Mrs
Simpson. Already she was cut off from nearly all her old friends.
Now she realised that even her solicitor was tainted with the
brush of her enemies. Yet Goddard had organised her divorce.
She had had close contact and intimate conversation with him. It
was a thought that made her recoil in horror.

Even the weather was against her. The rains of the Riviera
came and went. The skies were dark. There seemed no single ray
of light anywhere.

CHAPTER XII

Climax and Defeat

THE events of the previous chapter were all crowded into the hours of Mrs Simpson's life from Sunday afternoon to Tuesday morning. Tumultuous as they were, they were paralleled by events in London, where the conflict shifted and merged and was past before the newspapers could comprehend its scope or significance.

On the Monday Winston Churchill rose in the House of Commons and was howled down. It was, as *The Times* said, the worst rebuff in modern political history. Baldwin had successfully crushed an incipient Parliamentary King's Party. He had put the autocratic Government Whip, Captain David Margesson, on the track of Conservative M.P.s whose sympathy seemed to be with the King; officially Margesson set out merely to sound opinion; in fact he diverted it firmly into line with Baldwin. This was a job at which Margesson was unsurpassed, and he succeeded. Nobody rose to support Churchill who, gesticulating defiantly, his voice lost in the uproar, finally slumped back in his seat defeated. Many observers of that scene believed that Churchill's career was finished.

Next morning Fleet Street was still coping with Wallis's statement to the press. *The Times* treated it with uneasy contempt, and the editor was clearly determined that the King was not going to wriggle free in this manner. They printed the story in small type under the Parliamentary debate. Under the story of Wallis's offer to withdraw and linked to it by a row of dots, they ran the following paragraph without headline: 'Thelma Viscountess Furness arrived in Southampton in the liner *Queen Mary* yesterday from New York.'

It was an acid joke for a society in acid mood. But Dawson

quickly decided that either the joke was not funny or else it was too funny. After the first edition the item was moved to a less explosive part of the paper.

Geoffrey Dawson's editorial on the adjoining page was the most withering of the lot, and ripped to shreds the last remnants of Mrs Simpson's aspirations. Answering a last plea for morganatic marriage by the *Daily Mail*, Dawson wrote:

> 'There has, as Lord Rothermere says, been no suggestion at any time and from any quarter that the lady for whom the morganatic exception is recommended should become Queen. Yet in law—apart from the fact that she is not legally free to re-marry—there is nothing to bar her from becoming Consort and Queen in the full sense. The disqualification here is not, as on the Continent, one of law, but of fact. What is demanded is statutory recognition of the fact that she is not fitted to become Queen. The Prime Ministers of the Empire are to be asked to propose, and the Parliaments to accept and ratify, a permanent statutory apology for the lady whom the King desires to marry. The Constitution is to be amended in order that she may carry in solitary prominence the brand of unfitness for the Queen's Throne. . . .'

Lord Beaverbrook, in London, could see all round him the collapse of the King's cause, and he was aware of the hash being made of the conspiracy on the Riviera. His handling of Mrs Simpson's statement was in significant contrast to *The Times*, and typified the conflict of the press.

Beaverbrook went all out on the statement. Making a mountain of propaganda out of a molehill of news was a familiar game to him. He had done it many times in the past and he did it again now. The *Daily Express* brought out its blackest type for the headline 'End of the Crisis'. The words were ironically chosen.

The crisis was indeed almost over, and ending on a note of din and confusion. Yet inexplicably, as events succeeded, overlapped and crossed each other during these last hours, Stanley Baldwin began to have last-minute alarms, and appears to have feared an eleventh-hour reversal. It was probably the result of the strain of the previous weeks and the victory that now seemed so very close. Some time earlier Baldwin's Cabinet had sent an address to the King, saying:

'Ministers are reluctant to believe that Your Majesty's resolve is irrevocable, and still venture to hope that before Your Majesty pronounces any formal decision Your Majesty may be pleased to reconsider an action which must so deeply distress, and so virtually affect, all Your Majesty's subjects.'

To this the King had replied: 'His Majesty has given the matter his further consideration but regrets he is unable to alter his decision.'

It seemed safe enough, but Baldwin was not so sure. Mrs Simpson's statement had attracted wide attention, and the Simpson press, as it was being called, was making a lot of noise about it. Baldwin was due to see the King that evening (Tuesday), and he was determined not to let him get off the hook. 'Only time I was frightened,' Baldwin admitted later, 'I thought he might change his mind.'

He need not have worried. Edward, he found, was calm and inflexible, almost gay, in spite of *The Times* editorial. But next day the King received the worst news of all. Mrs Simpson was on the line to him, her resolve once more stiffened to leave him. Goddard had been followed at the Villa Lou Viei by Esmond Harmsworth (how Lord Rothermere), who was adding his voice to all the others urging Wallis to renounce the King. Throughout the crisis Harmsworth had been one of the truest and most unswerving friends of the King.

Lord Brownlow's plans for escape still stood ready, and Harmsworth had strengthened her for one last effort. She realised that one telephone call stood between her and the end of the ordeal. At the end of it a Prime Minister would be frustrated and a King would remain King. So Wallis had picked up the telephone and implored the King to let her go.

In this call it is clear from the King's Memoirs that the scene was a climax of emotion, and it culminated in the King's steady warning that wherever she went he would follow. Mrs Simpson was beaten. The King's love, as Theodore Goddard told Baldwin, was too much for her, and she threw in her hand. The brief tempest of conjecture which had followed Wallis's statement died, and with it the last hopes of the British Empire that it would keep its King.

It was all over. There was no longer any issue. Baldwin, content, could look forward to the accession of Edward's brother. The British Monarchy, so serene and majestic eleven months ago, had been saved from disaster by the Prime Minister and guided through the valley of the shadow of death. Tomorrow it would be delivered pale but still breathing into the safe and dedicated hands of King George VI.

The last assault on the nerves of Mrs Simpson and the King was made on Wednesday, December 9th. A seventy-four-year-old solicitor's clerk named Francis Stephenson, of Ilford, Essex, 'intervened' at the Divorce Registry at Somerset House and said he had reason to show why Mrs Simpson's divorce should not be confirmed. It was exactly as Baldwin had forecast in his warning to the King the week before. Had it happened a day or so earlier, when Baldwin feared the King might be wavering, the intervention might have altered considerably the character of the crisis, as it sought to prevent the King marrying Mrs Simpson, on the throne or off it. Now, however, the crisis was too far gone for anything to be done about it.

On this same Wednesday the skies opened over Cannes and the rain came down in sheets, drenching the thousands of sight-seers waiting outside the Villa Lou Viei. The following day the King abdicated.

A few more scenes were still to be played before Edward left for his exile. He had drafted the notes for a short farewell speech to the British people, calling in Winston Churchill and his unfailing muse for the final polish. The meeting between the defeated King and the apparently beaten statesman was a moving one, and gave Churchill the moment to invest the whole crisis past and present with its one note of sheer nobility.

As he said good-bye, tears in his eyes, he recited half to himself, tapping out the rhythm with his stick, the words which Andrew

Marvell wrote to a king who lost not only his throne but also his head:

> *He nothing common did or mean*
> *Upon that memorable scene.*

It was utterly Churchillian to go out into a future which would seem black enough to embitter any man, his parting words being a little couplet in tribute to the man in whose cause he had given everything he had. And if Churchill was at his most magnificent, Edward recaptured for a flash the boyishness of his Prince of Wales days.

He picked up the autographed photograph of himself that he had given Churchill and tore down the drive after him. 'Hey, Winston!' he shouted. 'You've forgotten the picture.'

That evening, all his bags packed, he said good-bye to Fort Belvedere, the place where he had been young in love. Away from his sight dust-sheets were already being put over the furniture, and the chintz curtains were being taken down.

He was driven to Windsor Castle, where he was to have dinner with his family before making his broadcast. As a farewell meeting it went off better than it might have done. The ex-King probably did not realise how completely he had been written off by his family. Perhaps the family did not realise it either just yet. The crisis had been so sudden and cataclysmic that it was difficult for members of the family to adjust themselves to it. Although the sceptre had passed from David to Bertie, neither could reconcile themselves to their new positions, and tonight David was still the senior, Bertie the junior. The ex-King talked little about the job he had given up. He recommended his valet to his brother, 'a good fellow', and chatted about family matters. George VI was polite, possibly unaware himself of the depth of his anger. The Duke of Kent, a young man of high intelligence and artistic imagination, was the least composed and closest to breaking down. Gloucester was distrait and showed most resentment. He had made a career of the Army, and now realised he would have to give it up to help his brother, the new King, in his task. Queen Mary was impassive, invulnerable. Her bitterness was the deepest of all, but tonight she revealed the least. The dinner marked the last time in which Edward was admitted as part of the family. So far as the Royal Family was concerned, the story was finished. For the rest of the world, waiting by their radiosets, the emotional climax was about to come.

*　　*　　*

A limousine travelled through the night along the Great West Road from London to Windsor. In the back sat Sir John Reith, a steely handsome Scot, head of the B.B.C., and a good man for the part he now had to play.

Windsor Castle was ominously black and strangely deserted. There were no sentries or guards to be seen. Reith's car passed unchallenged, unrecognised, under the main archway, and pulled up at the foot of the private apartments. Reith got out, but was given no opportunity to knock. He had hardly reached the doorway when the door opened silently and the light from the corridor streamed out into the courtyard. The superintendent admitted him without a word. The housekeeper stood in the corridor, her eyes on his face. Reith was shown up to the King's modest three-room apartment in the Augusta Tower. The engineers had done their job, the B.B.C. was ready, and Reith settled down in the King's bedroom to wait. A servant came in and put a match to the fire, and Reith stared into the flames.

He was interrupted in his reflections by the arrival of the superintendent who said that the King was approaching—the 'former King' he meant—and would Sir John go down to welcome him. Reith thought it hardly correct to welcome the ex-King to his own apartments, but a glance at the servant's distraught face made him cut short his refusal. Edward did not seem at all surprised to see him. He wore his famous coat with the astrakhan collar, and puffed at a big cigar.

'Good evening, Reith,' he said amiably. 'Very nice to come over yourself for this.' Walter Monckton was by his side and was introduced.

What was there to say? Reith decided to act as though nothing had happened. He discussed the broadcast cheerfully. 'Madrid has just called,' he said. 'Civil War or no Civil War, they want permission to relay your broadcast.' Edward laughed.

The former King walked into his suite, and saw some of the furniture was under dust-covers. For a moment the thin veil of aplomb dropped, and his face went grey. So soon? Then he recovered himself. He remembered he had personally ordered the furniture to be covered. He had planned some redecorations and had not expected to leave so abruptly.

There were still some moments to go. Reith suggested a routine voice test, and handed the former King a newspaper to read from, tactfully turning the front page down to the table and presenting him with the sports page. But the Abdication was in the news everywhere. Mechanically the ex-King started to speak, and found he was reading a speech by Sir Samuel Hoare who that day had told a tennis organisation that the new King was an enthusiastic tennis player. Involuntarily Edward stopped, looked up at Reith, and grinned. Reith noticed that the typescript of Edward's speech had been untidily prepared with many corrections and erasures. He recalled that Edward, as Prince of Wales and King, always pasted each page of his speech meticulously and personally on to large sheets of cardboard.

The red light went on. 'This is Windsor Castle,' Reith said to the listening world, 'His Royal Highness Prince Edward.' Reith then slipped out of the chair and Edward took his place, banging his foot against the table leg as he did so and making a noise that perplexed millions. Reith left the room noiselessly. Monckton was waiting for him outside. 'Glad you behaved as you did,' Monckton whispered. 'Pretending nothing had happened. Right approach.' Reith looked at Monckton, and saw the tired eyes behind the rather owlish glasses. He remembered the haggard face of Godfrey Thomas in his office the week before. He realised how utterly the King's men had given themselves to the cause that had been lost that day.

'At long last,' the ex-King said, 'I am able to say a few words of my own. I have never wanted to withhold anything, but until now it has not been constitutionally possible for me to speak. A few hours ago I discharged my last duty as King and Emperor, and now that I have been succeeded by my brother, the Duke of York, my first words must be to declare my allegiance to him. This I do with all my heart. You all know the reasons which have impelled me to renounce the throne, but I want you to understand that in making up my mind I did not forget the Country or the Empire, which, as Prince of Wales, and lately as King, I have for twenty-five years tried to serve.

'But you must believe me when I tell you that I have found it impossible to carry the heavy burden of responsibility and to discharge my duties as King, as I would wish to do, without the help and support of the woman I love, and I want you to know that the decision I have made has been mine and mine alone. This was a thing I had to judge for myself. The other person most nearly concerned has tried, up to the last, to persuade me to take a different course. I have made this, the most serious decision, only upon the single thought of what would in the end be best for all.

'This decision has been made less difficult to me by the sure knowledge that my brother, with his long training in the public affairs of this country and with his fine qualities, will be able to take my place forthwith without interruption or injury to the life and progress of the Empire, and he has one matchless blessing, enjoyed by so many of you, and not bestowed on me, a happy home with his wife and children.

'During these hard days I have been comforted by Her Majesty, my mother, and by my family. The Ministers of the Crown, and in particular, Mr Baldwin, have always treated me with full consideration. There has never been any constitutional difference between me and them, and between me and Parliament. Bred in the constitutional tradition by my Father, I should never have allowed any such issue to arise. Ever since I was Prince of Wales, and later on when I occupied the Throne, I have been treated with the greatest kindness by all classes wherever I have lived or journeyed through the Empire. For that I am very grateful. I now quit altogether public affairs, and lay down my burden. It may be some time before I return to my native land, but I shall always follow the fortunes of the British race and Empire with profound interest, and if, at any time in the future, I can be found of service to His Majesty in a private station, I shall not fail.

'And now we all have a new King. I wish him and you, his people, happiness and prosperity with all my heart. God bless you all. God Save The King.'

It was probably the most emotional night in the history of radio. An American woman correspondent arriving in London that morning had been warned earlier by a British politician friend to stay out of the West End as the police expected trouble. The politician under-estimated the receptivity of the British people. London, far from exploding, seemed uncomprehending. The crowds outside Buckingham Palace stood silent. Later the arguments stilled by the King's speech were resumed in homes and public-houses, sometimes with heat but rarely with violence. Sadness, coupled with wonder and relief at the quietness of one's own reactions, seemed to be the national note. From two friends of King Edward, two authentic quotes of the time were preserved.

One, from a man: 'We have seen in him the last of the Stuart charm in the Royal Family. History may never be able to estimate its loss.'

And the second, from a woman: 'I loved Edward with all my heart, and I would have died for him. But when a King fights Parliament, Parliament always wins—thank God.'

Wallis Simpson sat the speech out at the Villa Lou Viei with Herman and Kitty Rogers and Perry Brownlow. She was dry-eyed, but the moment the speech was over she went silently to her room and closed the door. Ernest Simpson listened to the speech in a friend's home in the West End of London. As Edward ended with the words, 'God Bless you all. God Save The King', the radio rumbled into the sonorous tones of the National Anthem, and Ernest Simpson rose to his feet and stood to attention.

Edward left the microphone as though he were in a daze. He had not the slightest idea what was going to happen to him next. He did not even know where he was going and there was some vague impression in his mind that he was going to Zurich, although Mrs Simpson had made plans for him to go to Austria.

King George VI had created him Duke of Windsor. Together the four brothers walked to the door and shook hands. A butler helped the Duke on with his coat, and he disappeared into a night that was raw and wispy with mist. With Walter Monckton waiting for him and Slipper, Mrs Simpson's small dog left behind in her flight to France, snuffling on the front seat, the Duke climbed into the car which started off in the direction of Portsmouth. He had declined the sympathetic offer of Samuel Hoare to accompany him and to give him whatever ceremony was fit for an ex-King. He wanted to slip away quietly and undetected at night, so that he could be out of the country by the time his brother was proclaimed King next day.

The arrangements to receive him at Portsmouth were makeshift and went wrong. At first some official at the Admiralty had arranged for the former King to go to France in the naval yacht the *Enchantress*, which had taken Samuel Hoare to the Mediterranean some months before. But it was hastily felt by some other official that the name was ill-chosen in the circumstances, and switched orders to the destroyer *Fury*, of the 6th Flotilla, Home Fleet, without, however, informing all the officers on the dock, who were in some confusion.

None of the newspapers had heard of the King's impending departure, which was a relief, but on arriving at Portsmouth docks he was driven through the wrong gate. While a small guard of honour was chilled to the bone waiting for him at Unicorn Gate, the Duke's car had passed through Main Gate guarded by a single stamping sentry. The sailor recognised the former King and straightened into a salute which the Duke acknowledged. The car continued into the dockland and got lost. A passing watchman was asked the way and gave incomprehensible directions. The Duke thanked him.

A policeman who had seen the car pass phoned Admiral Sir

William Fisher, Commander-in-Chief, Portsmouth, waiting with the guard of honour. Fisher got into his own car and drove off in search. He found the Duke's car stopped, the chauffeur baffled. Smiling, the Duke apologised.

Fisher led the Duke back to *Fury*. It must have been difficult for the admiral to know what to say, but he found words. 'Your broadcast, Sir, was deeply moving,' he said hesitantly. 'It must have made a great impression on all who heard it.'

The Duke smiled slightly. He waited cheerfully on the dock while Slipper attended to necessary matters, then carried the dog under his arm up the gang-plank. On board ship the last remnants of King Edward's court were assembled. Sir Piers (Joey) Legh, his equerry, was to accompany him to Vienna, with Storier of the Yard, and a valet. Sir Ulick Alexander and Sir Godfrey Thomas were to cross the Channel with him. Walter Monckton was saying good-bye to him in Portsmouth.

Admiral Sir Roger Backhouse, Vice-Admiral Sir Dudley North and the commander of the ship, Commander C. L. Howe, welcomed him aboard. The Duke went immediately down to his cabin, and invited the flag officers to join him. The officers protested. 'You must be terribly tired, Sir,' said Backhouse. 'Perhaps we should say good-bye now.' But the Duke insisted they come down. 'Just for a moment,' he said. The officers did and farewells were made.

The night had become clear and calm as *Fury* sailed at 2.00, Monckton, a solitary figure in civilian clothes among the impersonal blue and gold of the Royal Navy, waving good-bye from the dock. *Fury* anchored for the night in St. Helen's Roads, and that morning at 6.30 set out for Boulogne. Meanwhile the dawn of a new day and a new reign was breaking over London.

The former King had succeeded in leaving his realm quietly. A combination of love and bluff had done for him. On the windy wharf at Boulogne he said good-bye to his friends, and summed up the events of the preceding months simply and frankly. 'I always thought,' he said to one of his friends, 'that I could get away with a morganatic marriage.'

He failed—but he can rest in peace and so can the woman for

whom he sacrificed so much. This great adventure has sealed the places of Edward VIII and Mrs Simpson in history.

Love is a great preserver of names. Love is the reason why Lord Nelson's life is richer than the Duke of Wellington's; Browning's than Tennyson's. Love will make Edward VIII a hero to future centuries when abler kings are mere names and numerals. Whether this is a comfort, we do not know. Only the principal concerned can ever know whether the consciousness of his immortality is a consolation for present suffering.

Edward's was not the only last word on the subject. Stanley Baldwin, characteristically, made two.

His narrative to the House of Commons describing the events of the crisis and his efforts to dissuade the King from marrying Mrs Simpson provided him with the greatest triumph of his career. At the end he looked up from what he called his 'scrappy notes' and said: 'I am convinced that where I failed no one would have succeeded.'

A few weeks later Lord Brownlow returned to London and called on the Prime Minister. Brownlow had also failed in his mission to separate Mrs Simpson from the King, but he was in good conscience. He had done his best, and he could have used Baldwin's words to the House of Commons as his own. He told Baldwin the whole story. The Prime Minister, puffing his pipe, listened silently. At the end he said jovially, 'My boy, if you'd succeeded in your mission, I'd have clapped you in the Tower of London.'

PART II

THE WINDSORS

CHAPTER I

The Morning After

———

THE Duke must sometimes find himself bewildered at the proliferation of marriages surrounding the Duchess. He is her third husband, and her two previous husbands have between them had eight wives. The Duchess's mother had three husbands, and the situation is complicated still further by the fact that Mary Kirk Raffray's second husband was also the Duchess's second husband, Mary divorcing Jacques Raffray and marrying Ernest Simpson after Simpson had been divorced by Wallis.

It was the Duke's misfortune. Behind him in England the waters closed, and so smoothly did the new reign take over that the Abdication, which some feared might produce a revolution and the disintegration of the Empire, was quickly made to look almost unimportant.

In Berlin, Hitler complained to his ministers that Edward VIII had been squeezed out because he was pro-German. Apart from this gem of top-level Nazi thinking, the world reactions to the Abdication were somewhat inconsequential. Mayor Howard W. Jackson of Baltimore offered the couple the keys of the city, and in Washington Don Felipo Espil, now Argentine Ambassador to the United States, clucked admiringly. 'My! My!' he said. 'Who'd have guessed our little Wallis would come so far!'

Americans were as divided as the British on the subject. Sinclair Lewis in the *New York Post* begged Edward to come to the United States. 'We are a funny people, David Windsor,' said Lewis unctuously, 'because we believe in righteousness. We believe that a man must have his own conscience and his own life. We believe perhaps that the most important thing that has happened in the last one hundred years is whether David Windsor should have his own life or not.' William Allen White, distinguished editor of the *Emporia* (*Kansas*) *Gazette* said that Edward should have told the British people from the balcony of Buckingham Palace, 'You are all a bunch of white-livered hypocrites.'

H. L. Mencken, the American sage—and a Baltimorean, more-over—took a different view. 'The King is an idiot,' he said, 'and the Abdication showed it. He ought to go to Hollywood. If he is too dumb to make good there, he could go to Washington.'

From Jamaica Lloyd George cabled the Duke: BEST CHRIST-MAS GREETINGS FROM AN OLD MINISTER OF THE CROWN WHO HOLDS YOU IN AS HIGH ESTEEM AS EVER AND REGARDS YOU WITH DEEPER LOYAL AFFECTION DEPLORES THE SHABBY AND STUPID TREATMENT ACCORDED YOU RESENTS THE MEAN AND UNGENEROUS ATTACKS UPON YOU.

Later Ribbentrop's wife claimed to have heard Winston Churchill say at a supper party at Lord Kemsley's: 'Had Lloyd George not been abroad they would never have succeeded in making Edward VIII abdicate. Alone I was too weak.'

The Baroness Ravensdale, that most perceptive critic of British gentlefolk and their habits, returned to England shortly after the Abdication and was amazed at the tone of the conversations she heard. Remembering the mighty sway which Mrs Simpson had held only a few weeks earlier over society, she commented: 'I was nauseated by the hostesses of London turning on Mrs Simpson as if they scarcely knew her, and calling her every name under the sun.'

Ernest Simpson, goaded for the first and last time out of his silence, sued a well-known society woman for alleging at a dinner table that he had been paid to accept the divorce. An unqualified apology was made, and Simpson let it go at that without claiming damages.

A mood of introspection settled on the people of the British Empire. Even the newspapers were muted after the Abdication. But quite suddenly into this valley of calm poured an extraordinary assortment of high dignitaries of the Church of England howling in pursuit of the former King.

At the microphone, March 1936. His first broadcast as King.

Fort Belvedere.
"My home during my last days in Britain."

It was headed by Dr Cosmo Lang, the Archbishop of Canterbury, in a statement of such unChristian-like vindictiveness that the Church has still not shaken off the painful effects of it. He condemned the King for wanting to marry a woman who had divorced her husband, and rebuked his friends whose ways of life he said were 'alien to the best interests of the people'.

Other bishops scurried in to get into the act. The Bishop of Durham said hopefully that if the marriage were taking place in the diocese of Durham, he would consider himself in duty bound to inhibit any clergyman within his jurisdiction from officiating in it; though there seemed little reason to think that the Duke had even momentarily contemplated Durham as the place in which to get married.

Then the Bishop of Fulham made a statement which carried more bite. He controls the chaplains on the continent of Europe, and he told reporters with urbane obscurity that his 'directions to them had been followed with complete loyalty'—his instructions being not to marry the Duke to Mrs Simpson.

Such remarks stung some people to reply. In Parliament John McGovern, Glasgow Socialist, bawled: 'Let the bishops get out and deal with the means test instead of kicking a man when he is down.' And H. G. Wells commented that he thought Mrs Simpson would be 'a far nicer-minded and altogether cleaner house companion' than the Archbishop of Canterbury.

The Archbishop was, in fact, disconcerted at the unfriendly impact of his speech, so he hastily made another one urging people to forget the Abdication, after which he did his best to woo some of the more outspoken British correspondents away from their hostility with a Gargantuan banquet of pheasant in Lambeth Palace.

Throughout the incident the Archbishop kept his piety for his private diary. 'My heart aches for the Duke of Windsor,' he wrote. 'Remembering his childhood, the rich promise of his services as Prince of Wales . . . I cannot bear to think of the life into which he has passed.' Later he admitted he was unwilling to crown King Edward. He saw King George VI and wrote: 'For an hour we talked together with the utmost ease about "the crisis", about the poor Duke of Windsor and then about arrangements for the Coronation. What a relief it was after the strained and wilful ways of the late King to be in this atmosphere of intimate friendship, and instead of looking forward to the Coronation as a sort of nightmare to realise . . . that to the solemn words of the Coronation there would now be a sincere response.'

Fort Belvedere, the Duke of Windsor's old home described so movingly in his Memoirs, was left deserted except for a housekeeper. Weeds grew and choked the rhododendrons he had tended with such care, and the lawns, unmown, became a derelict jungle. For a long time the Duke kept the furniture under dust-covers, but as the years passed and the possibilities of his return became more and more remote, he moved the furniture out bit by bit, so that today it is scattered over the Windsors' homes everywhere from Paris to the Waldorf-Astoria.

The real-estate aspect of the Abdication involved others besides the staff and trustees of Fort Belvedere. Shortly after the Abdication the charming D. B. Merryman estate with five hundred acres (five times as many as Fort Belvedere), at Hayfields in the Washington Valley near Baltimore, was put up for sale. As Mrs Simpson was related by marriage to the Merrymans, the estate agents put out a few feelers in the direction of the Duke to find out whether he would like to buy it. And up in Alberta, Canada, the manager of the EP Ranch (EP = Edward Prince), the Duke's own ranch, wondered whether it would be spruced up for the arrival of the owner and his bride for permanent residence. It was a decrepit windy shack, but the Duke had always been proud of it and it was the only home he had left. But neither the quiet respectability of the former nor the dedicated discomfort of the latter made any appeal yet to the Windsors, and from the Duke came no word.

Ernest Simpson crossed the Atlantic to be united with Mary Kirk Raffray, now divorced. To his surprise and alarm he found himself a hero in America, and momentarily disappeared under a squealing swarm of bobby-soxers. He escaped to Connecticut, where he married Mrs Simpson's childhood friend.

An idyll—tragically short—began with both Simpson and

Mary really happy. To the delight and mild surprise of friends, all of whom liked Simpson a lot but scarcely thought of him as the life and soul of the party, it was seen that Mary adored him. She also fell in love with England in a way that Mrs Simpson had never done.

Mary made no secret of the fact that she was determined to give Ernest Simpson a son to make the marriage a success. She did so in 1939 when she was forty-three. Mary went to New York in 1940 to take her baby out of the way of the bombs. There she learned that she was suffering from an incurable illness and said simply: 'I want to die in England.' She was given a priority passage back to blacked-out Britain, and a few months later she died. She is buried in a cemetery at Wells, in Somerset.

Simpson was deeply affected by her death. He rejoined the Guards in World War II, and served for three years in India. It was not until 1948 that he married again, for the fourth time but to his first English wife. The fourth Mrs Simpson was the beautiful former Mrs Avril Joy Leveson-Gower, younger sister of the famous Mrs Barney, who was found not guilty on a charge of murdering a Chelsea artist in a famous case in the early 'thirties and died some years later in a Paris hotel room. The Simpsons live happily today in Kensington, Simpson wealthy both by the bequests of parents and by his own commercial efforts.

The Duke of York was proclaimed King George VI. No man ever stepped into a more terrifying job. He had to prove not only himself but also the institution of monarchy which had been sprung on him. Shy as he was, he possessed enormous courage both moral and physical, and also a remarkable, unconscious charm. In the new King, with his diffident manner, his distrustful smile, his sudden expression like that of a startled stag, his reverence for his own position and his single-minded determination to live up to it, there was an atmosphere of goodness and refreshment. His apple-cheeked wife and darling daughters helped. Baldwin's forecast was quickly justified. The Yorks did it very well.

*　　*　　*

Before returning to the story of Mrs Simpson, one incident remains to be cleared up to wipe the slate of England clean of the Windsors' affairs. It was a strange incident, the ultimate secret of which is wrapped up today in the mind of an incredibly old man.

Francis Stephenson, the seventy-four-year-old solicitor's clerk, had 'intervened' with the King's Proctor slightly more than twenty-four hours before the Abdication, stating that he was going to show why Mrs Simpson's divorce decree nisi should not be made absolute. The intervention was pushed to some extent into the background by the other sensations of that memorable day. But even after the Abdication the matter remained on the books, and until it was removed Mrs Simpson could not obtain her decree absolute and marry.

The act of intervention was a little-known fact of law, yet during the Abdication crisis it had occurred to at least two people. Baldwin had warned the King that someone might take advantage of it. A week later Stephenson, coming from nowhere, known to nobody, did take advantage of it. The revelation of the power of a private citizen in a divorce case was startling.

The British people heard, most of them for the first time, that any person can interfere in any divorce. He simply goes to the Divorce Registry at Somerset House in the Strand. He pays half a crown and states he has reason to show why a particular decree should not be made absolute. His 'appearance' is noted, and notice of it is sent to the solicitors of the petitioner (the petitioner in this case being Mrs Simpson). According to law the intervener must file an affidavit within four days giving his reasons, though even if he fails to do so his 'appearance' remains on the records, and the decree cannot be made absolute until it has been formally removed in court.

In order to get it removed, the King's Proctor—the man who 'polices' divorces to make sure there is no collusion between the two parties—has to appear in Court and ask for directions. The petitioner's lawyer must also appear and request the 'appearance' to be removed from the register. Altogether it is quite a business, and it remains, with alterations, on the books today except that the period between the decree nisi and the decree absolute has been cut from six months to six weeks.

Francis Stephenson turned overnight into a world-famous and, to some, a sinister figure. He made his 'appearance' and filed his affidavit, and then when the matter came up in the Divorce Court in March 1937, he withdrew as abruptly as he had intervened.

The Attorney-General, Sir Donald Somervell, K.C., was in court for the occasion. He represented the King's Proctor and applied to Sir Boyd Merriman, President of the Divorce Court, for directions in the case. Sir Donald pointed out that the King's Proctor had seen Stephenson, and Stephenson had no evidence to support his allegations and that they were based on rumours which he had heard from friends and news which he had seen in the press.

Stephenson stood up in court, a stooped, insignificant man with drooping moustaches, but confident and precise. He announced that he withdrew his notice, and Sir Boyd Merriman ordered it to be struck out. Stephenson's affidavit setting out the reasons for his intervention was not read out, but several interesting facts emerged during the hearing. One was the first mention in court of the name of the woman named in the Simpson suit, Mrs E. H. Kennedy.

Another was the frank discussion of why Mrs Simpson had moved to Felixstowe before the divorce, the reason allegedly given by Stephenson being that she hoped to slip the divorce through quietly without the publicity which would have attended a London divorce. Mr Norman (now Lord Justice) Birkett, K.C., representing Mrs Simpson, said hastily on this account: 'I think it only fair and right to say at once that as far as Mrs Simpson herself is concerned in all matters of procedure she acted on advice.

'Expedition was the primary consideration. Mrs Simpson at the time was suffering from ill-health. A very great nervous strain was imposed upon her. The matter of expedition was carefully considered by her advisers—I don't mean by her solicitors only, I mean solicitors and counsel' (meaning Birkett himself). 'Reading was the appropriate assize town. The adultery alleged was at

Bray. It was ascertained that at Reading there would be no divorce suits. Ipswich was considered and a residence was taken at Beach House, Undercliff Road, Felixstowe, where Mrs Simpson resided during the trial and intended to reside for some time afterwards. After the trial certain circumstances arose. . . . Mrs Simpson cannot expect to be free from those things [rumours and gossip], but if it is in anybody's mind at any time that the reason for removal of this trial to Ipswich was to avoid a London trial, I am here to say that the only reason for removal was that of expedition.'

Sir Boyd Merriman acknowledged Birkett's explanation: 'You have put it quite frankly that the Felixstowe residence was taken in order to qualify for trial. I understand.'

With the intervention withdrawn, the way was cleared for Mrs Simpson to get her divorce made absolute, and the storm in the tea-cup died. Stephenson retreated into the endless jungle of London suburbia, leaving behind him two questions still not properly solved. Why did he intervene originally? and, having intervened, why did he so quietly withdraw?

Stephenson was no ordinary crank. He had a good brain, an above-average knowledge of the law, and a self-confidence which enabled him to have his say without either losing his head or being frightened by the uproar he created.

In the beginning he gave out a story that he was 'so moved' by the King's Abdication speech that he felt he could not continue with the intervention. Later he admitted bluntly: 'I withdrew because I was told to.' Next the question must be asked, 'By whom?'

The answer to that is locked in the old man's mind. Stephenson, nearly ninety, and a widower, today lives in a single room in a boarding-house in the wilderness of fading stucco known as Tulse Hill in South London.

'One of the newspapers sent a pretty girl to me a few years ago,' he is fond of telling friends. 'She handed me a blank cheque and said I could fill it in if I told her the inside story of my intervention. But what do I need money for at my age?' And the leading character of one of the oddest and most futile incidents of the Abdication clings with complacent glee to his secret.

CHAPTER II

Forlorn Wedding

———————

MRS SIMPSON remained in Cannes. Edward travelled quietly to Vienna, where he was greeted by the British Ambassador, Sir Walford Selby.

The Vienna police had made elaborate arrangements to make sure that the Duke of Windsor was not pestered by photographers, but the Duke saw them and said patiently, 'Let them come.' Afterwards he set out escorted by police into the Austrian countryside, and to the Castle Enzesfeld, twenty-five miles from Vienna.

It was the home of the Baron Eugene de Rothschild and his American wife, the former Kitty Wolff. During the war it was occupied first by the Germans, then by the Russians, but is now restored to the Baron minus a few art treasures. As soon as he arrived the Duke was on the long-distance telephone to Cannes and Mrs Simpson, still cloistered in the Villa Lou Viei. From now until May, when Mrs Simpson's decree nisi became absolute, the telephone would be their only means of communication. They dared not see each other, and risk another incident like that created by Francis Stephenson. It was going to be a heartbreaking separation, but both Mrs Simpson and the Duke were exhausted by the events of the previous weeks, and for several days they did little in their respective retreats but sleep, venturing out only occasionally, and hardly bestirring themselves except when the time came for their two long-distance calls every day.

As the weeks passed Mrs Simpson found herself occasionally able to wander into town on shopping expeditions without being buffeted by sight-seers and newspapermen. She appeared pale but self-possessed, and was beginning to regain the ten pounds she had lost in the anxiety of the Abdication. Gradually in her telephone talks to the Duke their wedding plans began to form, although the difficulties in the way seemed endless.

Difficulty number one was the matter of the church service. The Duke was desperately anxious to have the wedding blessed by the Church of England, but there seemed to be no way round the Church's 'hands-off' attitude. Difficulty number two was the alarming business of Francis Stephenson and the King's Proctor. Difficulty number three was to find a place where the marriage ceremony could be held, and difficulty number four was to find another place for them to make their home.

This was the testing time for Mrs Simpson. She was alone with an exhausted ex-King, hundreds of miles away, relying on her decisions. Even Lord Brownlow was gone. Problems concerning her wedding had to be solved and solved by her alone.

Her best move was when she found an ideal place to live. She entertained Sir Pomeroy and Lady Burton to dinner. Burton was an American-born, British-naturalised newspaper executive who died in 1947, aged seventy-nine, and Wallis arranged to rent from them their Riviera home, the Château la Cröea, radiant tropical house near Antibes with stone terraces grading gently down to the Mediterranean. This she planned to occupy as a holiday home. For a town house she opened negotiations with agents in Paris.

Next she turned her attention to the wedding itself and in so doing she quickly came in contact with two extraordinary personalities, the Reverend Robert Anderson Jardine and Charles Eugene Bedaux, the first an aggressive, independent little man of God, Vicar of St. Paul's Church, Darlington, the second a business tycoon who later became a traitor to both the country of his birth and the country of his adoption. Both the vicar and the industrialist had one point in common which brought them together with the Windsors. They had a total disrespect for authority.

Bedaux first. Of all the many unfortunate acquaintances which the Windsors have made, Bedaux was by far the most unfortunate of the lot. It afterwards turned out that he was a notorious adventurer, openly pro-Nazi, and detested by the group with which he was most in contact—American labour. A French-born American citizen, he was a business operator of the E. Phillips Oppenheim school to whom frontiers and trade barriers seemed to present no obstacle.

He had perfected in the United States a scheme of industrial efficiency which made him millions in all sorts of countries—and Bedaux preferred travelling with large chunks of currency of whatever country he was in, rather than rely on orthodox bank accounts. Bedaux has been classed with operators like Ivar Kreugar who turned matchsticks into a gigantic financial empire, went bankrupt in 1932 and later shot himself; Serge Stavisky, whose frauds involved nearly £10,000,000 and who was found shot in 1934, whether by suicide or not was never settled; Alfred Loewenstein, the iron and coal magnate who fell out of a cross-Channel plane in 1928.

All died violently, and Bedaux followed the rule. He was picked up in Africa by the liberating Americans in 1943, taken to Florida to be tried for treason for trading with the Germans, and there he poisoned himself.

The attractiveness of his way of life in 1937 could not be denied, however. He owned a story-book castle in Touraine, a grey, turreted place called the Château de Cande, built on a hill slightly more than eight miles from Tours, amid woods thick with lilies of the valley, violets and wild strawberries.

Bedaux had met Herman Rogers and his wife two or three times. He had followed the Abdication with the same avidity as the rest of the world, and had a special sympathy for Mrs Simpson and her sufferings at the hands of the press. Bedaux had had similar trouble himself. A few days after the Abdication, Bedaux, being in New York at the time, cabled Rogers and offered them and Mrs Simpson the Château de Cande as a holiday home and a refuge. It would be empty, he pointed out, as he did not plan to return until the following March. There was no reply to his cable and Bedaux, as thick-skinned as he was philosophic, forgot all about the matter.

Rogers's omission was not due to bad manners. The Abdication and Mrs Simpson's flight to his home had given him a trying time. He was harried by the press, between whom and Mrs Simpson he was acting as a combination of public-relations officer and buffer. Though he was handling his job well, there were moments of confusion, and this was one of them. Mrs Simpson was not so much thinking in terms of a holiday home as of some place in which she could possibly get married.

She had received more than one offer—Sir Pomeroy Burton had put the Château la Cröe at her disposal for the ceremony, and an American called Gerald Murphy, who had been to Yale with Herman Rogers, offered his house at Cap d'Antibes. Both offers were appreciated, but it was the sixteenth-century castle in Touraine that appealed to Wallis.

Bedaux was somewhat taken aback when he found belatedly that his castle which he had offered to Mrs Simpson and the Rogers for a holiday had been selected over his head as the place where Mrs Simpson should marry her Duke. But the times and circumstances being unusual, he readily understood the confusion, and he received the news of his honour with delight. He hurried back to France from New York to prepare for the event.

It was stipulated at first that Wallis would have the Château to herself and that the Bedauxs should stay elsewhere. That, however, did not prevent Bedaux from being there to greet her and hand over, so to speak, the keys.

When Mrs Simpson arrived at the end of March with the Rogers and Aunt Bessie, Bedaux's thirty servants, in their most satiny uniforms, were lined up to greet her. The Bedauxs waited at the top of the stone steps. Mrs Simpson was shown to a suite which included, apart from antique furniture worth a fortune, a pink marble bathroom with gold attachments. Comfortably ensconced in the château the party said good-bye to the Bedauxs who were off to stay in Paris, and settled down to wait for the Duke, who would join them as soon as Mrs Simpson's decree became absolute in another six weeks. If they thought they had seen the last of the Bedauxs, they could not have been more wrong.

But first there was a poignant incident. Mrs Simpson had brought with her Slipper, the cuddly little Cairn terrier. He had been a gift of the Duke when he was King, and when the uproar began the happy little dog seemed to represent peace and contentment to the harassed couple.

Gambolling with the charming foolishness of small dogs in the grounds of Cande, Slipper was bitten by a viper and died. Coming as it did after the strain which Mrs Simpson had borne so resolutely, it was the last straw and she was deeply distressed.

It was the kind of situation in which Charles Bedaux appeared at his best. He bought her another dog called Pooky, which, in time, came to take Slipper's place in her affections, and spent a long, muddy lifetime rolling happily in every piece of dirt he could find.

Bedaux had reappeared rather quickly on the scene to which he was supposed to have said farewell. Actually Mrs Bedaux had been in the habit of driving to Cande on occasional weekends to take things back with her to Paris. Herman Rogers recalled later that Mrs Simpson's kind heart was troubled at the inconvenience to which her affairs had put the Bedauxs. In the end they were invited to return. They protested, but did so.

Though Wallis was upset by Slipper's death, she quickly recovered her composure. In the ebb and flow of life she had learned the virtues of patience. Not so the Duke of Windsor who fretted at Enzesfeld, and who had to be restrained by all the powers of Rothschild's persuasion from catching the first train to Mrs Simpson, without whom he had scarcely made a move in three years. The reunion dominated his thoughts. Forgotten were the years of service as Prince of Wales and his brief illumination as King. His Abdication hardly recurred to him. He thought only of his intended bride. But the period of waiting did him good. The Duke had always had a valuable recuperative gift of sleep, and Major Edward Dudley Metcalfe, his aide, coming into his bedroom one morning and seeing the window open, the snow blowing in and the Duke of Windsor asleep like a tousled boy, marvelled at the stresses which the human spirit could survive.

The Duke moved out of Enzesfeld at the end of the winter and rented a house, the Villa Appesbach, on the lake at St Wolfgang, near Salzburg. Here he ruled with a passionate economy. He signed an agreement paying rent of £20 a week, but stipulated that he did not want the house's tennis-court or private motor-launch, which would have involved something extra.

The lid was finally lifted on May 3rd, 1937, and from then on the events which had been blocked ever since the Abdication started to move swiftly. On this date Mrs Simpson's decree was made absolute, and the Duke was at last free to join her. Mrs Simpson's lawyers hurried from the Divorce Court in London to the telephone, and at 10.33 a.m. they were through to her with the good news. At 10.50 a.m. she was connected with St Wolfgang, and at 4 p.m. the Duke was racing for Salzburg Station by car, followed by other cars piled high with eight trunks, two golf-bags and a litter of suitcases.

An aide, left behind to settle the accounts, goggled slightly at the telephone bill, then recovered himself and paid—£940.

At 4.45 the Duke was occupying three private suites in the Orient Express bound from Salzburg to Paris. With him were his equerry, Captain Greenacre, Chief Inspector David Storier of the Yard, with an assistant named Gattfield. Dotted along the train were a dozen or so British and American correspondents, typing madly.

At 9.23 on the morning of May 4th, Mrs Simpson's Buick was waiting at Verneuil, thirty miles from Paris, to pick up the Duke when he arrived. An interesting transformation: twelve months before it was the King's car and the King's chauffeur which called to collect Mrs Simpson. Now the former King waited for Mrs Simpson's car and driver. The train was on time, and soon the Buick was travelling along the dusty lanes of Touraine to Cande. There a squad of five French detectives under an inspector and a Scotland Yard man prowled the grounds. Reporters were encamped around the gates as they had been ever since Mrs Simpson arrived, kept at bay by gendarmes reinforced by the powerful figure of Madame Robinet, the concierge, at the lodge of the château.

For the occasion the resident reporters had been joined by plane-loads of the hard-eyed women correspondents which British and American newspapers invariably select to specialise in stories of true love and romance. The local hotels were jammed with as many as three correspondents per room. One or two of the French journalists raised a cheer as the Duke shot through and were acknowledged by a fleeting wave.

At the top of the stone steps leading into the château the Duke and Mrs Simpson were reunited for the first time since Mrs Simpson's flight from England six months before. As the Bedauxs and the Rogers supervised the Duke's tower of luggage, the Duke and his intended Duchess walked arm in arm into the château, Pooky, the gift of the Bedauxs, savaging at the Duke's heels as they disappeared from the sunlight into the castle shadows. They had much to talk about.

He had brought her gifts from Austria; a Tyrolean costume, wooden ornaments—and an engagement ring, that glittering little band of good intentions which had signified so much in the Abdication crisis, but had somehow been forgotten in the substance until now.

After lunch the Duke and Mrs Simpson walked through the woods of the estate, making plans that now they were together seemed easier, Mrs Simpson stooping once to pick him a button-hole.

On May 8th a statement was issued from the château announcing that the marriage would take place on June 2nd. On the same day Wallis changed her name by deed poll to Mrs Wallis Warfield, a move rather plaintively designed to free herself from the association of the name of Simpson. It failed. Even the name of the Duchess of Windsor failed to do that.

On May 12th a silent party sat in the gun-room of the Château de Cande and listened on the radio to the Coronation of King George VI. The Bedauxs were there, Aunt Bessie, the Rogers and Dudley Forwood, the Duke's new equerry, a distinguished public school man. Side by side on the couch sat Mrs Wallis Warfield and the Duke of Windsor. There was much good in this little band of international sophisticates, even in the potential traitor Bedaux, and among the others was represented not only wealth and ambition but also loyal friendship and selfless generosity. Yet they seemed in this setting to be isolated from a rejoicing world.

They went on listening as the voice which was to become familiar to every hearth throughout the Empire was heard for the first time as the voice of the King, hesitant, apprehensive, but deeply moving.

Somewhere in the castle a telephone rang. It was a reporter wanting to know if the Duke of Windsor cared to comment on his younger brother's speech. The Duke asked Rogers to pass on a brief message to say that he thought the speech was inspiring. The occasion was too great for pat speeches of praise.

The excitement of the Coronation died gradually away. Sixteen days later, Lord Brownlow, accompanied by a mutual friend, Brigadier Michael Wardell, arrived at Cande, having flown from London with bad news. He carried with him an official notice which was to be formally published in the *London Gazette*. The notice read:

> 'The King has been pleased by Letters Patent under the Great Seal of the Realm bearing date the twenty-seventh day of May, 1937, to declare that the Duke of Windsor shall, notwithstanding his Instrument of Abdication . . . and his Majesty's Declaration of Abdication Act, 1936, whereby effect was given to the said Instrument be entitled to hold and enjoy for himself only the title, style or attribute of Royal Highness, *so however that his wife and descendants, if any, shall not hold the said title, style or attribute.*'

It was the concluding statement which caught and held the attention. 'The Duke is not going to like this intelligence,' Brownlow had said to Wardell on the way, and indeed dinner at the château that night was a depressing meal. No one could think of anything else to talk about. Wallis, when she married, would be entitled to the forms and addresses appropriate to the wife of a Duke. She would be addressed as 'Your Grace'. She would not be entitled to the address of 'Your Royal Highness', and she would not be entitled to a curtsy on formal occasions. The discussion went back and forth endlessly, but it is doubtful if any of the people at that table realised how profoundly the fortunes of the Duke of Windsor and his intended bride had been changed by the announcement.

The Duke's consideration of this ruling, however, had to be put aside under pressure of arrangements for the marriage. And now the second interesting character of the period turned up, the Reverend Robert Anderson Jardine, Vicar of St. Paul's Church, Darlington. In his parish Jardine conducted four services every Sunday and had become known as 'the poor man's preacher'. He was a small man and moved by a feeling of deep irritation at the ways and affectations of bishops. He also enjoyed publicity, and the two combined to the point that when he heard that the Church was bringing pressure to prevent the Duke's marriage being blessed by the Church, he sat down and wrote to Herman Rogers offering his services to the Duke.

By this gesture Jardine thumbed his nose at the bishops and satisfied his conscience. He expected no answer and forgot the matter. To his surprise he received almost by return a telegram from George Allen, the Duke's legal adviser. The telegram read:

'Reference your letter to Herman Rogers at Château de Cande. Will you please telephone me at West Wittering, Sunday, about 1.30. A. G. Allen.'

It is depressing to list the Windsors' category of mistakes, but here was another one. It was all very well to appreciate the offer of a clergyman to come forward despite the Church's ban, but was that what they really wanted? What kind of a man was it who could blithely defy the bishops? In Church of England circles Jardine was unpopular and regarded, even before this incident, as something of an opportunist. It would have been better, perhaps, to have sought in Canada or the United States for an Episcopalian clergyman who could perform the ceremony without involving an act of rebellion against Church heads.

Soon Jardine was on his way to the château, where the Duke and his intended Duchess were absorbed in wedding plans that seemed to get steadily more complicated and unhappy. The Duke, anticipating snubs, had decided to issue no invitations at all. He relied on his trusted friends to turn up if they could. He quickly heard that no member of the Royal Family was to be present, nor was any official of the British Government, though the British

Ambassador in Paris had said soothingly that somebody might come down 'in an unofficial capacity'. An impressive list of reasons why they could not come were given by friends whom they had expected. Even friends who had stood by them during the crisis were sending their regrets.

The excuses depressed the ex-King profoundly, more so perhaps because he understood that the confusion and conflict of loyalties among his old friends was genuine and mortifying to them. Many of his most trusted allies from his old Court had now accepted appointments with the new. And in the new Court suspicion against the Duke of Windsor and his intentions had a real force. The thought that some Britons might still look to him as their leader rather than the new King was a worrier. His remark 'something must be done' to the Welsh miners was still remembered.

The attitude was shown in strange and un-English ways. One of the Duke's friends who wanted very badly to attend the Windsors' wedding wrote personally to the King to ask his advice. He received no answer. This puzzled him until later he became convinced, for reasons that satisfied him at least, that a scheming courtier had intercepted the letter on its way to the proper authorities and destroyed it.

Other friends of the Duke turned for counsel to the various elder statesmen who knew more about the background of the Abdication. Baldwin, Churchill, Lord Beaverbrook, Lloyd George were all approached for advice. One perplexed British peer approached two of those gentlemen for their opinion. One told him emphatically 'Go'. Another said, 'Whatever you do, don't go'. Which left the peer not noticeably clearer in mind.

At the château the ceremony seemed likely to be rather makeshift, a likelihood which increased when Jardine arrived and saw what he had to use for the Holy Service. The castle was not equipped for the convenience of the Protestant Church, so Bedaux put his services at Jardine's disposal to improvise a suitable setting for the ceremony, and a most unlikely alliance sprang up between the two men.

Bedaux, the humorous cynic, took an immediate liking to

Bride and Bridegroom. The wedding day picture.

At a castle in Hungary. Mr. & Mrs. Charles Bedeaux.

Jardine. They understood each other from the start, and both recognised implicitly the fact that they were there for all they could get out of the Windsors' wedding. When Jardine announced that he needed a holy table Bedaux and he scoured the house, and Jardine ultimately settled on an oak chest. More rummaging was necessary to find a piece of cloth to cover it, and it was Mrs Simpson who emerged dusty and breathless from her boxes with a piece of embroidered silk which Jardine proclaimed satisfactory.

Next there was the problem of the cross. Jardine did not have one. Bedaux gave a wave of the arm that encompassed the entire château and said with an agnostic grin, 'Take your pick.' But Jardine's Puritan mind shuddered at the Catholic crosses with vividly coloured figures of the Lord crucified, and declined. A plain cross, he insisted, no crucifix. Bedaux shrugged and set to work. Finally he located a Protestant church in the vicinity and the problem was solved.

And so the ex-King of England was married to a woman who had two former husbands still living by an itinerant clergyman in a room of a castle owned by an international scoundrel. The pathetic nature of the ceremony was felt by the guests, some of whom had been friends of the groom when he was the most idolised Prince on earth; a time which must have seemed an eternity ago, but which in fact had come to an end when he became King less than eighteen months before.

The wedding itself went without a hitch, in spite of the confusion caused by friends not knowing whether to come or not. Sixteen guests turned up in all, more than half of them American friends. The guests included the Rothschilds, the Bedauxs, the Rogers, Sir Walter Monckton, George Allen. There was also Lady Selby, wife of the British Minister in Vienna, Dudley Forwood and a few others. Aunt Bessie was Wallis's only relative present. Only one friend of the Duke's deliberately defied an official ban. He was Hugh Lloyd Thomas, a former secretary of the Duke's then with the British Embassy in Paris.

Mrs Simpson looked suitably charming in her long 'Wallis blue' dress made in Paris. A brooch of clustered sapphires and diamonds was at her throat, and a crucifix dangled from a bracelet of gold and sapphires. Her earrings were of sapphires.

She carried no flowers, but there were flowers by the hundred in the huge, high-ceilinged drawing-room.

According to French law, the Duke and Mrs Simpson first had to go through the civil ceremony, which was performed by Dr Charles Mercier, the Mayor of Monts, superb in an outsize tricolour sash. At this ceremony the Duke slipped on to his bride's finger the ring of Welsh gold traditional at British royal weddings. By French law they were now married.

After that they walked hand in hand down the corridor to the music-room, where the Reverend Robert Anderson Jardine waited to bless their marriage in the Church of England. The Duke had fought hard for that blessing as he has fought hard for everything concerning the prestige of the woman he married for love. This was one of the few battles in which he could claim the victory. Herman Rogers had been selected to give the bride away. Major Edward Dudley ('Fruity') Metcalfe supported the Duke as best man. Waves of organ music were heard throughout the ceremony, played by Marcel Dupré, one of France's leading organists, on the organ which Bedaux had earlier brought over from America at a cost to him of £10,000.

People who were there remember that both the Duke and his bride looked pale and tense. The Duke's reply 'I will' to Mr Jardine was so high-pitched that the guests in the music-room were startled. Mrs Simpson faced the occasion better. Her response was soft, almost inaudible, but with no trace of nervousness. The words of the wedding service were spoken in full. The Duke and Mrs Simpson knelt on the château's brocaded satin cushions, and at the end the organ gently toned the hymn 'O Perfect Love'.

The business was over. There was the usual escape of tension as the champagne corks popped. The Duke gave his bride a tiara of diamonds, and Bedaux turned up with a statue representing 'Love' sculptured by Fanny Hoefken-Hempel, a popular German artist. Neither the Duke nor anybody else kissed the bride. Outside, Madame Robinet, the gatekeeper, hurled a bottle of champagne against the gates in accordance with a local custom, to christen the marriage, and the patient newspapermen outside the castle gave Herman Rogers a gold fountain-pen in token of his tactful liaison work over the past six months.

Mrs Simpson was now Her Grace, though not Her Royal Highness, the Duchess of Windsor. It was the cue for the hard-eyed sisterhood of the press to go up in a spray of platitudes. 'Prince Charming and the beggar-maid'; 'Cinderella'; 'Wed in exile'; 'Off to live happily ever after'; 'The King who gave up everything for . . .'; etcetera.

The Duke and Duchess said good-bye to their guests and climbed into the Buick with good old George Ladbrook at the wheel, off on a honeymoon to the Castle Wasserleonberg in Carinthia, home of Count Paul Munster, an Austrian nobleman who married Peggy Ward, cousin of the Windsors' friend, the Earl of Dudley. Wasserleonberg was to be followed by a three-month honeymoon schedule taking in Salzburg, Venice, Budapest, Prague, Paris.

They were fairly well cushioned against the exigencies of exile. Reporters counted 266 pieces of baggage, including 186 trunks, loaded on to the train to arrive ahead of them. The habit of travelling much and travelling heavy became a characteristic of the Windsors in the years that followed.

CHAPTER III

The New Life

THE Duchess had lost a throne. She now began the long lonely saga which even today shows no sign of ending. The tide of the Abdication had receded leaving her stranded, and her life assumed a harsh pattern of isolation with no connection at any point with her previous experience. At the height of her power she had been an obscure figure. Now she had lost her power and was world-famous. Once she had been genuinely popular, the great houses of England open to her. Now she was an outcast. She had married a King and lost her social position.

A terrifying future yawned ahead of her. Her husband knew nothing of the ways of ordinary people. She was totally responsible for his well-being and happiness, and the world would not tolerate failure on her part. It was the Duchess who had to make the decisions, run the establishment, find friends and rebuild a new life from the ruin of her own and her husband's fortunes. If she failed she would be condemned. If she succeeded, the Duke would be praised. It was a battle which the Duchess could not win but which she might avoid losing.

She set to work. Fortunately money was no object. The exact facts of the Windsors' varying financial fortunes are available only to their accountant, but this much is known. As Prince of Wales the Duke drew an income of £70,000 a year from the Duchy of Cornwall and £43,000 a year from the Duchy of Lancaster.

King George V left him nothing that was not entailed. The King's fortune was divided among Edward's three brothers, the Dukes of York, Gloucester and Kent. George V did, however, leave the palaces of Sandringham and Balmoral to Edward on a lease for life, together with various entailed treasures such as the royal heirlooms and the incomparable royal stamp collection.

Edward, when he became King, also took charge of the £410,000 a year Civil List which Parliament granted the sovereign to look after royal expenses.

The Abdication created many legal puzzles. Edward might conceivably have claimed to remain lessee of Sandringham and Balmoral even after he abdicated, but instead he sold his leases and indeed everything to which he was entitled to King George VI. He also received on Abdication a settlement from King George VI's personal funds, amounting to £25,000 a year. Altogether, after the Abdication the Duke of Windsor was worth about £1,000,000 and could rely on an income, probably tax-free, of something like £70,000 to £80,000 a year.

On Abdication he automatically lost Fort Belvedere, which was Crown property, and also the incomes from the Duchies of Cornwall and Lancaster. The Cornwall income normally belongs to the heir to the throne, or to the King when there is no direct heir (today Prince Charles gets it). However, the Prince of Wales was always careful with his money, and the capital he piled up from the many years during which he drew the income from the Duchies must have been large. After he married he settled on the Duchess an income of £10,000 a year.

The Windsors' fortune, which was to be looked at rather enviously in later years by the hard-pressed British Royal Family, was their one major asset, and it helped considerably to ease their path. The Château la Cröe was an impressive home, and the Duchess had taken on a superlative chef. The water which flowed into the gold, swan-shaped bathtub was kept admirably hot, and the household comforts were many.

The Duchess's friends took a good look and began to re-emerge, and it was not long before she was once more the centre of a thriving circle. Her new friends were not quite the same as those she had known in England. Most of these had faded away. The only ones left were a few people with an obstinate sense of loyalty, like the Earl of Dudley. Among her new friends the most enthusiastic and possessive, of course, was Charles Eugène Bedaux, who six years later was to commit suicide rather than face the basest of all charges—treason. The other new friends and admirers were cosmopolitan and attractive, beautiful and witty, and all eager for invitations to Cröe.

The Duchess had done a magnificent job on the château's redecoration. In many of the rooms the Duchess played on the contrasting effect of blues and whites, and in doing so made a lasting impact on Riviera fashion. The rooms had a blue and white motif. The cocktail bar at the top of the house was blue and white, and cocktails were served in blue and white glasses. The breakfast trays which the servants brought to the guests' bedrooms would be white with blue cups or blue with white cups.

The Duchess invariably wore blue and white, and although she was much too good a hostess to try to influence her guests in their choice of dress, they soon realised that it made her happy if they joined in the game, and soon her women friends were arriving at the château in blue and white. The fashion persisted after the Windsors left, and even today there is a tendency among fashionable Riviera women to wear a standard day-time dress of white blouse and blue skirt or vice versa.

It was a typical inspiration of the Duchess's, the kind of idea which had always made her so stimulating a companion. There was no doubt whatever that the Duke was utterly happy in her company. He sloshed away energetically at golf-balls, and began to putter conscientiously in his garden in an attempt to build at Cröe something as much like Fort Belvedere as possible. 'I am a very happily married man,' he told the Anglo-American Press Club gaily in Paris, 'but my wife and I are neither content nor willing to lead a purely inactive life of pleasure.' For their first Christmas together Herman Rogers let them have the Villa Lou Viei while Cröe underwent decorations. The Duke had never before lived in such a small and intimate home, and he revelled in it. He invited Winston Churchill to dinner and showed him with delight Rogers' new American furnace for the central heating, pressing the button so often to demonstrate its workings, that it was never quite the same afterwards.

Circumstances might now have improved had the Duchess's personality been different. But it seemed to many that with her elevation in society she left her middle-class common sense behind her, and her attitude to life often seemed no closer to earth than her husband's.

The question of her title was unceasingly humiliating. The title of 'Royal Highness', the right to a curtsy, are the tiny cankers of tragedy which eat into the soul. In this case the Windsors had every reason and excuse to fret over a patent injustice. The problem of recognition was one of the most curious of all strange problems which have complicated the life of the Duchess of Windsor, and one fundamental fact must be understood. In specifically denying the Duchess the title, the British Court acted contrary to custom and damned the flow of royal tradition. The Duchess of Windsor has been singled out of history for this act.

'Royal Highness' is not a title that is conferred or denied. It is assumed automatically by women whose husbands are entitled to that distinction.

Endlessly the Windsors fretted over this discrimination against the Duchess, asking themselves—and all their friends—'Why?'

Was it those divorces? But divorce was far from unusual in London society, and a title is not a sort of Ascot Enclosure, a privilege restricted to the undivorced. Besides, the Duchess of Windsor was the guiltless party in both her divorce actions.

The unsocial layman may ask: 'What's in a name?'; but in this case there was more at stake than a mere dispute over a form of address.

With the title goes the Duchess's standing in British society.

Bar her from the title, and she is effectively barred from Court. Bar her from the Court, and her husband will bar himself, too.

In their opinion this means they are barred also from England. The refusal to recognise the Duchess is the reason why they remain in exile.

'The Duchess', the Duke was heard to say once, 'is interested in courtesies, not curtsies'—a statement sufficiently epigrammatic to sound as if it originated with the Duchess. Officially protocol was satisfied by a curtsy to the Duke and a handshake to the Duchess, but this angered the Duke and has continued to anger him. Among the Windsors' friends there was total confusion. Grace Moore, the opera singer, was seen to drop the Duchess a curtsy at a party, and it started an international controversy.

Society became divided into those who did and those who did not. The Hon. Mrs Helen Fitzgerald, a loyal friend of the Duchess's, did not. Lady Brownlow did not. Mrs Colin Buist did not. These three had been in the old *Nahlin* party.

Mrs Martin Scanlon, wife of the United States air attaché in Paris, did; Mrs Euan Wallace (now Mrs Herbert Agar) did; Lady Diana Cooper, wife of Duff Cooper (afterwards Viscount Norwich) did, and continued to do so even after her husband had become British Ambassador to France, thus starting a French tradition whereby Frenchwomen invariably curtsy to the Duchess. Lady Pembroke, one of the bluest bloods in English society, did not and went further. When she heard that Lady Diana and Mrs Wallace had curtsied to the Duchess, she was annoyed and told them so in front of their husbands.

Many people have wondered if there was a particular enemy at Court, who was preventing, by a mere formality, the Duke and Duchess from making a reasonable life together on their own standards in England. Queen Mary, until her death, was widely believed to be the person most unrelentingly opposed to the Duchess. Certainly there could be no point in minimising the old Queen's hostility. She hated her American daughter-in-law, and when one of her relatives asked why she did not relent for the sake of her son's happiness, she declared flatly that she would never tolerate seeing the Duchess of Windsor walking ahead of 'my dear Duchess of Gloucester and my dear Duchess of Kent'.

The opposition of King George VI to the Duchess was less clear-cut than that of his mother. He seemed to hate the whole subject, and avoided it as much as he could. Whenever the problem was presented to him, he met it with either silence or evasions. It was the weakness of this attitude which probably frustrated the Duke most, particularly as he had a solid suspicion that the King had no legal or historical justification for taking the attitude he did to the Duchess.

The Duke determined to do something about it. In January 1938, eight months after the publication of the letters patent which denied the Duchess the right to the title of 'Royal Highness', he invited Lord Jowitt to Paris to discuss it. Jowitt was one of the nation's most outstanding lawyers. He had served in the Government as Attorney-General under Ramsay MacDonald from 1929 to 1932. The Duke asked him what he thought were the legal aspects of recognition of the Duchess.

Jowitt took time to think it over, and in due course delivered his opinion in writing. It was an opinion which illustrated the doubts and indefinables surrounding the whole matter, but it was optimistic enough to fill the Windsors with hope.

First of all Jowitt considered it obvious, from the express terms of the Letters Patent of May 1937, that the Duchess could base no claim to the title, style or attribute of 'Her Royal Highness' on this document alone. But did that conclude the matter? What if the Duchess had a claim entirely independent of these letters patent?

Jowitt proceeded to discuss first the legal position of the Duke and then of the Duchess as the Duke's wife. In the course of his reflections, he traced at least one earlier issue of letters patent dealing with this very subject. It was dated February 5th, 1864, and it said:

'The Queen [Victoria] has been pleased by Letters Patent under the Great Seal, to declare her Royal will and pleasure that besides the children of Sovereigns of these Realms, the children of the sons of any Sovereign of Great Britain and Ireland, *shall have and at all times hold and enjoy* the title, style and attribute of "Royal Highness", with their titular dignity of Prince or Princess prefixed to their respective Christian names, or with their titles of honour . . .' etc.

Here was a starting-point. It was clearly laid down that the title of 'His Royal Highness' was to attach to any son of the sovereign and to any grandson of the sovereign throughout the male line. Now nothing was more certain than that the Duke of Windsor was the son of George V and the grandson of Edward VII. He was therefore plainly entitled to the title of His Royal Highness under the letters patent of Queen Victoria, which contained no exceptions and no qualifications.

It was well known that if the son of the sovereign were to become a Roman Catholic, he would consequently lose his right to accede to the throne—but there was no ground, it would seem, for asserting he would also lose his right to be styled 'His Royal Highness'. Similarly, in the event of abdication, he would lose his throne but he remained his father's son. The letters patent of 1937 assumed that because he abdicated he also ceased to hold and enjoy the title, style or attribute of 'His Royal Highness', for these letters patent purported to confer the title on him and on him alone. In other words the letters patent were giving to him something that could not be taken away from him. Nothing in the letters patent of 1937 seemed to alter or cut down the provision of the earlier letters patent.

Was it possible that those responsible for the drafting of the letters patent of 1937 were not aware of the letters patent of the Victorian age? Or if they knew of them, why were they not referred to? Was it inadvisable to make it clear that the letters patent of 1937 were taking away from the Duke that which he already had? Were the letters patent of the Victorian days implicitly though not expressly repealed by the letters patent of 1937?

Jowitt was reluctant to accept the doctrine of implied repeal, and emphasised that the whole matter was in urgent need of clarification. His argument so far helped to establish the position of the Duke. Now, how was the Duchess affected by it?

It had to be borne in mind, Jowitt said, that when any one of the King's sons contracted a legal marriage his bride automatically became on marriage 'Her Royal Highness'. When, for example, the Lady Elizabeth Bowes-Lyon married His Royal Highness the Duke of York (later George VI), she became by the mere fact of marriage 'Her Royal Highness the Duchess of York'. She did *not* have this title conferred on her by any special order or decree. When, therefore, His Royal Highness the Duke of Windsor married, did not his wife by the mere fact of marriage become entitled to the style of 'Royal Highness'?

It was one thing to say to the Duchess, you shall not have any claim to the title, style or attribute of 'Royal Highness' under the letters patent of 1937. It would have been another more far-reaching thing to add that any claim to the title which derived from a wholly different source was to be invalidated.

Hence the uncertainty, the confusion, and hence the problem which confronted women who found themselves presented to the Duchess. Should they curtsy or not? All these doubts would have been so easily set at rest by an official pronouncement—but no such pronouncement was made. The only guidance was that given by the letters patent of 1937—and these seemed to have been based on the fallacious reasoning that by reason of the Abdication the Duke of Windsor had ceased to be His Royal Highness. In reply it could only be said that the Sovereign, no doubt, is the fount of all honour, and in matters such as this his subjects would bow to the royal wish.

That summarised Jowitt's views. The Duke must certainly have impressed this opinion on his brother as vigorously as he could, but to no effect. Nothing was issued to alter or clarify the letters patent of 1937, and a nice legal tangle was bequeathed to future historians.

The Duchess, despite the best legal opinion in the world, therefore, was helpless.

Her position was literally agonising. She was like a prisoner holding the key to a door which could be opened only from the other side.

All reason, all legal argument, all precedent, all that and Christian compassion too, urged that she was entitled to be styled 'Royal Highness'.

But she was not 'Her Royal Highness'. The Duke insisted that his servants call her 'Your Royal Highness'; the Duchess could, with justice, claim to be called 'Your Royal Highness'; but when she opened her eyes it remained make-believe in the light of the harsh facts.

So the Duchess was obliged to accept the position with as much dignity as she could. The Royal Family had shown that it wanted no part of her. Their wedding, so ostentatiously boycotted, proved it. The King's refusal to give the Duchess the title they sought, confirmed it. His indifference to the publicity created established the fact beyond all doubt. Few wives have been so emphatically and publicly ignored by their husband's relatives.

Perhaps the Royal Family was right to resent a King who shook a love affair like a sabre in the face of history, the dynasty and the British Empire. Perhaps it was wrong to turn its back on the tradition of family charity; many a family in every class and period has taken to its heart a daughter-in-law or sister-in-law whose existence was repugnant to it. The problem is a matter for instinct and defies analysis.

What is beyond doubt is the fact that the Royal Family's attitude set up a formidable barrier in the Duchess's efforts to make a contented life for herself and her husband.

Formidable, that is, but not impossible. In the years between the wedding in 1937 and the war in 1939 feelers were put out by both sides, by the British Government and by the Windsors, probing for a means of *rapprochement*. The opportunity did exist for the Windsors to win their way back.

The great tragedy of the period, in my judgment, is that the frail bridge back to Britain was destroyed.

Bad judgment and bad luck both played a part in turning mutual good-will to mutual distrust, and the result was that the British Government completely lost interest in the Windsors; while the Windsors could feel, with justice, that they had been very badly treated by the Government.

Yet in Britain before the war, despite all the rumours, the con-jectures and the half-conceived fears about the Windsors, a great fund of good-will remained. A Gallup Poll was taken in Britain in January 1939, asking whether people would like the Duke and Duchess to come back and live in England. The result was:

Yes — 61 per cent.
No — 16 „ „

Many people would have liked to see the Duke given a responsible job. The reasons were mixed: there were still rem-nants in England of his former popularity. There was curiosity to see what talents an ex-king is able to bring to civil life. There was

a suspicion of abuse of the national sense of thrift that a man who
had spent so many years training in public service at the tax-
payers' expense was now making a full-time career of getting a
sun-tan on the Riviera.

But there was little chance of a job for the Duke. His activities
had attracted too much criticism, and there was the ever-recur-
ring obstacle of the Duchess's two former husbands which could
not be kept down. A rumour circulated that the Duke sought the
post of Governor-General of Canada. He might have made a
good Governor-General, and gone on to do other things, thus
avoiding the sad drift of his later years. But the Windsors' stock
with all the Dominions governments was low, as Neville
Chamberlain personally discovered.

In 1938 Chamberlain had replaced Stanley Baldwin as Prime
Minister, a change that was of debatable benefit to Britain.
Chamberlain had many friends in the country, and still has his
defenders, but even his best friends do not give him the credit of
having much of a clue about personalities.

Chamberlain had been one of Baldwin's lieutenants during the
Abdication crisis, but he had no strong personal feelings against
the King or against Mrs Simpson. At first he was shown by his
private papers to have been anxious at all costs to avert the
Abdication and also to give Edward a chance of happiness. Later
he reached the personal conviction that the King would use
morganatic marriage simply as a stepping-stone towards making
Mrs Simpson Queen, and came out most solidly on Baldwin's
side.

Chamberlain visited the Windsors in France in 1938. In the
course of a pleasant chat, he suggested that the Duke bring his
wife to England on a visit. The Duke, as always eager to advance
his cause in Britain, agreed enthusiastically. Chamberlain returned
to London and mentioned the proposed visit in the course of
official business. The reaction was such a loud and unanimous
chorus of disapproval that Chamberlain was rocked. He realised
for the first time that the Windsors were a problem to which
there was no easy solution.

After pondering how to get out of the mess into which he had got himself, Chamberlain had a somewhat questionable idea. He sent for Beverley Baxter, the smoothest and most literate of all the journalist M.P.s in the House. As indirectly as a Prime Minister must do to suggest anything so unethical, he gave Baxter the impression that he would not mind seeing an article in a London newspaper to the effect that it would be a very bad idea for the Windsors to come home at present. Baxter, just as evasive, hinted that such an article would be most interesting, but that he was hardly in a position to write it himself. He gave several reasons, but did not mention the fact that at that very moment the Windsors were threatening him with an action for libel for something he had already written.

In the end Chamberlain was obliged to do it the hard way, and tell the Duke directly that the moment was ill-chosen and that his idea had not been a good one. The Duke, rebuffed once more, retired into his cocoon on the Riviera.

CHAPTER IV

Bedaux, Bedaux, Bedaux

I N the Labour magazine, *Forward*, at the end of 1937, Herbert Morrison, M.P., then leader of the London County Council, wrote, wonderingly it seemed rather than in anger: 'The choice before ex-kings is either to fade out of the public eye or to be a nuisance. Who are the Duke's advisers? I do not know, but either they are very bad ones or he will not take good advice.'

Morrison said apologetically that he was not criticising because he wanted to. What stung him to such an attack was the Windsors' visit to Germany a few months after they were married, an ill-starred trip from the start which did probably more than anything else to cost the Duke of Windsor the confidence of the British Government.

His plan was to tour first Germany and then the United States to study labour conditions. Every sane counsel urged on him the foolishness of an official Nazi-sponsored visit to Germany, including, it must be suspected, the secret, suppressed counsel of his own mind. The Germans had not troubled to mask their arrogance even to the Duke personally; the German press had ignored his wedding because of the presence of Jewish guests.

But the Duke was set on the trip, and Charles Bedaux was the man responsible.

Bedaux, of course, was overjoyed at the windfall which had dropped the two famous lovers in his lap, and he looked forward to a glorious future of business coups while he hid behind the Windsor name. Bedaux had a twofold idea for a great Windsor comeback.

First of all the Duke should visit Nazi Germany and then the United States.

The Windsors fell for both projects, but their remaining friends in London were appalled at the idea of the ex-King of England visiting the country of Hitler and the Nazis.

The Duke had said innocently that he merely wished to study labour conditions in Germany, but it was apparent that such a visit must have the most dangerous repercussions.

The Windsors must have felt a twinge also, because the Duke went to the extent of consulting Lord Beaverbrook about the trip. They were staying at the Meurice Hotel in Paris at the time and they sent Brigadier Michael Wardell to ask Beaverbrook to come to Paris and discuss it. The newspaper proprietor flew from London in his private airplane.

It was Wardell who later recalled the arguments Beaverbrook used to try to talk the Windsors out of it. Beaverbrook was dead against the trip to Germany.

First of all he suggested that the Duke consult Winston Churchill, and offered to send his plane back to England to bring Churchill over.

Beaverbrook knew that Churchill, too, would be emphatically opposed to the trip, and he, if anyone, would be able to convince the Windsors of its folly. (Perhaps the same idea occurred to the Duke because he said 'he did not want to bother Churchill.')

Next Beaverbrook suggested that the Duke should ask the advice of the Foreign Office. When that suggestion came to nothing, he advised the Duke to go to America first and to Germany afterwards, hoping probably that what was delayed might then never happen.

The Duke would not be swayed. He was set on the trip, and all Beaverbrook's apprehensions were justified.

Everywhere in Germany the Windsors were treated with discourtesy and exposed to the assault of Nazi propaganda.

They arrived in Berlin on October 11th, 1937, under the sponsorship of Bedaux's good friend Dr Robert Ley, the Nazi Labour leader, who was almost invariably drunk throughout the tour.

Neither Goebbels, boss of Berlin, nor Ribbentrop, the Foreign Minister, could spare the time to greet them, and each sent along a minor official instead.

This behaviour was coldly deliberate, because Hitler was actually fascinated with the Duke. It was inconceivable to Hitler, a man to whom power was everything and women were nothing, that a man should give up all his power for a woman.

Hitler had followed the Abdication eagerly day by day and had even sent to his Embassy in London for further details. The Embassy had obliged, and sent him two short, uncensored films which Hitler watched repeatedly. One showed Edward VIII looking over preparations for his father's funeral. Hitler reportedly giggled all the way through.

The other film showed Edward and Mrs Simpson sporting in swim-suits in the Adriatic in the course of the *Nahlin* trip.

Hitler was furious at the Abdication, as he believed that Edward was Germany's best friend in England. 'An hour with me and he would never have abdicated,' he commented.

The interview when it finally happened amounted to very little. The talk was mostly in generalities. The Duchess spoke little, but Hitler seemed more impressed by her than with the Duke.

'She would have made a good Queen,' he told his interpreter, Paul Schmidt, when they had gone.

The British press hardly mentioned the visit, but the American press did. Men of the calibre of Edward R. Murrow, William Shirer, and Albion Ross were covering Germany at the time, and their despatches reflected their bewilderment at what had possessed the Windsors to hobnob with such a crew of bandits. Albion Ross cabled the *New York Times*:

'The Duke's decision to see for himself the Third Reich's industries and institutions, and his gestures and remarks during the last two weeks, have demonstrated adequately that the Abdication did rob Germany of a firm friend, if not indeed a devoted admirer, on the British throne. . . . He has lent himself, perhaps unconsciously but easily, to National Socialist propaganda. There can be no doubt that the tour has strengthened the [Nazi] regime's hold on the working classes.'

On October 16th the *New York Times* reported that the Duke was 'continuing to give a modified Hitler salute'. This was a controversial gesture, even though Britain and Germany were not at war at the time.

Alas for the Windsors, the poison of their German visit was spreading through the United States. Americans who genuinely wanted to greet them now hesitated, puzzled. America's Jews were furious at the Duke's association with the Nazis. America's trade unionists were furious at his association with Bedaux.

Unaware of this swelling hostility, the Windsors began to make plans for their American adventure with undiminished enthusiasm. The sadness of this controversy lay in the fact that neither wanted to make political capital out of the trip. They simply wanted to go to the United States. The Duke adored America and the American achievement.

For the Duchess it was something more—it was home—and no home could ever have seemed sweeter. It was the end of the road, a long road of suffering and tears, triumph and downfall, through an alien Europe which had flayed her emotions and tossed her ruthlessly to her lonely destiny.

Now she was about to set her eyes once more on the New York skyline and the cool pure light which bathes the Manhattan towers in the fall.

Soon she would be back in her home-town, Baltimore, Maryland, with its languorous, hilly avenues, reunited with childhood friends whose minds were innocent of the passions of international intrigue.

And her man was by her side, a man who but for her would be King of England, now nobody, but who looked at her with eyes that said: 'I am a contented man. I would not wish it to be any different from what it is.'

The Duchess longed to savour the joy of the homecoming. Her husband's home had cast him out. This, she wanted to tell him, can be your new home, as it has always been my home and always will be.

Unfortunately it did not happen like that.

The Windsors booked passage in the *Bremen*, a German liner. This was the lighted match. The explosion followed.

The trip to Germany in which the Duke had praised everthing he had seen . . . the sponsorship of Charles Bedaux . . . finally the *Bremen*. It was too much.

Bedaux, going on ahead to make the arrangements, was almost stupefied by the chorus of fury which greeted him.

The Windsors had not been the only dreamers. This was to have been Bedaux's masterstroke. Instead, it was catastrophe and the bitter ruin of his soul.

From the depths of his failure he cried to the Windsors in a telegram to release him from the trip—and went off to have a nervous breakdown. He never recovered from this blow to his ego.

The Windsors were baffled, dismayed, rocked at the furore. Stumbling like the blind, they sought a way of escape, and blundered again. The trip was cancelled and the Duke issued a statement in which he 'emphatically repeats that there is no shadow of justification for any suggestion that he is allied to any industrial system, or that he is for or against any particular political or racial doctrine'.

Dr Paul Schmidt, Hitler's interpreter, in his book about Hitler, also considered this to be the Duke's outlook.

A Prince must be above politics, but this kind of impartiality was unlucky in its choice of words.

It meant that he was neither for nor against Germany that was persecuting its Jews, obliterating its internal freedom and frightening its neighbours.

In time the storm died away. The Windsors abandoned their hopes of seeing America, and it was not to be for another three years that their desire was rewarded.

War was now very close—and so was the next major error by the Windsors.

After a visit in the spring of 1939 to the old battlefields of Verdun, the Duke thought it would be a good idea to broadcast a world-wide appeal for peace. The appeal would be aimed principally at the United States, as the country with the greatest potential power for preventing war.

Once more the painful question had to be asked: Why? The

words of Herbert Morrison after the Germany trip came back: 'Who are the Duke's advisers?'

The time for an appeal to peace was past. Munich had come and gone. The annexation of Czechoslovakia had killed appeasement dead, and the British Government was girding the country for war.

But there was an aspect of the broadcast that was even worse than the fact that it was out of tune with British policy. King George VI, at that moment, was on his way with Queen Elizabeth to America on a good-will mission requiring the utmost tact.

Quite obviously no connection dawned on the Duke between his broadcast to America and his brother's visit. But in England a few old skeletons seemed to rattle in the cupboard. Was this a move of 'the King across the water' trying to take over in the absence of the crowned King?

Of course it was not, but there was an uncomfortable stirring of the fears that had arisen after the Abdication. There was a murmur of protest when the news was announced of the Duke's proposed broadcast.

This was when Beaverbrook intervened—to the anger of the Windsors. The press lord directed an editorial attacking the idea of a broadcast.

'The decision of the Duke of Windsor to broadcast to the United States today is to be regretted' [said the *Daily Express* opinion column on May 8th, 1939].

'The moment is unhappily chosen. The King is on his way to America. Any word spoken in the United States at present should come from him. It would have been better for the Duke to wait.

'It is reported that the Duke will make an appeal for peace in his broadcast. Such an appeal would have been uttered more appropriately after the King's peace mission had been brought to a conclusion.'

The whole incident became a mess.

The B.B.C. refused to relay the Duke's speech, and Beaverbrook swung round on the B.B.C. with an even harder editorial fulminating against censorship.

The New York *Herald-Tribune* chipped in and called the speech 'ill-timed'. Once more the Windsors, with the best intentions in the world, were involved in a bitter and totally unnecessary controversy.

In an hotel bedroom in Verdun the Duke persisted doggedly with his broadcast. The Duchess sat by his side while he made it. His previous broadcast in December 1936 was something the world would never forget. This one flopped painfully.

It was sincere, pious, indistinguishable from many other speeches that were being made by people dismayed by the state of the world that Hitler menaced. The speeches were ineffectual. Hindsight shows that the cause of peace would have been better served had Allied statesmen listened more closely to the warning growls of a man like Winston Churchill.

Both the Duke and the Duchess blamed, and still blame, Beaverbrook for the failure of the speech.

In fact, the Windsors could blame nobody, not even themselves. It is conceivable that the Duke who had moved the world once on the radio might move the world again, this time to stem an apparently inevitable war. It is a credit to his courage in the face of criticism that he tried. But once again his lack of worldly experience proved his undoing.

The Windsors were two confused, ingenuous people dangerously prominent in a complicated world; obstinate only to be misled, well-read only to misinterpret what they read.

The Duke needed the harness of royal duties under which he had performed so admirably as Prince of Wales. Without it he was uncertain of himself and insecure.

The Duchess did not understand. European politics were hard enough for experts. They could consume amateurs and suck them dry.

However happy the Duchess made her husband's life—and this she did utterly—she was contributing little to his political stability.

By 1939 the Windsors' stock at Whitehall was depressingly

low. Then in September of that year Germany invaded Poland, and the Windsors, with the rest of humanity, went to war.

It is a curious fact that in the lives of the Duke and Duchess of Windsor nothing is quite simple or straightforward. The war which caught them up started a chain of adventures as sensational, desperate and mad as any they had endured so far.

CHAPTER V

On the Run Again

A N anonymous destroyer was tied up in Cherbourg Harbour.
Its name, concealed against the eyes of enemies, was later to
thrill England—the *Kelly*.

It was a fine sight for the Duke and Duchess of Windsor when
they arrived, tired, after the long drive from the South of France.

With Major Edward Dudley Metcalfe they had left the Château
la Cröe, and it was now tea-time, September 12th, 1939, an
eventful date for the Windsors, the date they were to return to
England together for the first time as man and wife.

The war, which the Duchess had dreaded so deeply, was nine
days old, and she had realised she was not frightened. Rather she
felt a sense of exhilaration, of expectancy.

It changed everything. It seemed to wash the past clean. It was
so enormous a calamity that it obliterated all that had gone before; even perhaps an abdication with its legacy of distrust and
hatred.

With a steadily mounting excitement the Duchess prepared to
return to England, that strange, complicated island, the judge and
the jury of her life, which had ravaged her with so many conflicting
emotions of love and hate, and made her at once resent it and yet
desire its love. All the old suspicions and vendettas could—and
surely must—be forgotten now in the face of such awful danger.
And so it must have seemed as she first set eyes on the pulsing,
breathing, ugly little destroyer, waiting only for her to step
aboard to be off.

The Navy was here for her and her husband alone. Her exile
was over. Across the dark and choppy sleeve of water embattled
England lay. At the heart stood Buckingham Palace, indestructi-
ble; at the head, King George VI and Queen Elizabeth, unafraid—

her brother-in-law and sister-in-law. She was on her way home,
and home was England.

And now there came bustling to greet them a figure which
filled her mind with memories, sweet and bitter, out of her past.

Lord Louis Mountbatten, commander of the *Kelly*, smiling,
confident, supremely sure of his own personal destiny, greeted
them warmly as though the years that separated them had been
no more distant than the party of the night before.

Once, Lord Louis and his wife and the Prince of Wales and
Mrs Simpson had been inseparable. Since the Abdication an iron
curtain had divided the Mountbattens and the Windsors. They
seldom saw each other any more. That, too, was forgotten for
this moment.

The atmosphere in the wardroom was carefree and hilarious as
the *Kelly* sped full speed for England. Mountbatten was a superb
conversationalist, the Duke a master anecdotalist, the Duchess a
first-class wit. They were made for the same circle. They were,
in fact, an unusually interlocked group. The Duke had been
Mountbatten's best man, Mountbatten had been Metcalfe's best
man, and Metcalfe had been the Duke's best man at their respective weddings.

The *Kelly* reached Portsmouth about nine o'clock that night.
The Windsors' first view of England was a dark mass in the
blackout, and as the *Kelly* slipped gingerly up to the wharf they
could see a dim, blue harbour light directed downwards to a
stretch of red carpet and gleaming here and there on the brasses
of the naval band assembled to welcome them.

The unaccustomed darkness and a strong ebb-tide made dock-
ing a treacherous business and the *Kelly* had to be edged in gently.
But Mountbatten was a remarkable sailor and his directions were
sure. The first to congratulate him as the ship was finally tied up
was the Duke of Windsor.

Mountbatten and Metcalfe followed the Windsors ashore. 'It's
nice to be home again,' the Duke said as he put his foot on English soil for the first time since the Abdication. Behind him the
Duchess trod carefully down the gang-plank, with the assistance
of a naval officer. The first person to greet them was Sir Walter

Monckton. Lady Alexandra Metcalfe, wife of Major Metcalfe, and the Commander-in-Chief, Portsmouth, were also there. The sailors, lined up on the deck of the *Kelly*, gave the Windsors three cheers, and the band played a welcoming march. Both the Duke and the Duchess were sincerely moved by their welcome.

They stayed that night at the Commander-in-Chief's house, and the following morning said their good-byes to Lord Louis Mountbatten, who was taking the *Kelly* back to sea. (She was sunk off Crete in 1941.)

Did Mountbatten notice that the enthusiasm had fallen from his two old comrades? Did he see a drooping of shoulders, and where last night they were exuberant, now they were forlorn? Perhaps not; Mountbatten had a ship to command and a war to fight. A brilliant, purposeful future lay ahead of him. His path did not cross the Windsors' path again.

There was no reception, no welcome-home or invitation from Buckingham Palace. Nothing was forgotten, nothing forgiven. A cold dawn of disillusion had taken the place of the Windsors' gaiety.

They travelled to the Metcalfes' modest home at Coleman's Hatch, in Sussex; an interesting example of the fleeting montage of war. Only a matter of hours before they had been in luxurious Cröe.

The Duke did not allow his misgivings to depress him. He unpacked at Coleman's Hatch, then drove to London to call on the Prime Minister, Neville Chamberlain.

Chamberlain passed him on to Hore-Belisha, the War Minister. The Duke emerged from the War Office with a brighter smile on his face than people could recall in a long time. A beaming Hore-Belisha saw him to the door and shook him warmly by the hand.

At long last the Duke had succeeded in getting a job from the British Government. Censorship referred to 'an appointment overseas', but did not specify what it was. The Duke often wondered during the months that followed.

The Windsors then returned to France, Metcalfe accompanying them as A.D.C. to the Duke. England had been as chilling to the Duchess as ever. She wanted so badly to be accepted, but it seemed impossible. England would not soften.

Left to her own resources, the Duchess now began to seek this way and that for an outlet for her own restless energies.

She was full of ideas. She discussed the idea of turning the Château la Cröe into a convalescent home for wounded officers and talked about it to Herman Rogers.

Rogers was still around, still living at the Villa Lou Viei. As a neutral American, opportunities for him to help in the war effort were limited, but he had joined the Red Cross and was agreeable to the Duchess's suggestion that he should supervise the convalescent home once it was established.

To do a job like that one needed a uniform, and the Duchess speedily appeared in the trim uniform of the French Women's Ambulance Corps. . . . She appeared in several uniforms, in fact. She looked very good. No woman in the world could carry clothes better than the Duchess of Windsor, and her figure lent itself to uniform. Soon she was adding a unique military chic to the smart restaurants of Paris.

She had plenty of time to spare for such relaxations, all the time in the world, in fact. The British had shown no interest in her projects. In the face of official indifference, she abandoned the idea of a hospital at the Château la Cröe.

She tried other activities, but met with little more success. Women's memories are long and the Duchess of Windsor was paying the penalty for too many witty sayings made in the past, too many good jokes at other people's expense casually thrown out but relayed from dinner table to dinner table.

Wit is a treacherous dart. It is perhaps the only weapon with which it is possible to stab oneself in one's own back.

As discouragement deepened once more to despair, the Duchess had to turn from her own problems to those of her husband.

Nothing had come of his job. He was attached to the French G.H.Q. in Paris and he had a desk. What he was called on to do he did efficiently, but his responsibilities were few.

So this storm-tossed couple, finding life bursting like bubbles whenever they tried to grasp it, sat out the twilight war in Paris eager to help but with nothing to do, all dressed up, as it were, in uniform but with nowhere to go. Days and nights passed in futility.

Fortunately the Duchess was able to keep her social life agreeable.

As her hopes grew dimmer, her parties in the world of gloom became more of an escape. That Christmas season marked a magnificent party in her town house on the Boulevard Suchet. Noel Coward was there; another eager soul who was finding it hard at the time to adjust his soaring patriotism to a paralysed war.

Coward played the piano and sang 'Tropical Heatwave'. The Duke, wearing the kilt, walked downstairs playing the bagpipes, a difficult feat and a standard test for the expert player.

On January 23rd, 1940, the Duke made a secret trip to London to try to get himself a better job. He called on General Ironside, Chief of the Imperial General Staff. It got him nowhere, and he returned, frustrated, to Paris.

The German invasion of France changed everything. The Duke sent the Duchess to Biarritz out of harm's way, and every morning at four o'clock he went north with Metcalfe to visit the collapsing French front.

The Duchess became frightened for her husband. He must not risk capture by the Nazis. He would be far too important a prisoner. From Biarritz the Duchess called repeatedly, urging the Duke to escape south before the Germans captured him. *Sauve qui peut.*

One night, after a visit to the front, the Duke decided to go. He left the deserted house in the Boulevard Suchet, climbed into his car and travelled south to the Château la Cröe. Metcalfe managed to get back to England. A few days later the Germans were in Paris.

It was all over so quickly, and confusion on the Riviera was utter. No real news was coming through from Paris or the battlefronts, and the wildest rumours were believed. All round the Windsors the British colony was packing up and hastily departing by whatever means it could. One large group—Somerset

Maugham was in it—boarded a Polish coal-boat which had put into Cannes and ultimately reached safety after a nightmare voyage.

The Duchess had arrived at Cröe from Biarritz, and with the Duke wondered what to do next. They were informed that Paris had fallen and that France had surrendered, and it was clear that they could not stay on the Riviera as the Germans might turn up at Antibes within a matter of hours.

But the Duke refused to be panicked. He remained calm and assured anxious friends that there was nothing to worry about. 'There is no reason for alarm,' he said on several occasions. 'If we were in any danger the British Government would send a warship.'

They had been at Cröe together for a few days when Captain George Wood, a big, humorous, but harassed Army officer, joined them with his Austrian wife, Rosa. The Windsors had known the Woods in Austria, and Wood was shortly to take an appointment as the Duke's aide. Wood had been in Vienna when the Nazis had swept through, and his daughter, who was married to Prince Hohenberg, second son of the murdered Archduke Franz Ferdinand of Austria, had just disappeared somewhere under the holocaust of the *blitzkrieg* (they were both discovered undernourished but safe in Austria when the war ended).

Major Grey Phillips, the Duke's comptroller, followed the Woods to Cröe on the evening of June 18th, and a long conference was held to decide the next move. The Duke himself was in favour of staying put, feeling that to leave would look like running away. Phillips agreed. Wood, who had seen the Nazis enter Vienna and was touched more closely than the other two by the Nazi menace, was for getting out. In the end the Duke decided he could not rely on the British Government for help and that he had better leave. His liaison job to the French Army had disappeared along with the French Army, and there was nothing to keep him on the Riviera except the physical difficulty of getting away from it with the Germans closing in from the north and Mussolini's Italians holding the east only a few kilometres away. The whole thing must have seemed quite unreal to all the characters caught in the trap of this sun-drenched paradise, the luxury hotels and millionaires' villas disgorging wealthy refugees of all nations, panic, anxiety everywhere, only the blue sea unruffled, the Germans, for all anyone knew for certain, on the other side of the superb mountain coastline.

The Windsors began to pack and by June 19th, several days after the French surrender, the Cröe party was ready to move. The Duke had contacted the British Embassy, which had been evacuated from Paris and was trying to maintain some kind of fugitive organisation at Bordeaux. In spite of all their other problems, the British officials were relieved to hear the Duke's voice, and more relieved still to hear that he was about to make a bid for safety. Already the Foreign Office had been anxious about the possibility of the Windsors being taken prisoner by the Nazis. The Bordeaux officials asked him to keep in touch, and promised to try to help him to get into Spain.

A high wind was blowing as the Windsors, now changed out of uniform into civilian clothes, prepared to say good-bye to Cröe, a home that had been a happy one for them. One obstacle, however, had still to be overcome before they could finally leave. The large entrance-hall was crammed from ceiling to floor and from wall to wall with trunks, crates, bags, boxes. The Duke had hired a lorry to carry the stuff, but it looked at first as if it would be too much for half a dozen lorries. Somehow it was all squeezed aboard in the end, and the party was almost ready to go.

The Windsor Buick was the first in line, with George Ladbrook at the wheel and the Duchess's maid beside him. Behind sat the Windsors and Phillips. Then came Wood's Citroën with Wood at the wheel, Mrs Wood and her personal maid. A luggage trailer bumped along behind. In the rear was the lorry driven by a hired man. That completed the human roster. There were also four dogs. Mrs Wood's Sealyham was already curled up in the car. All that remained was to catch the Windsors' three Cairn terriers —'my three little princes' the Duke used to call them—which was not so easy. The terriers thought the whole thing a fine frolic and disappeared into the brush, and the party was delayed fifteen minutes while they were collared, yapping in amusement, one by one.

For the second time in her life the Duchess of Windsor now set out in flight. First it had been from the British, and now it was from the Germans, a combination of enemies that would have daunted a weaker woman. Progress was fairly good along the roads that afternoon, although it was inevitably slowed because of the difficulty the heavily-laden lorry had in keeping up with the two cars. The war had not yet reached the Riviera (the Germans did not, in fact, appear for another two years), and though there were quite a lot of refugees there was not enough to bother them seriously.

It was not until they reached Arles that evening that the full impact of the French disaster really struck them. Here was a city literally shuddering with war, with tanks and gun-carriers clattering through the streets, soldiers everywhere, airplanes flying constantly overhead. With difficulty the party managed to get accommodation for the night, the Windsors in a large, old-fashioned bedroom with a double-bed.

The electricity supply at Arles had been cut off two days before and the town was in total darkness. The royal party ate a dismal meal that night by the light of two smoky yellow candles. This was war, a harsh, flickering war-commentary which may have reminded the Duchess ironically of one of her most sparkling peace-time maxims that at dinner 'a woman over forty looks her best by candlelight'.

Next day on the road from Arles to Perpignan the little convoy ran into hordes of refugees, most of them soldiers of several nations, who had lost both officers and organisation, and were wandering helplessly not knowing where to go or what to do next. In spite of frequent hold-ups the Windsors showed no impatience and were unflaggingly cheerful, almost as if they were on an outing in the country. After several delays in traffic-choked villages, the Duke developed a simple but apparently effective way of breaking through. Whenever the convoy was forced to stop he would get out of his car, wave his arms and say in his abominable French, 'Moi, je suis le Duc de Windsor'. His popularity had survived even the French defeat, for invariably there would be a feeble cheer, and cries of 'Vive le Duc de Windsor!' occasionally 'Vive le Roi!' and the road would open to let the party pass.

They arrived at lunch-time at Perpignan, a French town on the border of Spain crammed with British refugees trying to escape into neutral territory. By now the royal party had been joined by two worried British consular officials also fleeing from the Germans.

The Spanish frontier was closed tight and held by troop re-inforcements, and rumours, started probably by fifth columnists, kept rippling through the bursting town: the Germans were only twenty miles away; Perpignan had been picked out for devasta-tion by the Luftwaffe. Bordeaux, however, on the phone to the Duke, was reassuring. Visas had been obtained for the Windsors and were waiting for them at the Spanish consulate.

So there were—two of them, one for the Duke, one for the Duchess. The Duke looked at them blankly and demanded, 'How about the rest, Major Phillips, Captain and Mrs Wood, the two consuls and the servants?'

The Spanish consul, a big-built impassive man, just shrugged. The Duke argued, but the consul was immovable. Only two visas had been granted. After getting nowhere the Duke refused to accept them and pushed his way back to the hotel to ring the British authorities in Bordeaux. The official with whom he spoke promised to do what he could and advised the Duke to return to the consulate. The Duke did so, but there were still no visas. He went back to the hotel to call Bordeaux yet again. Now one member of the party had suddenly discovered that his British passport was marked 'not valid for Spain'. On the Duke's recommendation he climbed into a car and streaked to the nearest British consulate. There he found one French assistant remaining alone, burning papers and rubber stamps. A stamp marked 'Valid for Spain' was salvaged, impressed on to this passport, and he returned as fast as he could to Perpignan.

He need not have hurried. The Duke had made no progress. The Spanish authorities refused to grant him further visas. The

Duke refused to desert his friends. Three times he had travelled back and forth between the consulate and the hotel.

Only once did the Spanish consul appear to soften in any way. As the Duke was leaving after another fruitless argument, the consul said awkwardly, 'Excuse me, Your Highness. My little daughter collects autographs. Would you give me yours?' He took an autograph book from a drawer and held it out.

The Duke, in his ebullient way, grinned. 'I tell you what,' he said. 'Let's swop signatures. I'll sign your daughter's book if you put your signature on the visas for my party.' The consul's face instantly hardened and the proffered book was withdrawn.

The Duke may have felt he had done himself no good with his little attempt to be pleasant. 'Oh, come on,' he said. 'I was only joking. Give me the book and I'll sign it.'

It was almost certainly a coincidence, but on the Duke's next trip back to the consulate, he found the Spaniard's manner had changed completely. He was smiling broadly and held out visas for the entire party, including the member whose passport mark 'Not Valid for Spain' had been only unconvincingly obliterated. Watched by hundreds of envious British refugees, the convoy rolled over the border towards Port Bou on June 20th, at 5.30 p.m., after which the gates which divided safety from danger snapped shut behind them. The party sighed with relief at the abrupt escape of tension.

There was a long delay while they unpacked the lorry which was not allowed to travel through Spain. They hired a Spanish lorry and headed for Barcelona. It was a long and rough drive, and the party was tired, but there were no stops except for a picnic dinner of tea and sandwiches by the roadside.

Barcelona was reached very late that night and accommodation was found at the Ritz Hotel. For the first time in several weeks the refugees were able to sleep with a feeling of security without wondering whether the Germans would be at their front door by the time they woke up. The Windsors rested for three days in Barcelona, leaving finally on the morning of June 22nd. Their saga was not yet over. All day they travelled through the killing heat of a Spanish summer day, and arrived at Saragossa that night, running right into a big Spanish fiesta, the fiesta of the Virgin of la Pillar. While the Windsors slept that night in the Gran Hotel, there was dancing in the streets outside all night, until the festivities were stopped by a rainstorm.

Next morning the Duke and Duchess visited the cathedral at Saragossa, and it was not until 12.30, the rain still falling heavily, that they got on the move again with Madrid next stop. They reached the capital seven hours later, and moved into rooms found for them by the British Embassy, at the Ritz Hotel.

They celebrated with a quiet dinner party in the hotel garden restaurant. The food was as good as anything one could find at the time in Spain so soon after the Civil War was over, but one thing spoiled their appetites. At the other end of the restaurant, a man in evening clothes, his head close-cropped, stared at them unblinkingly and with an almost frightening malevolence. Who, they wanted to know, was that?

That, a waiter told them, was Doktor Eberhard von Stöhrer, Hitler's Ambassador in Madrid.

Von Stöhrer maintained a regular table at the Ritz, and every evening the two parties, British and German, dined at the same time in the same room, never acknowledging the existence of the other, although sometimes a mutual friend would stop first at one table and then at the other, and it would produce a feeling of shock as though two electric currents had been suddenly joined. The German Ambassador had a part to play in the adventures that were to come.

Sir Samuel Hoare, now Lord Templewood, had just become British Ambassador in Madrid, and the Duke saw him several times. War throws the most unlikely people together, and it must have been a reunion with the most dramatic undertones, as Templewood had been one of Stanley Baldwin's chief lieutenants during the Abdication crisis. Yet in this time of collapsing alliances and dreadful menace, how far away the Abdication, and even the world in which it happened, must have seemed at that moment in battered, hostile Madrid.

As in his reunion with Mountbatten at the beginning of the war, so now with Templewood, the Duke of Windsor showed no rancour for past differences, and his sessions with the Ambassador were very friendly.

The Windsors were in Madrid for a little over a week and seemed quite content to stay there until the government decided on a job for the Duke. In London, however, there was anxiety over the aggressive German activities in Spain, especially in Madrid, and instructions were sent to the Duke to move westward into the friendlier atmosphere of Portugal. Bags were packed and the little party set off for Lisbon, heading, though they did not know it yet, for a month of adventure as strange as any they had ever encountered in their strange lives to that date.

CHAPTER VI

'The Mouth of Hell'

THE Windsors made their way across the Iberian Peninsula under the fascinated eyes of the Nazis. They were watched out of Spain by the agents of Dr Eberhard von Stöhrer, German Minister in Madrid, and they were watched into Portugal by agents of Baron Oswald von Hoyningen-Huehne, the German Minister in Lisbon.

At the border the Germans might even have seen the Duke lose his temper for the first time on this eventful journey. With the Duchess he had taken every previous development in his stride with cheerfulness. Now, on arriving at Mérida near the Portuguese border with rooms booked for him at a Government rest-house, he discovered that the lorry had taken a different route via Badajoz, and was temporarily lost somewhere along with the Duke's pyjamas and shaving-kit. The Duke hit the roof and had to be content to borrow the necessary accessories from his aides.

On the morning of July 3rd, 1940, the Windsors crossed into Portugal and, accompanied by a British Embassy official named Hogg, they drove into Lisbon, making the last stretch of the journey by ferry-boat. They were then escorted out of the city to a mansion in the romantic little village of Cascais just outside Estoril, the home of their host, Dr Ricardo de Espirito-Santo Silva, a Portuguese banker and connoisseur. Espirito-Santo means 'Holy Ghost', and he named his house 'O Boca do Inferno', which means 'The Mouth of Hell', the name being taken from a cavernous rock formation in the vicinity.

The man responsible for this arrangement was Sir Walford Selby, the British Ambassador in Lisbon. Selby, as British Ambassador to Austria, had greeted the Duke in Vienna immediately after the Abdication. An old-school Englishman, Selby was a wise and experienced Ambassador, and he and the Duke were close friends. When Selby heard that the Windsors were on their way he asked Espirito-Santo if the Duke might stay at his house 'for a night or two', and the banker had willingly agreed. The Windsor party was expected to arrive by tea-time, but there were various delays and it did not turn up at Cascais until shortly before dinner. In the conference that followed Selby was able to tell the Duke that an airplane would be ready to take him and the Duchess to England the following day, but the Duke would have none of this. The notice was far too short, he said, and he would not be ready to leave.

So it was agreed that the Windsors would stay a week in Espirito-Santo's treasure-crammed house in Cascais, while Espirito-Santo and his wife moved to another house which they owned in Lisbon itself. The Duke would then wait for his next assignment. It arrived in due course by telegram. He was offered the job of Governor of the Bahamas, a post so insignificant and so far away from the scene of battle that he was appalled. As a result, instead of staying only a few days he stayed a month at 'O Boca do Inferno', aptly named for a place where the Duke was forced to wrestle with his conscience, his aspirations and the German devil.

There is no doubt that the Germans entertained great hopes concerning the Duke of Windsor at this time. Walter Goerlitz, the German historian, has quoted the notes of Ernest von Weizsaecker, a permanent head of the German Foreign Office, relating to the period of July 1940, the month the Duke and Duchess of Windsor spent in Lisbon. These notes speak of letters to King George VI from Lloyd George and the Duke of Windsor in which plans for peace were referred to.[1]

The full facts of what happened next have not yet been revealed. They still lurk in private notes and in confidential files. However, Hoyningen-Huehne, the German Minister in Lisbon, was now brought in. The German Foreign Office wanted to know the prospects of the Duke of Windsor remaining in Lisbon 'inside the German circle of communications'. The Germans had hit

[1] *The German General Staff.*

upon the fantastic plan of keeping the Duke close in the wings of the great drama they were about to perform. Once Britain was invaded and occupied they would try—if it seemed politically advantageous to them—to restore the Duke to the throne as 'Friedenskoenig' or 'peace King'. A subsidiary part of this idea was to install Lloyd George as a puppet Prime Minister. There was even some softening-up propaganda on the Axis radio, the Italians sending out a broadcast that Churchill had ordered the Duke's arrest if he should ever land on British soil.

Around the Duke there now emerge two important men, important because it was their particular personalities which were largely responsible for deciding the course of the story. Had their characters been different, the Duke might never have reached the Bahamas. One was Ricardo de Espirito-Santo, a handsome cosmopolitan who spoke many tongues and knew many people. He was a personal friend to one degree or other of all the four sons of King George V, most intimately of all, however, of the Duke of Kent. In fact, Kent had been in Lisbon only a few days before on an official mission, and had spent some time at Espirito-Santo's house, returning to England hardly more than twenty-four hours before the Windsors arrived.

Besides his wide British background (he was once or twice rumoured as a likely Portuguese Ambassador in London), Espirito-Santo, through his bank, had commercial relations in Berlin and his bank held large Portuguese deposits of the Reichsbank. Dr Salazar, Portugal's Prime Minister, relied heavily on him for information both from Britain and from Germany. Salazar was pro-British, and though he quailed before the German might he wanted to do what he could to help his traditional ally. Espirito-Santo reflected entirely Salazar's attitude.

Espirito-Santo was a close personal friend of the second character involved in the affair of the Duke, namely Baron Oswald von Hoyningen-Huehne, who now had before him Ribbentrop's message about the Windsors and was digesting it without a great deal of enthusiasm.

Hoyningen-Huehne had been in Lisbon for many years, and had already decided to make it his home on retirement. He was an able, humorous, popular diplomat, a typically apathetic anti-Nazi in that he disliked Hitler but not enough to do anything about it. His mother was an Englishwoman. A cousin, George Hoyningen-Huehne, was and is one of New York's best-known photographers. A nephew married Nancy Oakes de Marigny in 1952.

So far as Hoyningen-Huehne was concerned, it was at least as important to remain in Salazar's good books as it was to remain in Ribbentrop's. He was not at all happy about the legion of German agents slipping unobtrusively from Spain into Lisbon, and he kept as remote from them as he could, particularly as he knew that British agents were also around keeping him under careful watch. Salazar, he realised, was not going to like the idea of the German Minister interfering with a member of the British Royal Family on Portuguese soil.

However, orders were orders, and something had to be done. Hoyningen-Huehne approached Espirito-Santo as a friend and asked him for his co-operation. Somehow a message was conveyed to the Duke about the prospects of his remaining 'inside the German circle of communications', which phrase seemed to be the key to the German idea.

That was all. But the sense of intrigue could be felt everywhere. At the Cascais mansion the Duchess, feeling that she and her husband were trespassing too long on their friend's hospitality, sent an aide to try to get some accommodation at the fashionable Hôtel Aviz in Lisbon. A British Embassy official heard about it and was startled. 'For Heaven's sake stay put and don't move into an hotel,' he told the aide. 'This city is swarming with German spies and there are rumours that they are going to try to kidnap the Duke.'

All the time the Duke, probably unaware of the tension he was creating in both London and Berlin, carried on, playing golf with Espirito-Santo in the afternoons, turning up once or twice at the Estoril Casino, and once at a bullfight, at which the Portuguese crowd, recognising him, rose to give him an ovation.

Boca do Inferno and its large staff of silent servants were at his disposal, and the servants were sometimes disconcerted by his simple ways. ('Madam,' the chef once said despairingly over the telephone to Senhora Espirito-Santo, 'I wish to prepare His Highness some of my finest dishes, but all he keeps asking for are sardines and salad.')

The world is always small for famous people, and the co-incidence is sometimes more the rule than the exception. Among the small group of people to whom the Windsors were introduced in Portugal was a beautiful young Frenchwoman, Mrs Lucy Fury Wann, wife of a senior officer of the R.A.F. Mrs Wann had escaped from France, and was now waiting for a chance to return to England and rejoin her husband. Some years later her husband died, and in 1949 the Windsors were witnesses when she married Herman Rogers, whose wife also had died.

The international developments revolving round the Duke went on quite unknown to him. All the same, the British Foreign Office feared for his safety. Despite the pious quotation of Queen Victoria ('There is no doubt in this house . . . the possibility of defeat does not exist', etc.) that was appearing on the walls of offices and public-houses all over Britain, the possibility of occupation was always present in the minds of the Government, and had even been given official voice by Churchill in one of his greatest speeches ('and even if . . . this island were subjugated and starving . . . we will never surrender'). Hitler had already made it clear that he preferred to keep the Kings of occupied countries on their thrones. He had been angry at the escape of Queen Wilhelmina of the Netherlands and of King Haakon of Norway. He was even now making use of patriotic men like King Leopold of Belgium and King Christian of Denmark. The British Royal Family was fairly safe and could be whisked to Canada if necessary. There was only one exception, remaining on the treacherous continent of Europe, alone and exposed—the Duke of Windsor. And the Duke was showing himself reluctant to accept the post that had been offered to him. In the end the situation became so serious that Churchill flew Walter Monckton out to Lisbon to settle the differences. Monckton arrived about July 28th, and was also put up at the home of Dr Espirito-Santo. With all his lawyer's powers of persuasion, he urged the Duke to accept the position. Espirito-

Santo also added his voice, and pointed out how potentially important the Bahamas were. For one thing, he said the islands were near the still-neutral United States to which the Duke was so closely drawn. For another thing, they were important strategically. For yet another they were a focal-point of Allied censorship (Espirito-Santo was wrong here; the central point was Bermuda). Reluctantly the Duke yielded on all points, and it was with great relief that the Colonial Office in London was able to announce:

'His Majesty the King has been pleased to appoint His Royal Highness, the Duke of Windsor, K.G., to be Governor and Commander-in-Chief of the Bahama Islands.'

The next few days were spent in a frenzy of shopping for clothes and equipment. Reservations were made on the American liner *Excalibur* sailing to Bermuda with a cargo-load of American ex-Ambassadors and wealthy American refugees. The Windsors reserved a verandah suite with six two-bed cabins. Eighty-five pieces of baggage accompanied them on their journey. No attempt at secrecy was made. It would have been futile, since Portugal was a neutral country and the *Excalibur* was a neutral ship. So the Duke and Duchess gave a noisy party for Lisbon newspapermen the night before the sailing.

George Ladbrook was invited to travel with the party, but his part in the story had finally come to an end. The bombs were beginning to tumble down on London, and Ladbrook felt his place was there beside his family. He said good-bye, and later one of his sons was killed in the R.A.F. Farewell was also made to the Buick, which had played such a big part in their adventures.

Even now there was a slight hold-up. On the morning the *Excalibur* was due to sail, the Duke asked Espirito-Santo if he could see Dr Salazar and thank him for his hospitality. The Duke and Salazar met in the President's house behind Lisbon's Houses of Parliament and chatted for an hour. This meant a last dash through Lisbon to get to the ship. The Windsors were the last people aboard. The gang-plank was pulled up after them, and the ship sailed half an hour late.

The German incident was over and Hoyningen-Huehne cabled

Berlin that the birds had all but flown. The Duke was able to leave Portugal unharmed, partly because of the influence of Ricardo Espirito-Santo, partly by Monckton's intervention, partly because of Hoyningen-Huehne's inert attitude.

When Salazar handed Britain bases in the Azores, Hoyningen-Huehne was almost the only diplomat in Portugal taken by surprise. Ribbentrop was so furious that he called him home and then arrested him. In his place he tried to send a hundred-per-cent. Nazi. Salazar, shocked, refused to accept him, and personally protested at the treatment of the popular Hoyningen-Huehne. Nevertheless, Hoyningen-Huehne remained under guard for the rest of the war in Germany. Today he lives contentedly in retirement in Estoril.

Had Hoyningen-Huehne been a different type of man, had he been an ardent Nazi, the result might have been different. The war was still young at the time, but already something had been seen of what determined cloak-and-dagger agents could do. Best and Stevens, two British agents operating secretly, had been seized in neutral Holland by the Germans and spirited across the frontier. Later in the war, when systems had been perfected, alert agents moved backwards and forwards across battle-lines with ease, and the culminating-point came when Mussolini was rescued from captivity inside the Allied lines by German paratroopers.

Under circumstances only slightly different it would have been a comparatively minor coup for specially picked Nazis to descend one night on Boca do Inferno and snatch the Windsors into Germany.

Fortunately it did not happen that way.

CHAPTER VII

Troubles in a Tropical Paradise

IN Bermuda the Windsors were transferred from the neutral *Excalibur* to a small Canadian passenger ship, *Lady Somers*, and a destroyer was detached to escort him on the last step of his journey to the Bahamas.

The whole town turned out with pomp and regalia to welcome the new Governor, and apart from the killing heat of the day, the reception went without a fault. The period of the Windsors' reign in the Bahamas was marked by many big and unexpected events. The Americans were given bases there. Controversial good-will visits were made to the United States. There was a riot and a fire. On the night of July 8th, 1943, the Windsors' circle of friends decreased violently by one. The Windsors still attracted criticism, but for a change they also received some well-merited praise.

The Duchess of Windsor spent in the Bahamas probably the greatest years of performance and achievement in her life. Some local politicians rate her among the greatest Governors' wives in the history of the colony.

She made no secret, however, of her dislike for the Bahamas. She complained in private and she complained in public, and about nearly everything. This offended many residents, but it increased in a way their respect and admiration for a strong-minded woman who could work so hard in the interest of a country to which she wanted only to say good-bye.

Even before she arrived the famous wit of steel had been turned on her husband's appointment. 'St Helena, 1940 fashion,' she commented to a friend in Lisbon. Later on she varied her place of exile. In letters to friends she sometimes crossed out the words 'Government House' at the top of stationery and wrote in 'Elba'.

This fact was drawn to the attention of King George VI, who totally failed to be amused.

One of her first remarks on landing was to complain about the heat and the mosquitoes. In 1940, shortly after arriving, she exploded so succinctly to an American woman reporter that a question was asked about it in the House of Commons. 'How can one expect the Duke to live here?' she reportedly demanded. 'I, too, wish to do our duty. But is there scope here for his great gifts, his inspiration, his long training? I'm only a woman, but I'm his wife and I don't believe that in Nassau he's serving the Empire as importantly as he might.'

But it has always been the Duchess's habit to say what she thinks, and it does not take a long experience of Nassau to sympathise, in some degree, with her position. Nassau is a village community with a compelling capacity for inspiring dislike. The climate is the least pleasant in the Bahamas. The prevailing wind is the Trade, which sometimes blows from the north-east, sometimes from south-east. Most of the Bahamas get this wind off the water, and it comes in cool and refreshing in the appropriate manner of the tropical paradise. But New Providence Island, on which the town of Nassau stands, is an 'in-island' (distinguishing it from most of the other islands, which are called out-islands). The waters which surround it, while superb for yachting, are warm shoal waters, and the humidity becomes intense. In Nassau, the water supply is low and it comes up dank. Nassau flowers in consequence have relatively little smell. Mosquitoes are only a minor problem, but the islands breed a virile sandfly which penetrates mosquito-nettings with ease and laughs in the face of DDT. There are few singing birds, and the whole atmosphere is like that of a painted post-card. Count Alfred de Marigny, the man who was acquitted of the murder of Sir Harry Oakes, gives a short bitter picture of the Bahamas in his skilful and plausible autobiography, *More Devil than Saint*.

'Mediocrity is the word for the Bahamas,' he writes. 'The country is mediocre in everything. There are no rivers, fresh-water lakes, mountains. Even from the earliest days the people were mediocre. After the American revolution, when the British

Government became tired of their demands for "compensation for the losses they had suffered on account of their loyalty to His Majesty during the late trouble in America", they developed a mentality which exists to this day—"The Nassau Pirate Mentality". They were not bold, daring pirates of song and story. They lived on the wrecks that were thrown up on the coral reefs.'

The town of Nassau itself can be traversed comfortably in a ten-minute stroll. The Government House is a chocolate-box affair, tiny, rather comic, with an heroic statue of Christopher Columbus at the entrance gazing down George Street towards Bay Street, the Nassau shopping centre, a street which visitors suddenly transplanted from London might forgivably mistake for a somewhat commercialised mews in Margate.

But its smallness, meanness and tourist-chiselling are only the surface irritants of Nassau. As a seat of government it presented problems which the Duke of Windsor was never trained to handle easily. Unlike most of the other outposts of the British Empire where the Governor, as the personal representative of the King, is expected to be above politics, the Governor of the Bahamas, like the Governors of neighbouring Bermuda and the Barbadoes, contributes actively to local political policy.

The Bahamas Legislature itself has three parts—the House of Assembly, the Legislative Council and the Governor. The House of Assembly is equivalent to the House of Commons, and it is guided in debate by May's *Parliamentary Practice*, which is the textbook of the House of Commons.

The Legislative Council is appointed by the Governor representing the King. This body of eight or nine members is presided over by a President, also picked by the Governor. It is equivalent to the British House of Lords, though it has more power.

The Governor convenes Parliament, signs Bills. He has veto powers over legislation, and often uses it. He can dissolve the Legislature, and sometimes does. He presides over an Executive Council, and acts in a way like a British Prime Minister. In effect his function is more similar to that of a President of the United States than as a representative of the King, in that he is both the head of the State and the initiator of policy.

In other words, of all the appointments far from home that the British Government could have handed to the Duke of Windsor, they handed him one in which his opportunities to utilise his impartial training as Prince were at a minimum. He now had to embroil himself in the party politics of a particularly inert community, comprising 70,000 people, eighty per cent. of them coloured, twenty-nine islands, most of them uninhabited, and a few thousand bays, coral reefs and sandspits. On the one hand, his job was made easier by the fact that there was little extremist urge in the islands—few Communists, fewer secessionists and a population lethargically content with its position in the Empire— but, on the other hand, it was made complicated by the population's sloth, its selfishness, narrow outlook, reluctance to pay taxes or to compromise in any way with its own comfort.

All Governors get criticised steadily in the Bahamas, and the Duke did not care for this either. He protested mildly to a Bahamas editor at one attack on some political proposal he had made. 'In Britain the newspapers do not usually criticise the Royal Family,' he said.

'Sir,' replied the editor, 'I would not dream of criticising you as a member of the Royal Family. I am criticising you as Governor of the Bahamas.' The Duke took the reproof in good part and laughed.

The Duke depressed the community no little in his first excellent speech when he warned darkly that it was not only in Britain that blood, sweat and tears must be shed. 'My wife and I will work as a team here,' he added. 'That is how I want all of us to work.' Happily for the Bahamans the Duke's bark proved to be worse than his bite. In the Bahamas community there was little blood or toil, infrequent tears though plenty of sweat.

On arrival in August 1940, the Duke and Duchess took adjoining offices in Government House and set to work. The first thing the Duchess did was to redecorate Government House, a cracked and flaking edifice which in the past had survived with about as much warmth and atmosphere as Wellington Barracks.

While she was still in Lisbon the House of Assembly had granted £2,000 to the Board of Works for the reconditioning of the Governor's residence 'so that it will be put in a befitting state' for the Windsors' arrival. The Duchess then cabled Nassau that nothing was to be done until she arrived. Once she was installed, she imported a New York decorator and detailed her ideas. She ordered softer lighting and arranged for candlelight in the dining-room. She had fun—three years in France had given her the craze that reaches its greatest frenzy among sophisticated French people, the craze for interior decoration, and with it a passion for moving furniture around. At the end of all the time and trouble the Board of Works added up the bills and found that expenditure had exceeded the authorised grant by £5,000. Instead of spending £2,000, the Windsors had spent £7,000, but the House passed the excess without comment, and the Governor's House was now so charming that the Duchess of Windsor has since been blessed by every succeeding Governor's wife.

The Windsors quickly became acquainted with a blue-eyed Swedish giant named Axel Wenner-Gren, a multi-millionaire, with an industrial empire ranging from Sweden to the United States and Mexico. He owned valuable real estate in Nassau, including the glorious Paradise Beach.

Wenner-Gren entertained the Windsors royally in his yacht the *Southern Cross*, and continued to do so until America entered the war. Thereupon the British and American Governments blacklisted him. Wenner-Gren had been a close friend of Hermann Goering, and had acted as a go-between in settling a truce to the Russo-Finnish war of 1940. The Allies felt at the time that he was excessively friendly to the Nazis.

The sense of doubt that troubled the Duke in Portugal followed him to Nassau. Both of the Windsors were appalled when Russia was grabbed by the scruff of the neck by Hitler and chucked into the Allied camp, but even before this happened, with Britain alone in the war, there was a note of anxiety in some of the Duke's statements.

'When this war is over,' he said in March 1941 in an interview with Fulton Oursler, then editor of *Liberty*, 'many strange things are going to happen. There will be a new order in Europe whether it is imposed by Germany or by Great Britain. Labour is going to get a more equitable distribution of the world's good things in this new order. The new peace will have to be as just a settlement as the human spirit can provide . . . there will have to be a world league with everybody in it, but this time it will be buttressed by police power. When this peace comes there is going to be a new order of social justice, and when that time comes what is your country going to do about its gold?'

In a free world everybody is entitled to his opinion, and in the Bahamas the Windsors made up for most things by the excellence of their performance. They were given a flying start when they were able to turn, at the beginning of their reign, a particularly unfortunate *faux pas* to their own advantage.

The story was revealed by *Life* magazine in 1940. It was at the Windsors' first social appearance in the Bahamas, at a ceremonial dinner. Sir Frederick Williams-Taylor, an elderly Canadian millionaire, formerly head of the Bank of Montreal, whose wife was the leader of what social set then existed in Nassau, presided and made a speech of welcome—to the Duke only. Somehow the name of the Duchess was left out. Williams-Taylor was a kind man and an old man, and it must be that this was un-intentional.

According to *Life*, the Duke, with the practised anger he, as a husband, reserved for any slur on the lady who is his wife, rose, stated that in Sir Frederick's prepared speech as originally sub-mitted to him, the Duchess had been included and that he, the Duke, wondered if the light were so dim that on reading his speech Sir Frederick had inadvertently made the oversight which he, the Duke, could not overlook. The Duke went on to give his own speech, which included the correct gracious references to Sir Frederick's spouse, known as 'Lady Jane', who was social leader of Nassau until the Duchess arrived.

Emerald Beach guests said that while the Duke was having his say was the most magnificently embarrassing moment of their lives. . . . Later the Duchess started to rise with the rest of the guests. 'You don't have to stand up for me, darling,' the Duke domestically advised her. 'It's a pleasure to stand up for you, darling,' she countered with double meaning.

Once installed, the Duchess assumed her duties energetically. She lent her name and her time to the Red Cross. She more or less took over the United Services canteen, and did hard work for the Y.W.C.A. and the I.O.D.E. (Independent Order of Daughters of the Empire). She discovered that many native children were suffering from deficiencies in their milk diets. She organised an office to distribute milk to the children. She opened clinics. One, built with donated funds at the Duke of Windsor's disposal, was given her name, and remains today a testimony to her vision.

Decisions were not always easy, nor were the problems concerned solely with the war effort. During the course of one Red Cross drive the fashionable ladies of Nassau were covered in confusion when Miss Sally Rand, the American burlesque queen, turned up and offered her services. Miss Rand was appearing in Nassau, and was eager to perform at the gala charity concert to be held that night. The Duchess was with other Red Cross committee women when the request came through. She laughed and commented: 'I am playing no part in this. You must decide,' and left. Sally Rand duly appeared and did her bubble dance. At the tables Nassau society, including the Windsors, watched stonily. Next day the Duchess asked a friend in delight, 'What are they saying in Nassau this morning?' Incidents like this tended to break the stuffiness of Bahaman life.

In the year of war in which England stood alone, many torpedoed seamen were being unloaded destitute from rescue ships. Responsibility for their welfare was assumed by the Duchess, who supervised their accommodation and equipped them with clothes and toilet articles. She and the Duke were the first to visit the celebrated Tapscott and Widdicombe, those two iron sailors who had established a record of two and a half months in an open boat, and who were later landed by rescuers at Nassau.

The U-boats were so audacious that they brought the Bahamas close to the front-line, and the Duke became concerned about the colony's defences, which were pretty much limited to some good rifles and old pirate cannon. He convinced the War Office that his uneasiness was justified, and a company of the Camerons was

transferred to Nassau from Curaçao, where it had been guarding
Dutch refineries.

The Services canteen in Bay Street was the Duchess's pride.
She would drop in at all hours of the day and evening to see how
things were going, and when necessary help out herself. One
night three tired American sailors, newly arrived in the Bahamas,
came into the deserted canteen and asked for food. It was 10 p.m.
'Sorry,' said the coloured girl behind the counter, 'we are closing.'

'We don't want much. Just give us a plate of eggs,' one of the
sailors said politely.

'Sorry,' said the girl with the unbudging deference to convention which is one of the most depressing characteristics the
Bahamans have inherited from the British, 'we are closing.'

The sailors became less polite. 'Eggs,' said one loudly. 'We'll
pay extra,' said another.

'No,' said the girl.

'Listen,' said one of the sailors, exasperated. 'This is the Duchess
of Windsor's canteen, isn't it? Well, the Duchess is an American
girl, and if she were here she'd kick you so fast into that kitchen
to get us some eggs, you would——'

At this moment the Duchess came into the canteen from the
street, and paused, startled by the noise. 'Hey, Duchess,' the sailor
yelled, 'this dame won't give us any food. All we want are some
eggs.'

The Duchess reached for an apron. 'How,' she asked, 'do you
want them?' Without more ado she went into the kitchen, took a
pan, and personally served the eggs to the delighted sailors.

Nassau, of course, was too small for much standing on
ceremony, and the Duchess had by now become a familiar,
though always formidable, figure in her light gay frocks driving
round in a rather dilapidated station-wagon. 'It's cooler than the
Governor's car,' she would say cheerfully in answer to the raised
eyebrows.

In 1942 a big fire broke out in Nassau. Both the Windsors
joined in to fight it and returned to Government House covered
in soot.

Meanwhile the Duke was also going about his own business.

He urged a minimum wage of six shillings a day for labourers, two shillings more than they were getting at the time. The Legislature resisted the move and after an acid debate rejected it. In 1942 labourers rioted over the wage the United States Government was paying them at the American naval base under construction. They marched through Nassau shouting and breaking shop windows, though there was little personal violence. The Duke, who was in Washington at the time, personally intervened with the American authorities, and managed better there than he had done with his own Legislature. The labourers' wages went up—by two shillings a day.

The Duke then tried to create an office to distribute jobs on government projects in the out-lands, and once more the Legislature, in its wisdom, booted the measure out. The Duke did manage, after a struggle, to get tariffs reduced on war-essential imports. But an attempt to draw the teeth of the 'Bay-street-pirate' merchants then sucking tourists dry got nowhere.

By and large the Duke was proving active enough, but he did not satisfy the Bahamas—few Governors ever do. The Legislature found him too liberally inclined for their own tastes. The coloured population, recalling his statement 'Something must be done' to the Welsh miners, did not find him liberal enough, and criticised his apparent lethargy and the modesty of such reforms as he tried to put forward.

Happily for the Bahamans the arduous wartime life which the Duke promised them did not materialise. It was too hot, for one thing. The Duke settled down after a very short while to an easier-going routine, which included golf and swimming most afternoons of the week. The Windsors continued to dress for dinner at night, the Duke often in the kilt, though evening dress had been socially barred in England for the duration.

Their problem was a delicate one. On the one hand, they represented a colony at war, demanding austerity in the local economy and sacrifices from the population. On the other hand, the Bahamas remained a favourite American holiday resort, and a certain amount of display and colour was needed to keep the dollars coming in.

The fact had to be faced that there was simply not a great deal of work to do in the Bahamas. There was justice in one of the Duchess's outbursts when she bewailed life in Nassau. 'I wish to do whatever is loyal and right,' she said. 'I will do everything I can as Governor's wife. But would any American wife be happy or satisfied if her husband were put in a position where there was little chance for him to do the big things of which she knew him to be capable.'

The Windsor's proximity to the United States, however, was a consolation. The Duchess had her clothes supplied by Mainbocher in New York. They made use of a large Criscraft-class yacht put at their disposal by an American friend, Arthur Davis, President of the American Aluminium Company.

But an unfortunate story was published in the American press that the Duchess had sent to New York to have a hairdresser flown down to her. The Duchess defended herself against the criticisms which the story aroused, and explained to a reporter what happened.

Harold Christie, a big Nassau real-estate man, told the Duchess that every year he brought down a hairdresser to Nassau to work through the season at one or other of his big hotels. The Duchess had been having hairdresser trouble, as her hair is very fine and soft and not easy to dress.

'Since you have no trained maid,' Christie reportedly said, 'I'll be quite happy to get the New York hairdresser to attend to you. Is there any hairdresser you prefer?'

'Antoine used to do my hair in Paris,' the Duchess said, 'and he has a place in New York. He is probably the best.'

So at Christie's request Antoine's sent down one of the firm's star hairdressers, Wayne Forrest, who now has a salon of his own on 57th Street in New York.

Once a week while he was in Nassau Forrest attended to the Duchess's hair, and in between times trained a Bahaman girl to do the job so that she could take his place when he returned to New York.

In 1944 the Windsors were criticised over a matter which must have taken them by surprise. It involved a sum of £532. The table in the dining-room had been riddled by termites, and the Duke asked for £532 to buy some new furniture and kitchen equipment.

Four years earlier the House of Assembly had approved an excess expenditure of £5,000 by the Windsors without a word of comment. Now, presented with a request for £532, some of the Legislators blew up. They said that the colony could not afford it, that sacrifices were demanded from everyone, *everyone*, and was the Governor aware of the fact that there was a war on? They scrutinised the request. They demanded to know whether the furniture was to be locally made or imported from the United States. In the end, grudgingly, the request was allowed. The Duke got his furniture, and with it a new illustration of the limits of his powers.

In spite of such incidents as these, the Duke's performance was, in the final count, very good. He made some good non-political speeches, and with his extraordinary adding-machine mind, in which names were as automatic as sums, he never forgot anybody he met, however briefly, and this made a gratifying impression on everybody with whom he came in contact.

As a tourist attraction alone he was worth his £3,000 a year salary. The year he arrived, Nassau's luxury hotels were packed to the maids' rooms for weeks beyond the normal tourist season, accommodating the hordes of American tourists pouring into the island for a glimpse of the fabulous Duke and his equally fabulous American wife. The local statistics office recorded in delight that the tourist influx was nearly fifty per cent. up on the previous year.

The tourists were not disappointed. The Duke really was incredibly attractive, with his serious boy's face and sad quizzical eyes, going about his tasks with the perfection of appearance that the world expected of him, in his general's tropical uniform. The Duchess was always smiling, always totally in command of herself. Or nearly always.

One American tourist was rewarded, according to a reliable account, with an incident that made her 1,000-mile journey worth while. Taking a stroll round the island, she saw the Government car whizzing past and the Duke serenading the Duchess in the back seat with his bagpipes, the Duchess clapping her hands to her ears and protesting through hysterical laughter.

Alone, the Duchess put the Duke's personal comfort above all other considerations. They read the papers from England and America. They worked out jigsaws and played patience and poker, the Duchess more ably than the Duke.

In December 1940, Lord Lothian, Britain's clever Ambassador to the United States, died. President Roosevelt had left America on December 2nd, in the U.S. cruiser *Tuscaloosa* for a Caribbean cruise. The Duke went out to see him, and met him on the ship just off the Eleuthera Islands. It was a well-known fact that the Duke would have dearly liked Lord Lothian's job, and it was assumed that he was asking the President to put in a good word, although all he would say to reporters when he boarded the ship was 'No comment'.

He did not get very far, and Roosevelt seemed to be in one of his elusive moods, for when aides broke into their private conversation the President was giving the Governor some sage advice on the administration of the Bahamas.

The Duke did not get the job. It went instead to Lord Halifax, an appointment that must have been a stroke of pure genius on Winston Churchill's part, for the man who had been one of Britain's less effective Foreign Secretaries quickly established himself as one of the greatest Ambassadors England ever sent to the United States.

CHAPTER VIII

America – and Murder

T HE Windsors finally succeeded in visiting America in
October 1941, and this time there was no Charles E. Bedaux,
and there were no hitches.

Ten thousand people lined the streets of Baltimore to greet
them. In Washington, while the Duke called on Cordell Hull, the
Secretary of State, the Duchess was mobbed by thousands of
screaming girls, and it was only after a quarter of an hour of
strenuous effort that the police were able to cleave a way through
the press of girlhood to rescue her. The Duchess emerged slightly
shaken, but intact.

They travelled to Calgary in Alberta to see the Duke's ranch,
a wild barn of a place. By early October the winds which sported
around its wooden buildings already contained the first warning
chills of the Canadian winter. However pleased the Duke was to
be back after so many years, the ranch obviously did not appeal
to them as a place in which to make any sort of a home after the
war was over.

After Canada, they visited New York and were smothered in
a ticker-tape welcome in the good New York tradition. The
Waldorf-Astoria played host to them, and gave them an entire
floor on the twenty-ninth storey of the Towers, the residential
side of the great hotel. This was more to the Windsors' taste
than the Canadian farm, and in later years they were to make the
Waldorf the most permanent home they had.

Everywhere there were invitations to parties, banquets, balls.
The Windsors, however, punctiliously reminded well-wishers
that there was a war on in England even if it had not yet extended
to the United States, and politely declined. Instead, they visited
the Bundles for Britain societies and the seamen's canteens, where

visiting British sailors were impressed to discover that not only
the Duke but the Duchess could toss a respectable dart.

Altogether it was a spectacular visit. Wherever they went they
ran into walls of cheering crowds. There were receptions and
speeches. The comparison between the tumultuous American
welcome for the Windsors and the icy British refusal to have
anything to do with them was so great it almost seemed self-
conscious. The crowds seemed to say: see how much we love you
in America, come back to us; and shouted a moral that seemed to
prove that in America, at any rate, the American woman was
welcome with her royal husband to make a new home whenever
she wanted.

That is what it seemed, but there were also indications that
approval for the Windsors, though vociferous, was not universal.
On September 9th, the British Embassy had announced that the
Duke and Duchess would visit Washington on September 25th,
and be received by President Roosevelt and Mrs Roosevelt. The
reception never happened. At first it was postponed for causes
beyond anyone's control. Mrs Roosevelt's brother died, so the
luncheon to be given in their honour was held over for two weeks,
the President receiving them alone and informally.

It was not until October 28th that the Windsors dined at the
White House in the manner originally planned, but once again
the President was alone. Mrs Roosevelt was 'unavoidably absent',
away on a lecture engagement in Chicago.

As the Windsors began to make more frequent trips to the
United States, enthusiasm tended to subside, and newspapers
began to lace their editorials of welcome with increasing criticisms.
The leader pages were particularly disapproving of their standard
of living and of the large quantities of luggage the Windsors
always brought with them. So long as America remained neutral,
this disapproval was academic or at least detached. Once Americans themselves had joined the war, they started to get rather
peeved, and as a result of one criticism the Duke was finally
goaded into a reply.

In June 1944 Helen Worden, the sob-sister-in-chief of the
Scripps Howard newspapers, wrote for the American *Mercury*

magazine an article on the Duchess the repercussions of which have still not disappeared. It told all the old stories of her attention to her wardrobe and her purchases, her influence with her husband, and her isolation from high society.

The article became a big talking-point in America, and in Nassau it had the impact of an earthquake. The Duke was so furious that, against the advice of some of his assistants, he sat down and wrote a letter in reply, an unusual course for royalty. It was the first answer he had ever made to the many attacks on his wife. The letter duly appeared in the American *Mercury*.

'Sir,' wrote the Duke, 'I have just read with considerable astonishment and some disquiet the article in your June issue entitled "The Duchess of Windsor". The writer, Miss Helen Worden, claims to have "observed the Duchess since 1936 and has talked with her on her recent visits to America". The fact is that the Duchess met Miss Worden once—at a formal press tea in New York—but beyond shaking hands with her on introduction had no conversation with her on that occasion and has never seen her since.

'Apart from the utterly fantastic and completely untrue stories of the Duchess's expenditure on clothes, jewels and furs, two references in Miss Worden's story are criminally libellous fabrications and call for categorical denial. These are statements that:

'(1) "The State Department foots the Windsors' bills on Lend-Lease arrangement."

'(2) "An autographed photograph of von Ribbentrop once hung over her toilet table at Nassau."

'A telephone call to the Department of State will immediately disprove the first allegation. I can only give you my personal assurance that the second is equally untrue, but both the Duchess and myself would be interested to know whether you or Miss Worden can name the "friend" who is supposed to have seen the picture.

'I have used the words "criminally libellous" to describe these two statements because the first accuses my wife of being a kind of black marketeer evading currency control regulations, and the second depicts her as a sympathiser with the enemy. These are extremely dangerous accusations to make against anybody in wartime, let alone the wife of a Governor of a British colony.

'I can well appreciate Miss Worden's dilemma in wartime, when, like all gossip-writers, she must find it difficult to unearth items of news that are readily discoverable in peacetime, but not so easy to come by nowadays because most people's lives are grim rather than glamorous. Not unnaturally, therefore, she falls back on her imagination. The surprising thing to me is that a magazine with the honourable traditions of the American *Mercury* should dignify these malicious flights of fancy by publishing them.

'Edward, Duke of Windsor.'

The Windsors did not allow the criticisms to curtail their American visits, and they became familiar wartime guests in the United States. The visits were a welcome escape for them from the tedium of the Bahamas, a tedium that, however, came to an end suddenly after three years of their reign.

* * *

One night in July 1943—appropriately enough on a night in which Nassau was whipped with rain and storms—there occurred one of the great classics in the history of crime. The murder of Sir Harry Oakes will not be told in detail here because it touches on the Windsors only in part, but even today when one thinks of the Oakes murder one almost instantly thinks of the Windsors, whose rule in the Bahamas was high-lighted by the crime.

Oakes was a crude, tough, able, generous, gold-mining tycoon of an almost legendary ferocity. He had been born in Vermont, travelled the world in search of gold, and found it at the age of thirty-eight when a train guard kicked him off a freight train on to some of the greatest undiscovered gold deposits in Ontario.

Oakes became a British citizen and a baronet. He married an

Australian girl who had waited twenty years for him to make his strike. Before World War II he had withdrawn from England to Nassau to avoid paying taxes, and at the time of his death was eyeing Peru as a possible home with the advantage of being farther away from the Chancellor of the Exchequer. Oakes laughed at the veneer of civilisation and hated wearing ties or formal clothes. His venom and his generosity were equally violent.

One of his chief delights was knocking down trees with a bulldozer. No tree was safe from his levelling mania. This charming habit did, however, produce one beneficial result for the Nassau community. He built Oakes airport on one spot after knocking down enough trees, and the airport was later taken over by the Government.

The Duke of Windsor has always been attracted to men who pioneered in the wilderness of the Empire. It was one of the characteristics which made him so popular as a Prince of Wales. He and Oakes became friends, and the Windsors visited Oakes's home, Westbourne, frequently while Government House was being redecorated. The Duke even managed to persuade the roughneck baronet to ensheath himself in morning dress on suitable occasions.

Oakes was sixty-eight when he died. He had given a small party for friends that evening. When everybody had gone home, the murderer slipped into Oakes's bedroom, bashed his head in, turned a blow-torch on him and sprinkled the body with feathers. He then left, without trace to this day.

As soon as Oakes was found, the Duke was informed at Government House. The Duchess was overwhelmed by the news, and her first breathless comment was, 'Well, never a dull moment in the Bahamas!'

In deciding what to do, the Duke took a step which he subsequently admitted was a mistake. Excusably he decided this was something too big for the Nassau police. The logical result of this conclusion was to call either Scotland Yard in London or the F.B.I. in Washington. The Duke did neither. He called Miami, and got in touch with a Captain Edward Melchen, a man who had been the Duke's bodyguard on one of his American trips and who had impressed the Duke with his efficiency.

The Duke reported that something terrible had happened. Melchen and an assistant named James Barker, flew down to Nassau with inadequate equipment. They believed they were investigating a suicide case.

In taking statements, the detectives' suspicions fell on Count Alfred de Marigny, a native of Mauritius, and husband of Oakes's eighteen-year-old daughter Nancy. Oakes and de Marigny had had some deadly quarrels, and once Melchen and Barker became convinced that de Marigny had committed the murder (he could not adequately account for his movements on the night of the crime, and his hands were burned, according to de Marigny, because he had lit storm-lanterns when the storm became violent), they went all out to convict him.

Meanwhile Nancy Oakes de Marigny had gone to New York and returned with Raymond Schindler, one of the best private detectives in the world. Although the trail had gone cold and Schindler was finding evidence mysteriously disappearing, not to mention letters addressed to him from New York and Washington mysteriously not arriving, he dug up enough to explode the case against de Marigny, who was acquitted, and deported as 'undesirable'. No new arrest has been made since. A few years afterwards, a woman who went to Nassau to try to discover the murderer was found dead in a ditch.

Barker was later dismissed from the Miami Police Force for manufacturing evidence. He was ultimately shot and killed in Miami by his son, and the coroner's jury returned a verdict of justifiable homicide. Schindler insists today that he knows the identity of the murderer.

It is possible therefore that an unconvicted murderer, of a particularly savage type, lives and works today in the tiny community of Nassau. Yet three succeeding Governors had made no attempt to reopen the case, although the stain of evil it has left behind remains a pervading and ominous force in the island, hampering its development and causing a deep degeneration in its communal character.

The Duke went on to do good work in the Bahamas, and was praised by a Parliamentary Mission which visited the Bahamas in 1944. Unexpectedly in March 1945—three and a half months before completing his five-year tenure of office—the Duke resigned his post as Governor. He broadcast a farewell message to the people of the islands, referring to 'an interesting and happy chapter in our lives'. The Duke was presented with an address of appreciation by the House of Assembly.

Both the Duke and the Duchess had lost weight and suffered in health during their stay in the Bahamas. The Duchess had declined from 110 to 95 pounds. Faults had been found, but one could count in their favour—and particularly in the Duchess's favour—solid and lasting achievements for which they are still remembered. Many women in the British Empire received high decorations for doing much less for the war effort. The Duchess of Windsor received nothing, not even a note of thanks.

The one fact that emerged most clearly as the Windsors said good-bye to the Bahamas and sailed for newly liberated France was that after five years of war service they had made no progress whatever in winning their way into official favour. In Buckingham Palace and Downing Street, the backs were still towards them.

CHAPTER IX

Her Friends and Her Enemies

THE Duchess of Windsor, in the autumn of 1945, experienced a new sense of hope from the Socialist Government.

She had caught the sense of excitement which simmered through Britain at the prospect of change, and which had resulted in the Socialists' unexpected and overwhelming victory.

The Duchess had suffered a lot under the Tories. With a new Government, new faces and new ideas in Downing Street, she hoped for a new deal for her husband and herself.

In the closing weeks of the war the Duke applied to Winston Churchill for another job, and the Prime Minister suggested the Governorship of Bermuda.

At this the Duchess was heard to comment: 'What, another St Helena?' The Duke said he was sick of the islands, and declined. Churchill had no other vacancies.

But now Churchill himself was out of a job, together with all his Tories, those who had supported the Windsors as well as those who had opposed.

It was not surprising, therefore, that the Duchess looked forward eagerly to the new regime, and in October 1945 the Duke travelled to London to see what kind of a job he could get.

The Duchess stayed in Paris, waiting and praying for good news, for a word of encouragement from the new masters of Britain.

She received word soon enough, but it was not of encouragement. It was a simple, uncompromising 'No'.

The Duke had called on Ernest Bevin at the Foreign Office. Bevin made no suggestions and had nothing to offer.

The Socialist Party dream was quickly over. The Socialists were clearly no more sympathetic to the Duke's aspirations than the Conservatives had been. But the Duke had one last card to play, a card he had been holding for seven years.

By an apparent stroke of good fortune the Lord Chancellor in the new Labour Government was his friend, Lord Jowitt, the man who, in 1938, had given his legal opinion to the Duke that recognition of the Duchess as 'Her Royal Highness' came automatically with marriage. By now the problem of recognition had become a dominating issue with the Duke. He called on Jowitt and reminded him of his opinion.

Here was a difficult problem dropped into Jowitt's lap from his days of private practice.

He told the Duke he would investigate the matter, and presumably he did so. But Buckingham Palace remained silent. No enlightenment came from King George VI.

Neither war, nor the Windsors' record in the Bahamas, nor yet the triumph of Socialism in Britain, had caused any unbending in the attitude of succeeding Governments. Yet again the Duchess, in France, was to hear from her husband the words that had been pounding on her brain ever since the Abdication.

No recognition. No job. No success. No anything. 'No' to everything.

In her humiliation the Duchess of Windsor possessed one rare jewel which will appear more perfect as the shadows of history lengthen. She had a husband of unquestioning loyalty, unbending before the repeated blows.

It must be remembered that he was not barred, like his wife. He could come home, see his brother, stay with his mother.

People were prepared to accept him who would not accept the Duchess. But these people maddened the Duke more than any others. He preferred open hostility to such a reflection on his union. The Duke may have given up everything, but he regretted nothing.

In October the following year the Duchess accompanied the Duke to England. They stayed together at Ednam Lodge, home of the Earl of Dudley in Sunningdale, near Ascot, a fine house on the southern rim of Windsor Great Park, not far from Fort Belvedere. This time the Duke's idea was to tackle the King rather than the politicians, and probably he hoped to persuade his brother to receive the Duchess—the two had not met since the long-ago holiday at Balmoral in September 1936, when the Yorks and Wallis Simpson were fellow-guests. The Windsors received a jarring welcome.

On the night of the 16th, while the Windsors were away, a nimble burglar climbed the drainpipe, forced his way into the Duchess's bedroom and made off with her jewel-box. The box itself was recovered by detectives in the lodge grounds, where it had been jettisoned by the thief. One or two important pieces of jewellery were also found. But the burglar got away with jewels worth £20,000. Valuable necklaces, bracelets, rings, earrings, clips and brooches were in the haul, and no trace was ever found.

It was a bold, spectacular robbery, one of many that were being carried out in southern England at the time. Robbery is an occupational hazard of the wealthy, but once more circumstances counted against the Windsors more than they would have counted against most other people. Only one month before, the British newspapers had been enlarged from their wartime ration of four pages a day to six. Not much, but enough for Fleet Street to start flexing its muscles a little. With the joy of youth renewed, the newspapers hurled themselves on the story. For six years there had been nothing but war news in the papers, and this was a first-class pre-war vintage robbery arriving just at the moment when the press was able to do it something like justice. The newspapers made the most of it. Reports of the value of the jewel haul soared, one newspaper estimating it at a solid £100,000. In the approaching winter of 1946, a year steeped to the depths in post-war austerity, the revelations, however inaccurate, of so many jewels made a profoundly painful impact on an austerely rationed people. King George ignored the incident.

The following year the Windsors returned yet again to Britain to celebrate their tenth wedding anniversary. It was spent quietly at Sunningdale. No members of the Royal Family were present. Later that year Princess Elizabeth was married to Prince Philip of Greece. The Windsors were not invited.

It was finally dawning on the Duke and the Duchess that their cause in England was close to hopeless, that they were viewed without favour by the Royal Family and aroused no interest in the statesmen of either party. Still the Windsors remained members of royalty, and had to be treated as such.

Up to this time the Windsors had tried to maintain a royal attitude of aloofness and silence, and it had achieved them nothing. They knew that the world was fun to people who were not constantly tied down by protocol. So they decided to give protocol a rest and really enjoy themselves. The money began to flow out, and stories of their now fabulous expenditures grew. Today the Duchess makes almost a full-time job of her appearance, but most people agree that the result at the end of the ministrations justifies the labour involved.

The Duchess of Windsor literally dazzles. She dazzles with jewels. She dazzles with sartorial and physical perfection. Not a hair is out of place, not a blemish on the cultured mask of beauty.

The super-luxury of the Windsors' living in a utilitarian world attracts attention, but the Duchess of Windsor is not to be censured. Her path has been a thorny one. There were no roses all the way for her.

She had tried to win approval and failed. Sometimes she had made mistakes. But sometimes she had *not* made mistakes. Sometimes she had performed splendidly. But it made no difference. She failed just the same.

Conscious that there was no longer a future for him in Britain, the Duke did what he would never have dreamed of doing if he had had any hopes left of official employment. He decided to break the silence which traditionally binds all members of the Royal Family and publish his Memoirs.

His material was the phenomenal memory he could apply to his past life as Prince and King, a past that had become very dear to him. It was obvious even before he started work that this past, so filled with incident and so dearly remembered, would provide a work of unique merit. An example of his attitude towards his own earlier life was shown some years ago when he met a cosmopolitan American woman whose hobby it was to collect pencils. In 1936 she had been in London and had bought a gross of twopenny pencils, adorned by portraits of King Edward VIII whose forthcoming Coronation was just beginning to plaster itself on the shoddier brands of British and Japanese trinketry. In 1948 she was carrying the last stub of the last pencil in her handbag when, quite unexpectedly, she found herself in the same room as the Duke and Duchess in New York.

'Sir,' said the woman, 'believe me, this is a complete coincidence, but I have a pencil here marking your Coronation.'

The Duke took the pencil and stared at it in fascination. 'It's me,' he said in ungrammatical amazement. 'Wallis, it's me.' Then an expression of melancholy spread over his face. 'But look,' he said sadly, 'I am almost whittled away.'

After several years the Memoirs came out, and the Duke buried himself on the Riviera 'for a long rest'. He made about £300,000 out of them.

This was a most auspicious success, and it came at the right time, for on the accession of Queen Elizabeth II to the throne the Windsors' income had changed its colour somewhat. The £25,000 a year settlement abruptly ceased. But by now the Windsors were full swing in the writing and press relations business. With his book still selling steadily all over the world, the Duke wrote a series of articles on his thoughts concerning the forthcoming Coronation of his niece. The Duke and Duchess also sold to the photographic agencies pictures of their country house and pictures of themselves. Almost £200,000 more has been earned from such subsidiary rights as these and newspaper and magazine serialisations.

The Duchess announced her intention of writing her own Memoirs—a further abdication of the Windsors' aspirations to be recognised at Court, but a decision likely to bring in another quarter of a million pounds.

The Windsors, in fact, have found an ideal consolation for not being recognised. They have become big business.

*   *   *

In the year 1953 the Duchess of Windsor became a clearer personality. It was as though she had emerged from a mist or been brought by a lens gradually into focus.

The impression at the end of the year was of a woman, tortured by a ruthless epoch, who had yet become the mistress of her soul.

Her eyes, those incomparable eyes, as much a legacy to legend as the Mona Lisa smile, so watchful, distrustful, seeking possible enemies everywhere, had nevertheless become the eyes of a woman finding peace within herself.

The Duchess in her own questing, darting way had begun, it seems, to have found the key to tranquillity at last, even though there has been no apparent change in her nomadic way of life.

July found her at Cannes completing arrangements for a Mediterranean cruise. The Duke was in Biarritz. Shades of his grandfather here—Edward VII had loved Biarritz, and the Duke, as he revealed in his Coronation articles, felt that his reign would have acquired something of the personality of Edward VII's had it run its course.

Cannes, of course, could not mean to the Duke what it meant to the Duchess—memories of a desperate dash across France a week before the Abdication; refuge in a pastel villa up in the mountains overlooking Cannes harbour. The Villa Lou Viei.

Up in those mountains, not twenty minutes away by car, Herman Rogers still sat, gruff, rocklike, reliable. He had a new house and a new wife. The Villa Lou Viei was up for sale. His first wife, the former Katherine Moore, had died some years before.

Rogers now lived in a smaller house with his second wife, a pretty Frenchwoman, the former Lucy Fury Wann, whose first husband had been killed in the R.A.F.

The Duchess, who never forgets such things, reminded the Duke that Herman Rogers and his wife were about to celebrate their fourth wedding anniversary. The Windsors asked them to have their anniversary dinner with them.

The reunion was perfect. The Duke was at his best; ebullient and full of anecdotes. The Duchess, slender as a rail from a close-to-starvation diet, was more inclined to be sentimental. She pointed out to the guests how good a friend Rogers had been to her for so many years (they had actually been close friends for thirty years).

'Not once but many times,' said the Duchess seriously, ' "home" to me has been where the Rogers were.'

The yachting trip followed, and then came autumn, a golden autumn untouched by controversy, and it marked a settling by the Duchess as two homes in France gradually became ready for habitation.

It was in this mood, almost of serenity, that she reappeared in December on the London scene.

Tactfully she waited until the Queen and the Duke of Edinburgh had left London on their world tour of the Empire. Then she came to London with her husband.

She arrived openly, not, as she has usually done on her rare visits to England, slipping in quietly and staying at the houses of friends in the country.

This time she stayed at Claridges. It was a move not without courage. The Duchess had endured many hard years, and she may have anticipated hostility.

Exactly the opposite happened. She was cheered wherever she went; cheered with all the Londoner's good nature and his unquenchable sympathy for the loser and underdog.

The visit was a complete success. The Duchess went shopping. Again she was followed and cheered. She and the Duke wandered over some of the scenes of their courtship, dining at the London restaurant and at the same table where they had dined when they were the Prince of Wales and Mrs Simpson.

There were some places, of course, they did not visit, places where even now the memory is too sharp. They did not visit Fort Belvedere, where they had been young in love. It was probably just as well. Today the gardens are overgrown, weeds flourishing everywhere.

They did not visit No 7 Grosvenor Square, the mansion of Lady Cunard, the American woman who called herself Emerald although her name was Maude; who sat the Prince and Mrs Simpson side by side at her candlelit dinner table and watched his love ripen.

An air of desertion was also on this house, which stood empty and derelict from the end of the war until 1955 when it was knocked down.

They did glimpse St James's Palace, the never-changing home of monarchs. Once on the balcony there, Mrs Simpson had watched heralds proudly and with the words of centuries proclaim Edward VIII King.

What a centre of interest she had been on that day! And where now, did she wonder as she sat at the table of a restaurant only a hundred yards away, were the men and women who surrounded her admiringly in those days.

As hard as those actors fought then for a smile, so later did they struggle to get out of the line of fire. The doors of town houses and country mansions banged shut behind beating hearts and heaving breasts, while Mrs Simpson was left alone in a Cannes villa with Lord Brownlow, Herman Rogers and his wife, 'Mrs Simpson? Oh, her we hardly knew.'

Calmer now, more confident in herself, reassured by the basic goodness of the English people, can she begin to recall with charity the heavy figure of 'Farmer' Baldwin; and 'Squire' Geoffrey Dawson, with his sensuous lips and cold eyes, and Archbishop Cosmo Lang, with his thin smile?

For Baldwin, after all, died forlorn. The hero of the Abdication, the imperturbable personification of John Bull, the man who received from the public the greatest ovation of all at the Coronation of King George VI in 1937, was perhaps the most unpopular man in England three years later.

His responsibility for England's military weakness had ruined him. '. . . This admiration [of the British people] converted to the bitterest hatred,' wrote G. M. Young, the man Baldwin himself chose to write his biography, Baldwin knew that 'far and wide throughout his own England men and women under the rain of death were cursing him as the politician who had lied to the people and left them defenceless against their enemies'.

The Archbishop of Canterbury, Dr Cosmo Lang, was surely one of the most unpopular incumbents to hold his high office in many years.

He died in 1942, and time has not mellowed his memory. He is remembered, despite his erudition and his culture, as a strangely un-Christian kind of man.

Geoffrey Dawson, autocratic editor of *The Times* through the 'thirties, moulder of public opinion in favour of Munich and the Abdication, was sacked in 1941. He knew some time before that dismissal was coming, and tried everything he knew to hold on to his job. But the blow fell, all the same.

He died in 1944, a complex figure of this century, and again, like his heroes, Baldwin and Lang, not popular, not well remembered.

What of the fortunes of those men who, moved by different policies and emotions, took the King's side during the Abdication crisis?

Winston Churchill at first was seriously hurt by his stand on the Abdication. His fortunes fell very low indeed, and many believed at the time that his political career was wrecked.

But now he stands massive and supreme among the statesmen of the world, the symbol and the repository of the glory of England.

Never in all the annals of British history was a war leader more idolised. His championship of the cause of the Duke of Windsor has been forgiven, and not only is he first in the hearts of his countrymen but first also in esteem and credit at the Court of St James's itself.

Then take Beaverbrook, the inimitable, twice a Minister of the Crown. He became for a time a great and heroic figure in the war.

Today he is unique, the most colourful of all the world's newspaper barons.

Faithful Walter Monckton—one senses the Duke of Windsor in his Memoirs softening whenever the name is mentioned—was King's Counsel in the true and literal rather than the conventional meaning of the term.

He was the confidant of Mrs Simpson. He is still a friend of the Windsors, but he has never quarrelled with their critics, and he retained his appointments with the royal household.

Monckton is at present the Minister of Labour, one of the

ablest and most popular members of the Conservative Government.

Sir George Allen never wavered in his devotion to the interests of the Duke and Duchess—or to the present Royal Family either. While he is no longer the Windsors' solicitor, his relations with them are intimate to a degree. But this attachment does not interfere with his association with the Court, and in 1952 Queen Elizabeth II conferred on him the K.C.V.O., a royal and not a political order.

Lord Brownlow—his career has been less spectacular than some of the others, but it, too, has been rewarding and successful. He remained Lord-Lieutenant of Lincolnshire until 1950, in spite of criticism of his friendship for the Windsors.

Brownlow, agreeable companion, generous friend, wealthy and enlightened landlord, has never swerved in his support of the Windsors. They are no longer intimate, however, and their relationship today is friendly but remote.

So Mrs Simpson, although she herself went down to defeat, has lived to see her enemies perish and her friends exalted.

This record of downfall and triumph is now an item of academic interest without moral or poetic justice, because the Duchess of Windsor is as distant from the misfortunes of the one as she is from the fortunes of the other.

Whatever irony exists in this situation is overwhelmed by the last strange irony of all.

For the way of life the Duchess has created to content her husband is nothing more than an imitation of the existence he once disliked so much.

Edward VIII used to be impatient of courts and the restrictions of court etiquette. He was contemptuous of courtiers, and he escaped from the formalities whenever he could—usually in the direction of Mrs Simpson. But he has escaped from one court only to find himself in another.

This is the international court, generally known as café society.

It is no exaggeration to describe this community as a court. The court procedure is meticulously observed. All the formalities which the Duke used to despise so much are there, the protocol, the rule of precedence by which a King enjoys the right to go first and sit at the head of the table even when he is a guest. This has always been the prerogative of royalty, and the Windsors adhere to it.

The throne-room is mobile; here a restaurant, there a night-club, now a rented house in France, next an hotel suite in New York; but the rules are rigid.

So the story ends in a mirage.

The throne, the Crown, the adulation of the people, the proud palaces, the carriages, the confidences of statesmen, all of which might have been rendered to the Duchess, have faded away.

All that remains is a court of sorts—that and a persistent and elusive feeling that had the Duchess lived in a period of more arrogant Kings she would not only have been Queen but a good Queen.

Bibliography

H.R.H. THE DUKE OF WINDSOR: *A King's Story* (Cassell).

History of the Times, Volume IV, Part 2 (Times Publishing Co.).

G. M. YOUNG: *Stanley Baldwin* (Hart-Davis).

LAURA LOU BROOKMAN: *Her Name was Wallis Warfield* (Dutton, 1936).

LORD BEAVERBROOK: B.B.C. Broadcast.

CLEVELAND AMORY: *The Last Resorts* (Harper, 1952).

JANET FLANNER: *Profile of Charles Bedaux* and other New Yorker pieces New Yorker).

Time Magazine on the Abdication.

KEITH FEILING: *Neville Chamberlain* (Macmillan).

LORD REITH: *Into the Wind* (Hodder & Stoughton).

LORD TEMPLEWOOD, VISCOUNT NORWICH, THELMA, LADY FURNESS: Articles in *Sunday Dispatch, Daily Mail, Sunday Pictorial*.

WALTER GOERLITZ: *The German General Staff* (Hollis & Carter).

JOACHIM VON RIBBENTROP: *Zwischen London und Moskau*.

J. G. L. LOCKHART: *Cosmo Gordon Lang* (Hodder & Stoughton).

FRANK OWEN & R. J. THOMPSON: *His was the Kingdom* (Barker).

BARONESS RAVENSDALE: *In Many Rhythms* (Weidenfeld & Nicolson).

THOMAS JEVES, C.H.: *A Diary with Letters* (Oxford).

ALFRED DE MARIGNY: *More Devil than Saint* (Beachurst Press).